SCHOOLCRAFT'S
OJIBWA LODGE
STORIES

Henry Rowe Schoolcraft
Courtesy of Marquette County Historical Society

SCHOOLCRAFT'S
OJIBWA LODGE STORIES

Life on the Lake Superior Frontier

Edited with a new introduction
By Philip P. Mason

Michigan State University Press
East Lansing
1997

Originally published in 1962
Michigan State University Press, East Lansing, Michigan 48823-5202

All Michigan State University Press books are produced on paper that meets the
requirements of American National Standard of Information Sciences—
Permanence of paper for printed materials ANSI Z39 .48—1984.

10 09 08 07 06 05 04   2 3 4 5 6 7 8 9

Printed and bound in the United States of America

Cover art is a black and white halftone from a painting entitled, "Shin-Ga-Ba-
Wossin: A Chippewa Chief." Courtesy of McKenney & Hall, *History of Indian
Tribes of North America,* 1848, 1:153.

Dedicated
to the memory of
John Johnston and his Chippewa wife,
Ozha-guscoday-way-quay, the *Woman
of the Green Valley*

CONTENTS

FOREWORD

SAULT STE. MARIE was no longer a thriving fur trading center when the U.S. government established a military fort and Indian Agency headquarters in the 1820s. The fur trade had declined drastically; no longer did hundreds of Indians and voyageurs return there each summer laden with pelts to trade with agents of Montreal and New York fur companies. Indeed, by 1825 most of the major fur companies had either stopped operations entirely or moved their headquarters to areas west of Lake Superior. The once powerful and dominant American Fur Company which had a major presence at Sault Ste. Marie and nearby Mackinac Island had not only curtailed its operation; but within a decade would close all of its fur trade posts and turn its attention to commercial fishing.

The construction of Fort Brady on the banks of the St. Marys River in 1822 along with the arrival of a garrison of more than two hundred soldiers helped revive the economic life of the small village. The new Indian Agency also had an impact, encouraging hundreds of Indians from villages in Minnesota, Wisconsin, and Michigan to travel there each summer to meet with the Indian agent and collect gifts from the U.S. government.

Despite these changes, Sault Ste. Marie remained a small frontier village. In 1827, a census taken of the Sault township counted 222 members of the Fort Brady garrison and 245 civilians. The majority of the residents were of French or mixed Indian blood. In addition, there was a significant Indian population located in tribal villages near the Sault. Across the St. Marys River was the Canadian Sault, also a small fur trade village.

Most of the residents of the Sault made their living from commercial fishing, maple sugaring, and supplying the needs of the Indian Agency and the garrison at Fort Brady. The newly established county of Chippewa created by the Michigan Territorial Legislature in 1826 also provided a number of positions.

In the 1820s the village was comprised largely of one-story, bark-covered log houses, many of which were unoccupied and falling into decay.

Several warehouses originally used by fur companies to store supplies and furs were located at the wharves along the river. By 1825, many of these buildings were empty and unused.

The oldest house in the village, located near the river, was owned by John Johnston. Built in 1770, it was large enough to accommodate the Johnston family and numerous visitors. It was in this residence that Henry Schoolcraft lived when he became an Indian agent in 1822. He remained there for several years, even after his marriage to Jane Johnston.

The social life of Sault Ste. Marie varied according to the season of the year. During the summer months hundreds of Indians arrived and camped along the river. With the coming of winter, the situation changed. From late November to May the following year ice and snow closed the lakes and rivers; the frontier post was virtually cut off from the rest of civilization. Mail delivery from Detroit by dog sled provided some contact with eastern settlements, but even this service was unreliable.

During the winter months village residents enjoyed social activities of their own making. The soldiers and their wives gave numerous parties, dances, and card games at the fort and citizens of both the American and Canadian communities often staged other social affairs for public amusement. Despite the efforts of the clergy, drinking and gambling were also popular pastimes.

Henry Schoolcraft did not participate in most of these social activities because he disapproved of heavy drinking and considered card playing a complete waste of time. In fact, he welcomed the solitude of the winter months since it gave him time to pursue his studies on the Natives. He worked diligently on his Chippewa dictionary and poured over the extensive material assembled during the previous summer months.

In December 1826, Schoolcraft formed a local reading society made up of several officers from the Fort Brady garrison, local government officials and friends in both the American and Canadian Sault. They met once a week to discuss books and other scholarly subjects and topics of local interest. In order to stimulate further discussion, Schoolcraft decided to publish a magazine for distribution to the members of the local reading society. Named the *Literary Voyager,* he described it "as one of the little means of supporting existence in so remote a place, and keeping alive at the same time the sparks of literary excitement." Written in longhand and consisting of an average of twenty-four pages, measuring 8" x 14" in size, he read each issue to the members of the literary society. Later, he circulated it to local residents and friends in Detroit and eastern cities.

The meetings of the Literary Society as well as the numerous visits from government officials and other prominent visitors convinced Schoolcraft that he needed a larger and more impressive residence, as well as a larger headquarters for the Indian Agency. With the support of the territorial governor, Lewis Cass, and his superiors in Washington, he received approval to build a new residence. Located on the banks of the St. Marys River, this imposing two-story "mansion," the largest residence in the village, consisted of fifteen rooms. The structure was surrounded by clusters of maples, elms, mountain ash, and other shade trees. Spacious lawns and gardens made the Indian Agency House even more impressive.

Named "Elmwood" by Schoolcraft, the entrance hall to the facility contained a large space for exhibit cases to display the numerous geological specimens, animal skins, stuffed birds, and "Indian curiosities" that he had collected.

The various "public" rooms were also elegantly furnished. According to the Reverend Jeremiah Porter, who visited Elmwood often, one room contained wallpaper, carpeting, and other furnishings "equal to any in his native New England town."

Completed in the fall of 1827, within weeks Elmwood became the social center of Sault Ste. Marie. The constant stream of visitors, many of whom were literary figures from Europe, visited Elmwood to meet with the Indian agent and Jane Johnston Schoolcraft, the granddaughter of a powerful Chippewa leader. Schoolcraft also used the house to meet Indian leaders who visited the Sault during summer months, conducting interviews regarding their history, customs, and legends.

The local literary society also met there to discuss various topics, especially Schoolcraft's interest in the Indians of Lake Superior.

Elmwood also provided excellent facilities for numerous dinners and social events hosted by the Schoolcrafts. They were described as "elegant and sumptuous." According to one visitor, the menus on two consecutive evenings included "eight varieties of meat, half a dozen vegetables, and eight desserts in addition to bread and butter, water, cider, beer, and wine."

During the winter of 1826-27, Schoolcraft produced fifteen issues of the *Literary Voyager*. Extra copies were circulated at the Sault and to friends in Detroit and New York. Schoolcraft retained a master set of the issues in his own archives; and, sometime after 1849, with the assistance from his second wife, Mary Howard Schoolcraft, edited it for publication in book form. It was never published, however, possibly because at that time he was deeply involved in the preparation of his monumental six volume *Historical and Statistical Information Respecting the History, Conditions and Prospects of the Indian Tribes of the United States.*

Following Schoolcraft's death in 1864, his widow gave his voluminous archives to the Smithsonian Institution in 1878. What happened to the collection after its arrival at the Smithsonian is not clear, but the complete set of the *Literary Voyager* was not retained in its original order. It is possible that some issues were removed from the collection and used by the staff of the Smithsonian for other research purposes.

The first installment of the Schoolcraft Papers were transferred to the Manuscript Division of the Library of Congress in 1897, and the remainder in 1942. Two issues of the *Literary Voyager*, intact in the 1850s when Schoolcraft prepared them for publication, were lost or misplaced.

Preface

The last decade has witnessed a renewed interest in the career of Henry Rowe Schoolcraft, the famous nineteenth century Indian agent, explorer, writer, and student of Indian life and customs. Although he wrote more than twenty full length volumes and hundreds of articles on the Indian, few of his major works are available except in rare book rooms of libraries and in the hands of private collectors. Starting in 1953, Michigan State University Press began an ambitious project to re-publish Schoolcraft's major studies and thus make them readily available to the American public. Mentor L. Williams edited the first two publications: *Schoolcraft's Narrative Journal of Travels . . . to the Sources of the Mississippi River in the Year 1820* (1953) and *Schoolcraft's Indian Legends* (1956). After Professor Williams' untimely death in 1956, the current editor continued the series with *Schoolcraft's Expedition to Lake Itasca: The Discovery of the Source of the Mississippi* (1958), which contained the extant diaries, journals, reports, and correspondence of the leaders of the expedition.

Even more important to the student of the American Indian than Schoolcraft's published works are the voluminous collections of his official and personal papers in the National Archives, the Library of Congress, and in other research repositories throughout the country. They contain a wealth of untapped source material about the aborigine and his culture. For Schoolcraft not only had a *sense* of the historic role he was playing as Indian agent and ethnologist on the frontier during a critical period, but he recognized the necessity of creating and preserving accurate records of his activities. He provided also that his voluminous collection of Indian materials should remain intact and be made available to future generations of scholars. Accordingly, after his death, his papers were given to the Smithsonian Institution and later to the Library of Congress.

With the active support of the National Historical Publications Commission and Michigan State University Press, the editor has commenced a series of publications of the "Papers of Henry Schoolcraft." The "Literary Voyager," a manuscript magazine produced by

Preface

Schoolcraft during the winter of 1826-27 was selected as the first publication. Later, the papers of Schoolcraft as Indian Agent and Superintendent of Indian Affairs for the Upper Lakes will be published.

Unfortunately, the Schoolcraft papers were hopelessly disarranged
after they were transferred to the Smithsonian Institution in 1878.
Part of the collection was transferred to the Library of Congress
prior to 1897 and the remainder in 1942. In the process, several
issues of the "Literary Voyager," which Schoolcraft was preparing
for publication in book form in the 1850's, were lost. I devoted two
years to a search of the major Schoolcraft collections for copies of
the missing issues before deciding to edit the incomplete set in this
book.

I retained the original text except for corrections of obvious copy-
ing errors. Schoolcraft's punctuation has been retained also even
though his practice of separating subjects and predicates with commas
is outdated. Some spelling changes have been made to avoid confusion
since Schoolcraft habitually used variant spellings of Indian names
even within the same paragraph. In the notes which appear at the
end of the volume, brackets are used to distinguish Schoolcraft's
original footnotes from those of the editor. The editor has attempted,
whenever possible, to identify the contributor of each article and
the informants of the Indian legends. Much of this information
was obtained from the Schoolcraft papers in the Library of Congress
which contain many of the original stories signed by the contributors.
There has been no attempt to make an anthropological analysis of the
Indian lodge stories published in the "Literary Voyager;" this is a
task for the professional.

I wish to acknowledge the assistance of many persons. Dr. Philip
M. Hamer, former Executive Director of the National Historical
Publications Commission, and Dr. Oliver W. Holmes, its present
executive officer, have supported the Schoolcraft project from the
beginning. Dr. F. Clever Bald of the University of Michigan and
Professor Leslie L. Hanawalt of Wayne State University have offered
many helpful suggestions. I am grateful also to Dr. Daniel J. Reed,
Library of Congress; Dr. James Heslin, New York Historical Society;
Mr. James Babcock, Burton Historical Collection; Miss Geneva
Kebler and Mrs. Elizabeth Rademacher of the Michigan Historical
Commission; Mr. Howard Peckham of the William L. Clements

Preface

Library, University of Michigan; Miss Myrtle Elliott and Mrs. Beulah Miller of the Chippewa County Historical Society; and Mrs. Esther Loughin of the Michigan State Library. Mr. George Wiskemann of Lansing generously made available to me his rare collection of Schoolcraft books. I wish to thank also Miss Patricia Proudfoot of the Wayne State University Archives for her assistance in proofreading the manuscript and her thoughtful suggestions. Finally, I wish to acknowledge the contribution of my wife, Henrietta, who spent many weeks transcribing the longhand issues of the "Literary Voyager."

This study was made possible through a grant from the American Philosophical Society. The Division of Graduate Studies and Research of Wayne State University assisted also in the purchase of photostats and microfilm.

Philip P. Mason

April 13, 1962
Detroit, Michigan

INTRODUCTION

THE FIGURE of Henry Rowe Schoolcraft loomed large in the gallery of men of learning in the mid-nineteenth century. He stood among a small and special group of scholars—those who made it their business to open up and elucidate for the rest of the world the newer parts of the new America: men who used as their daily tools not the serried books of a college library but the canoe, the Indian guide, and the gestures of sign-language. The nation knew him as explorer, Indian agent, and ethnologist.

From 1818 when Schoolcraft explored the lead-bearing hills of Missouri and the wilds of the Ozark Mountains until 1832 when he discovered Lake Itasca, the true source of the Mississippi in the heart the northern forests, he had a part in many important and often dangerous expeditions. As Indian agent for nineteen years—1822 to 1841—with headquarters at the half-Indian frontier posts of Sault Ste. Marie and Mackinac Island, he served the tribes of northern Michigan, Wisconsin, and Minnesota. During his agencyship, which witnessed the controversial and often painful federal policy of shifting the Indians west of the Mississippi, Schoolcraft visited all of the major tribes in his jurisdiction, consummated important treaties, and ministered to the homely needs of thousands of Indians.

In his twenty-five years on the frontier, Schoolcraft took advantage of his unique position to collect data on all aspects of Indian life and customs, recording in minute detail his anthropolitical observations on Indian culture—ceremonies, religion, superstitions, hunting and fishing techniques, dress, language, and village life. With the aid of interpreters, he recorded for the first time scores of lodge stories and tribal legends of the Chippewa. He made bales of notes from talks with fur traders, army officers, Indian agents, surveyors, and others who knew the Indian first-hand. The Schoolcraft Papers in the Library of Congress testify to his skill as a researcher and his perceptiveness as an observer of the American aborigine. Later, after his resignation in 1841 as agent, he continued his Indian studies under the auspices of the New York Legislature and the Congress of the United States.[1]

Unlike some of his contemporaries who studied the Indians but were content to accumulate facts in antiquarian fashion, Schoolcraft eagerly shared his findings with the American public in a series of publications. He penned hundreds of articles for popular and scholarly journals and newspapers of his day and wrote more than twenty volumes describing his explorations and the Indian.[2] His Indian lore was used widely by writers, notably Henry W. Longfellow, who based his epic poem, "Song of Hiawatha," on the legends from Schoolcraft's Algic Researches.

Schoolcraft's most famous Indian study was *Historical and Statistical Information Respecting the History, Conditions and Prospects of the Indian Tribes of the United States* published by Congress in six folio volumes between 1851 and 1857 at a total cost of over $150,000. Unfortunately, the author did not take time for careful research, thought, and organization, and left himself open to sharp criticism of future historians and anthropologists. But despite the shortcomings of the volumes, which were partly eliminated by the publication of an *Index*[3] in 1954 by the Bureau of American Ethnology of the Smithsonian Institution, they contain a wealth of valuable material on Indians. As one writer noted, Schoolcraft's six-volume study serves "as a monument to a great American explorer and ethnologist."[4]

In addition to his published works, Henry Schoolcraft presented some of his Indian knowledge to a select public in the odd form of manuscript magazines. Although now almost unknown except to a few bibliographers, these magazines were, in their day, widely circulated among students of Indian culture. The most informative of them was the *Literary Voyager* prepared weekly by Schoolcraft at Sault Ste. Marie during the winter of 1826-1827.[5]

This magazine, which Schoolcraft later gave the subtitle, *Muzzeniegun,* a Chippewa word meaning "a printed document or book," contained articles, poems, announcements, etc., on all aspects of Indian life and customs. The subjects included historic Indian battles, Indian ceremonies, superstitions, burials, fur trade, war chants and songs, totems, the effect of alcohol upon Indians, and the intertribal war between the Chippewa and Sioux. Of particular interest are biographical sketches of prominent Indian leaders, including Waub Ojeeg or the White Fisher, the famous war chief at LaPointe; and Shing-a-ba-wossin, head of the Chippewa band living along the St. Marys River.

Schoolcraft presented for the first time in the *Literary Voyager* some of the lodge stories that he himself collected and for which he later gained national recognition. Many of them he later published in *Algic Researches, the Red Race of America,* and the *Myth of Hiawatha.*[6] Material on the pages of the *Literary Voyager* was used by other writers as well as by Schoolcraft. Mrs. Anna Jameson, the well-known English author, examined the magazines in detail and extracted several of the Chippewa legends for her book, *Winter Studies and Summer Rambles,* first published in 1838.[7] Similarly, Dr. Chandler R. Gilman reprinted in *Life on the Lakes* several of the legends.[8] These books, however, do not give, as does the *Literary Voyager,* the source of each legend or the name of the informant. Later versions of several of the legends in the *Literary Voyager* were rewritten by Schoolcraft to reflect the romantic language more in vogue. The accounts were more spontaneous and written after only a few months from the time he recorded them from his Indian informants. Finally, several of the legends which appeared in the *Literary Voyager* are unique; they were not included in the later publications of Schoolcraft.

Although only a few copies of each issue, and indeed sometimes apparently only a single copy, were written, the *Literary Voyager* achieved wide distribution. Each issue circulated among the citizens of Sault Ste. Marie and then went to Schoolcraft's friends in Detroit, New York, and other eastern cities.[9]

The *Literary Voyager* is recognized as the first magazine produced in Michigan and one of the first of its kind in the frontier west. It has been hailed by one contemporary writer as "embryonically the first ethnological magazine in America."[10] The publication, incidentally, tells much about the early career of Henry Schoolcraft. It reflects his growing interest in studying all aspects of Chippewa culture and vividly illustrates how the young Indian agent brought a "spark of literary life" to a remote frontier outpost. And finally, the *Literary Voyager* reveals Schoolcraft's dependence on the John Johnston family of Sault Ste. Marie for their help in assembling data on the Chippewa.

Henry Rowe Schoolcraft was born in 1793 in the Manor of Rensselaerswyck, a small village west of Albany, New York. Even as a young boy, his scholarly accomplishments were well-known in the community. He supplemented his public school education with outside studies of his own and excelled in Latin, read widely in the classics, learned French from a tutor, and had taught himself Hebrew and German "with the aid only of grammars and lexicons." As one local resident observed, "he was generally to be found at home at his studies, when other boys of his age were attending horse races, cockfights, and other vicious amusements for which the village was famous."[11] this thirst for knowledge characterized Schoolcraft throughout his career.

His literary abilities were also evident early. Local newspapers and magazines first published his verse and essays in 1808, when he was fifteen years old. In 1809, he organized a literary society among the younger men of Hamilton, New York. It met to discuss contemporary literary problems and, with Schoolcraft as editor, produced in manuscript form a magazine, *The Cricket or Whispers from a Voice in the Corner.* It is not known whether this society flourished after 1810 when Henry moved to Geneva, New York, but he did continue to edit the magazine until 1818 under the title, *The Cricket or Parapetic Student.* Devoted to philosophy and literary subjects, it was obviously the forerunner of the *Literary Voyager* and other manuscript magazines that he later edited.

Henry Schoolcraft planned to complete his formal education at Union College in Schenectady but when the time came, his family could not afford to send him. Instead Schoolcraft went to work for his father who was superintendent of a glass factory in Geneva, New York. He must have learned the business well, for in 1813, he became manager of a glass factory in Salisbury, Vermont, and later accepted a similar position in Keene, New Hampshire.[12]

He might have remained in the glass-making business for the remainder of his life if an influx of British glassware after the War of 1812 had not forced the industry into bankruptcy. Thus in 1817, at the age of twenty-four, spurred on by popular accounts of opportunities in the West and with the hope that his knowledge of mineralogy would further his career, he left New York for the Mississippi region. This trip took him to the rich lead region of Missouri where he spent the following winter visiting mining operations around Potosi and making detailed notes of his observations.

Upon his return to New York, Schoolcraft's account of his survey was published under the title, *A View of the Lead Mines of Missouri.*[13] The book, hailed by scientists as the first reliable study of the "scientific resources" of the Mississippi Valley, boosted Schoolcraft's national reputation as a mineralogist. The study set forth specific recommendations for more efficient utilization of the nation's lead resources and advocated the immediate introduction of a number of mechanical improvements, including steam-driven pumps and up-to-date furnaces. His key proposal was for the establishment of a federal agency to supervise the lead mining industry.

The report attracted the attention of Secretary of War John C. Calhoun who was concerned about the exploitation of the nation's resources. At his invitation, Schoolcraft went to Washington, D.C., and presented his recommendations formally to President James Monroe, Secretary of the Treasury, William H. Crawford, and Calhoun. They, too, were impressed by the young scientist's observations and promised to work for congressional support of a government-sponsored program. Schoolcraft let it be known that he would be available for the position of superintendent of mines if Congress approved of the plan.

It is not known how much support the President and Secretary of War gave to his recommendations, but it is obvious that they considered him competent. Within a year after the Washington trip, Calhoun offered Schoolcraft a position as mineralogist for an exploring expedition under the direction of Lewis Cass, Governor of Michigan Territory. Schoolcraft readily accepted the position, not for the meager pay of $1.50 per day, but because the trip would provide an excellent opportunity for him to explore the natural resources of the uncharted wilderness of Lake Superior and Minnesota.

The Cass expedition, conducted during the summer of 1820, proved to be a turning point in Schoolcraft's career. His reports on the natural resources of the explored area, particularly concerning the copper deposits on the Keweenaw Peninsula, brought him further commendation from Secretary of War Calhoun and federal officials. His account of the trip, *Narrative Journals of Travels* published by Harper and Brothers in 1822, marked the young mineralogist as an explorer and writer. The friendships he made on the expedition with Lewis Cass, Charles C. Trowbridge, and other influential men served him well in later life.

Other government positions came to Schoolcraft through the influence of John Calhoun and Lewis Cass. In 1821, he served as Secretary to the U.S.

Indian Treaty Commissioners in Chicago. The following year, Calhoun offered him the position of Indian Agent for the Upper Great Lakes with headquarters at Sault Ste. Marie. His reactions to the latter appointment were mixed. He was deeply disappointed that Congress had not established a government department of mines with a position for himself therein, but on Cass' urging, he accepted the Indian post as a temporary position. At least his "taste for natural history might certainly be transferred to that point [Sault Ste. Marie] where the opportunity for discovery was the greatest."[14] Late in June, 1822, Schoolcraft left Buffalo, New York, by schooner for the Upper Lakes post.

Sault Ste. Marie was an ideal location for the new Indian Agency headquarters. Located on the rapids of the St. Marys River, it was naturally accessible to the Indians living in the northern Great Lakes area and for centuries had been a center of Indian settlement. In addition to a large band of Chippewa who resided permanently on the riverbank near the rapids, thousands of their fellow tribesmen gathered there every autumn to fish the rapids which teemed with whitefish.

The Sault had long been a favorite camping site for white men as well. Governor Samuel Champlain's young protegé, Etienne Brulé, stopped there as early as 1622 and later in the century, Father Jacques Marquette founded a mission near the foot of the rapids. The French government later utilized the strategic location to establish a permanent fort to control travel on the river. Fur trading companies made the Sault a rendezvous for traders who wintered among the Indian tribes west of Lake Superior.

The village continued to prosper after the British wrested control of North America from the French in 1760. By the close of the eighteenth century, several hundred families lived there—English, French, and half-breeds—as well as several bands of Chippewa. British influence remained paramount in the Sault even after the Untied States gained its possession in 1796. In fact, during the War of 1812, most of the Sault Ste. Marie's white settlers, and Indians as well, remained loyal to the British.

After the War of 1812, the U.S. government made plans to build a fort at the site and sent Governor Lewis Cass to Sault Ste. Marie in 1820 for a meeting with Indian leaders to reassert the American claim to Indian land along the St. Marys River preliminary to construction of the fort.[15] The negotiations took a dramatic turn when Sassaba, an influential Chippewa chief, denounced Cass and his mission and retired to his lodge where he hoisted the "Union Jack" in a crowning act of defiance. Acting courageously and decisively, Cass went alone to the lodge of the belligerent chief and removed the alien flag. Influential local citizens pacified Sassaba before blood was shed and the meeting ended with an agreeable settlement.[16]

As a part of the directive establishing a military post at the Sault, the War Department also authorized the placement of an Indian agency at the site, having jurisdiction over the tribes living in the northern parts of Michigan, Wisconsin, and Minnesota. Henry Rowe Schoolcraft became the new agent at the post and accepted the difficult task of gaining the Indians' cooperation as he carried out the enforcement of the policies of the Indian Bureau. In order to check British influence in the Lake Superior region, the War Department directed Schoolcraft to enforce rigidly the regulations which excluded foreign citizens from the fur trade, and to discourage visits of American Indians to British fur posts in Canada. The Department also warned him of the dangers of the growing rift between the Chippewa and Sioux and the effect intertribal warfare might have upon the safety of frontier settlements. Finally, Schoolcraft was told to prepare the Indians of northern Michigan for a peaceful cession of their land to the United States.[17]

The greatest handicap under which the young agent worked was his ignorance of the culture of the Indians. Although he had visited Indian villages on his expeditions to Missouri and Arkansas in 1818, and explored much of the territory within his agency on the Cass Expedition of 1820, he knew very little about the Indian and his ways. In fact, his boyhood experiences had given him the prejudiced stereotype of the Indian as a "bloodthirsty savage." He had listened often to the accounts of his father and other pioneers and they described their parts in the battles with the Iroquois during the American Revolution. "In these recitals," Schoolcraft wrote later, "the Indian was depicted as the very impersonation of evil—a sort of wild demon, who delighted in nothing so much as blood and murder. It was always represented as a meritorious act...to have killed one of them . . . thus ridding the land of a cruel and unnatural race, in whom all feelings of pity, justice, and mercy were supposed to be obliterated."[18]

Lewis Cass was probably the first to spark Schoolcraft's interest in studying Indian culture. Like Thomas Jefferson, Albert Gallatin, and a host of other statesmen, Cass was deeply concerned about the plight of the American Indian. As Governor and Superintendent of Indian Affairs of the Michigan Territory, he witnessed firsthand the disastrous impact of advancing white settlement upon the aborigine and his tribal customs. Although Cass was powerless to curb such forces, he did recognize the great traditions of the North American Indians and the urgent need to collect and preserve accurate data on their history and culture before it was lost forever. He personally undertook to collect such information from the Indian and persistently advocated a nationwide federal program to accomplish these ends.

In 1822, Governor Cass circulated a lengthy questionnaire, *Inquiries Respecting the History, Traditions, Languages, Manners, Customs and Religion...of the Indians Living Within the United States,* which he sent to Indian agents, fur traders, and others in a position to observe the Indian and his customs. It sought data on traditions, religion, government, medicine, music, birth, death and marriage customs, language, dances, and "peculiar societies."[19]

Schoolcraft received a copy of the document from Governor Cass when he stopped at Detroit enroute to his new post at Sault Ste. Marie. He was so impressed with the questionnaire and Cass' plan for further research on the Indian that he resolved to "be a laborer in this new field." He was convinced that the "analytical approach" which he had used to study natural history "could be used to study the Indian, especially his language."[20]

As soon as he arrived at the Sault, Schoolcraft plunged into the work of studying his new charges. He first concentrated on the Chippewa language because of its importance in his work. With the help of Indians, interpreters, and the half-Indian Johnston family, he compiled an "Ojibway Vocabulary" and prepared declension tables of verbs of the Chippewa tongue. Within a few years, he had won national recognition for his research on the grammar of the Ojibway.[21]

As his contacts with the Indians increased, so did his curiosity about other aspects of the Indian's culture. His childhood image of the "brutal savage" disappeared and in its place he came to have great understanding and sympathy for the Indian. "It was amazing," he wrote in his diary in 1824, "to find him [Indian] a man capable of feelings and affections, with a heart open to the wants and responsive to the ties of social life. But the surprise reached its acme," he continued, "when I found him whiling away a part of the tedium of his long winter evenings in relating tales and legends for the amusement of the lodge circle."[22]

The legends of the Chippewa tribes fascinated the Indian agent and in the years that followed, he collected scores of such lodge stories. While thus engaged, he conducted what was probably the first "oral history" program in America. He interviewed hundreds of Indians who visited in his agency headquarters in large numbers every summer, and took advantage of his numerous exploring expeditions into the interior to talk to isolated natives. Treaty meetings at Prairie du Chien, Butte de Morts, and Fond du Lac also brought him in contact with prominent Indian leaders.[23]

Despite Schoolcraft's dedicated study of Indian culture and the unexcelled opportunities afforded him by his positions as Indian Agent and from 1836-1841 as Superintendent of Indian Affairs, he could have accomplished little without the assistance of the Johnston family of Sault Ste. Marie. From the day of his arrival at this frontier post in 1822 until he resigned from the Indian Bureau in 1841, he was closely associated with this remarkable family. They were his chief informants on Indian life and deserved substantial credit for furnishing Schoolcraft with the data and legends which he later published.

John Johnston was a strong self-sufficient individual who wielded great influence among the settlers, fur traders, and Indians in the Lake Superior area.[24] Born in 1762 in Ireland, the son of a wealthy Scotch-Irish landowner, he came to North America in 1790 to obtain a government position in Canada. He abandoned these plans, however, and accepted an invitation from an old family friend, Andrew Tod, a prominent Montreal fur trader, to go to Mackinac Island. Although he planned to spend only a few months there helping Tod with his business, Johnston eagerly accepted his friend's offer to manage for a season the trading post at LaPointe on Chequamegon Bay, Lake Superior.

Johnston's first winter at LaPointe would have been enough to discourage even a seasoned fur trader. His assistants deserted him as winter approached and took with them most of his supplies and equipment. Rival fur traders refused to help him and the Indians at LaPointe could offer no assistance for they too faced starvation. It is a credit to Johnston's stamina and ingenuity that he survived the winter at all. Yet, not only did he manage to provide for his own needs, but by spring, he was conducting a profitable trade with the Indians.

Despite the first season's difficulties, Johnston decided not to return to Montreal. He was struck by the wild beauty of Lake Superior and was enjoying his first taste of success as a trader. Furthermore, he had fallen in love with Ozha-guscoday-way-quay, the youngest daughter of Waub Ojeeg, the famous and powerful chief of the Chippewa at LaPointe. Although the chief distrusted the motives of most fur traders, he consented to Johnston's offer of marriage. The following year, Johnston took his young bride, whom he renamed Susan, to Sault Ste. Marie where he established a temporary home on the bank of the St. Marys River. Within a few years his own fur trading business became so lucrative that he built a beautiful house which stood for decades as the finest in the whole "north country."

He outfitted scores of independent fur traders and, through his wife's influence, did a thriving business directly with the Indians along the St. Marys River and the southern shore of Lake Superior. In fact, Johnston was so successful in the fur trade that he received offers to join forces with the powerful Hudson's Bay Fur Company, and later its arch rival, the American Fur Company.[25] His connections in government circles in Montreal and Quebec also proved indispensable to him. By 1814, his assets were valued at nearly $100,000, a respectable fortune for an "independent" trader.[26]

The War of 1812 had ruinous effects upon Johnston's business interests. Because of his active loyalty to England, American troops pillaged his home and fur depot, destroying property valued at over $40,000. Although their action violated international law, Johnston was never able to collect damages from either the United States or British governments, and never fully recovered from this financial setback.[27]

In the years following the war, Johnston did manage to win the approbation of the United States government, even though he still remained friendly with the English. On several occasions, he saved the lives of American government officials by warning them of impending Indian attack. In 1820, during his absence, his wife and children helped avert an attack on Governor Cass by hostile Indians. The United States government later rewarded the Johnstons by granting them land near the Sault.[28]

The children of John Johnston and his Indian wife, Susan, played prominent roles in the development of the Lake Superior region. Lewis Saurin, the eldest of the eight children, became a midshipman in the English navy and later was employed by the British Indian Department at Sandwich, Ontario. His untimely death in 1825 at the age of thirty-three ended his promising career. George, born in 1796, held numerous positions in the United States Bureau of Indian Affairs. He served as government interpreter to the Chippewa, and subagent to the tribes at LaPointe, Wisconsin, and Traverse City, Michigan. He attended several important Indian treaty meetings as an agent of the United States. William and John, the youngest sons, were engaged in the fur trade and noteworthy in the early history of Sault Ste. Marie. Four daughters, Jane, Eliza, Charlotte, and Anna Marie were equally active in the affairs of the frontier community. [29]

The Johnston children received their early education at home, for there were no schools at the Sault. Their father tutored them in literature, history, and the classics, and procured a large private library with a variety of source material for their studies. Mrs. Johnston also participated actively in the education of her children. In addition to the routine household instruction she gave her daughters, Mrs. Johnston indoctrinated all of the children in the customs and beliefs of her people, the Ojibway or Chippewa. They learned legendary tribal traditions, particularly the exploits of their grandfather, Waub Ojeeg, and his father, Ma Mongazida. All of the children learned to speak Chippewa fluently; in fact, Eliza used the native tongue exclusively, as did her mother. Later the formal education of the children was completed in private schools in Canada.

When Schoolcraft arrived at Sault Ste. Marie in 1822, the Johnstons invited him to stay at their home until his own quarters were built. He eagerly accepted the invitation for he disliked living at the nearby garrison and he warmed to the hospitality of John Johnston. In the following months, a close friendship developed between the two men as they found many common interests. The bond between them is reflected in the correspondence which they carried on until Johnston's death in 1828.

Schoolcraft established a more permanent relationship with the Johnston family in 1823 when he married Jane, their attractive and talented eldest daughter. Born in 1800, Jane became her father's favorite child and received special attention from him. She went with him often on business trips to Detroit, Montreal, and Quebec and in 1809, he took her to Ireland to complete her formal education. Schoolcraft found her well read in history and literature and eager to help him with his Indian studies.

After her marriage, Jane gained notoriety as the "northern Pocahontas" and was sought after wherever she traveled. Some writers, including Anna B. Jameson, Harriet Martineau, and Thomas McKenney made special trips to the Schoolcraft home to meet her. All were charmed by her gracious behavior, her wit, and her intelligence.

She helped her husband constantly in his research. She acted often as his interpreter and checked his studies of the Chippewa language. She assisted with the production of the *Literary Voyager* and contributed many of its interesting poems, accounts, and legends on the Indian. Jane Schoolcraft was handicapped by frequent illness and never fully recovered from the death of her first son, William Henry, who died at the age of two years in 1827. She bore a daughter and another son before her death in 1841.

Jane's brother, George, became one of Schoolcraft's closest friends and advisers during their thirty-year working relationship. He served in various official capacities on the Indian agent's staff and on the recommendation of Schoolcraft, he was appointed to other positions in the Indian Bureau. After Schoolcraft left his frontier post, he relied heavily upon George to corroborate data on Chippewa culture and to collect additional lore from Indians. The existing correspondence from 1825 to 1855 between the two men reveals the debt of gratitude owed George Johnston by Schoolcraft.[30]

The other Johnstons served Schoolcraft often as his interpreters and individually interviewed scores of visiting Indians.[31] Schoolcraft's most valuable informant, however, of all the Johnstons was Mrs. John Johnston, his full-blooded Chippewa mother-in-law. Although she gave up many of her tribal customs when she married, she never lost contact with her family or members of her tribe. She visited them often and always opened her home in Sault Ste. Marie to visiting Indian relatives and friends.

As a result of her lineal connection to Waub Ojeeg, the powerful chief of the Chippewa of LaPointe, and her marriage to a highly respected fur trader, Mrs. Johnston was esteemed by her fellow tribe members in the Lake Superior region, particularly those Chippewa living near Sault Ste.

Marie. She counseled them often and on many occasions she intervened in their deliberations. As previously noted, she helped persuade the Indians to negotiate with Lewis Cass in 1820. Thomas McKenney, Commissioner of Indian Affairs from 1824 to 1830, paid tribute to her in 1826 when he wrote: "As to influence, there is no chief in the Chippewa nation who exercises it, when it is necessary for her to do so with equal success."[32]

Mrs. John Johnston was always ready to aid Schoolcraft in his studies of the Indian. Using her sons and daughters as interpreters, for she could neither read, write, nor speak English, she gave him invaluable information about the Chippewa—their history, customs, and beliefs. She alone supplied accurate biographical accounts of Waub Ojeeg, Ma Mongazida, and other deceased Indian leaders. She recounted also many legends which had been passed on to her by Waub Ojeeg, who was known as "the greatest storyteller of his tribe."

Mrs. Johnston often arranged private meetings between Schoolcraft and certain politically important Indian leaders of the day. With her urging, they permitted the Indian agent to attend many of their ceremonies, some of which were secret and limited to tribal membership. From these contacts, Schoolcraft gathered for publication information on the history of the Chippewa, hitherto unknown, and enlarged his collection of lodge stories.

Mrs. Johnston's brother, Wayishkee or "The First-born," who resided with his own wife and children at the Sault, gave Schoolcraft much "reliable traditionary information about the Chippewa." Shingabawossin, the ruling chief of the Sault Indians, whose father, Naidosagee, had been noted in his day for his repertoire of "imaginary legends, allegories, tales and fables," also contributed material for the *Literary Voyager*.

Schoolcraft's debt to the Johnston family is best stated in the entry of his private journal, 28 July 1822: "I have in fact stumbled, as it were, on the only family in Northwest America who could in Indian lore have acted as my guide, philosopher, and friend."[33]

The Literary Voyager

No. 1.   Sault Ste. Marie   December 1826

CHIPPEWAS

This tribe of North American Indians, has been known from our earliest history, as a powerful body of hunters and warriors. They spread over a large area of the continent. They provided men, distinguished for bravery. The Indian pronunciation of this term is Od-jib-wa, the meaning of which is lost in antiquity. Like Illini & Lenopi, it appears to designate men. Some assert it to be, men *who are men,* basing this interpretation on the Indian term for nervous vitality. They speak the Algonquin language, in the purest form of it. Tradition asserts that they came from the East. The language has the greatest affinities with the Mohican of New England.

They had wars with fierce tribes whom they call Mundwas, Assiguns, and Nodowas. The French, on the exploration of this part of Canada about 1641 found them seated at the falls on the outlet of lake Superior, called Ba-wa-teeg, cascades or rapids. To this term, the missionaries put the nominative of Sainte Mary, in reference to the Virgin Mary. As this term is feminine, its abbreviation required that fact to be noticed, which is done by the abbreviation Ste. in Sault de Ste. Marie, or Sault Ste. Marie. The correction of the French dictionary demanded the letter "l" to be dropped in the word *Sault.* But with respect to geographical names, long in use, the "l" was retained. Hence Charlevoix and his contemporaries and followers, retain the abbreviation *Sault Ste. Marie.* The Indian term, is declined in the following manner—

Noun   Bauwateeg
Prepositional Bauwa-tiag-in, at, on, by.

LAKE SUPERIOR

Several unsuccessful attempts, were made by the French to name this lake. The Chippewas call it, Gitchi-gumi, or sea-water, since it is their term also, for the Sea. The Algonquin particle gum, denotes a liquid, without regard to quantity, as Mushcowagumi, signifies strong water spirits, as sometimes written, in connection with the particle *mee* making *gumee* or gomee. When the ocean is meant to be referred to, the adjective is duplicated; making the sense, great-great water—a not uncommon mode of marking the superlative, in Indian languages. A pretty, & distinctive name for this lake, may be made by prefixing this syllable Al, to Iomi, meaning Algonquin Lakes.

We are surprised, in examining these languages, to find the concrete made up of the simple. Has it not been so, with all languages? The ancients thought air, earth, and water to be elements. But the progress of chemistry has dispelled this delusion. Should philosophers be surprised to find a similar process in analyzing these wild languages?

The French were impressed with the magnitude of this lake, and bestowed, at separate times, several names on it, but none of them have survived. Taking the particle goma, to stand for a large body of water, and placing before it, the first syllable of the generic name for the tribes living on it, we have the more poetic and equally truthful term *Algoma*.

PEBON & SEEGWUN (WINTER & SPRING)[35]
A CHIPPEWA ALLEGORY

An old man was sitting alone in his lodge, by the side of a frozen stream. It was the close of winter, & his fire was almost out. He appeared very old, and very desolate. His locks were white with age, and he trembled at every joint. Day after day he sat in solitude, & he heard nothing but the sounds of the tempest, sweeping before it, the new fallen snow.

One day as his fire was just dying, a handsome young man approached & entered his dwelling. His cheeks were red with the blood of youth, his eyes sparkled with animation, and a smile played upon his lips. He walked with a light & quick step. His forehead was bound round with a wreath of sweet grass, in the place of a warrior's frontlet, and he carried a bunch of flowers in his hand.

"Ah, my son," said the old man, "I am happy to see you. Come in. Come, tell me of your adventures, and what strange lands you have been to see. Let us pass the night together. I will tell you of my powers & exploits, and what I can perform. You shall do the same. And we will amuse ourselves."

He then drew from his sack a curiously wrought antique pipe, and having filled it with tobacco, rendered mild by an admixture of leaves, handed it to his guest. When this ceremony was concluded, they began to speak.

"I blow my breath," said the old man, "and the streams stand still. The water becomes stiff & hard as clear stone." "I breathe," said the young man, "and flowers spring up, all over the plains."

"I shake my locks," retorted the old man, "and snow covers the land. The leaves fall from the trees at my command & my breath blows them away. The birds get up from the water, & fly to a distant land. The animals hide themselves from my breath, and the very ground becomes as hard as flint."

"I shake my ringlets," rejoined the young man, "And warm showers of soft rain fall upon the earth. The plants lift up their heads out of the earth, like the eyes of children first opening in the morning. My voice recalls the birds. The warmth of my breath unlocks the stream. Music fills the groves, wherever I walk, and all nature rejoices."

At length the sun began to rise. A gentle warmth came over the place. The tongue of the old man became silent. The robin and bluebird began to sing on the top of the lodge. The stream began to murmur by the door, and the fragrance of growing herbs & flowers came softly on the vernal breeze.

Daylight fully revealed to the young man the character of his entertainer. When he looked upon him, he had the white visage of ice of Peboan.[36] Streams began to flow from his eyes. As the sun increased he gradually grew less & less in stature, and soon had melted completely away. Nothing remained on the place of his lodge fire but the miskodeed[37] a small white flower, with a pink border, which is one of the earliest species in a northern Spring.

SUPERSTITIONS

The Manito Tree: There is a hill called by the French *La Butte de Terre* and by the Indians *Sat-tooke-wang* situated a mile from the Sault Ste. Marie, to which an Indian path connects. In the intermediate distance near this path formerly stood a mountain ash tree Amer. Sorbus, [Sorbus americana] from which the Indian tradition says, there issued a sound resembling that possessed by their own drum, during one of the most calm & cloudless days which have ever been witnessed in the country. This occurrence took place long before the French had appeared in their country, & in consequence of it, they supposed it the residence of one of their local manitos. From that time they began to deposit at its foot, small green twigs & bows, whenever they passed along that path, so that in time a high pile of these small limbs was collected. During a violent storm the tree itself blew down, & has since entirely decayed, but the spot was recollected & the practice continued to the present time, & would probably have been continued as long as any of the tribe had remained to observe it, had not an accident put a stop to it. In order to procure wood from *La Butte de Terre* for the use of the garrison, Col. [Hugh] Brady issued an order for cutting a road 60 feet wide from the cantonement to the hill. This road passed over the site of the tree, & the men without knowing it, removed the consecrated pile.—

Sault Ste. Marie   July 16, 1822.

Superstition respecting Mines: There is a superstition prevalent among the Chippewas & other Indian tribes, in regard to mines, the effects of which we have long witnessed, without knowing the cause. They are firmly impressed with a belief, that if they discover a mine to the whites, they shall be punished with untimely death, or overtaken by some disastrous circumstances.[38] This opinion, although certainly not a strange one, to be held by a barbarous race, has nevertheless its origin in the transactions of an era, which is not only well defined, but celebrated, in the history of the discovery and settlement of America. It is very well known that gold & silver were the objects which led Cortez & Pizarro into the interior of South America, & ultimately to conquer the country & to tax & destroy its inhabitants. It is equally certain that to escape the scenes of cruelty & oppression, which followed the conquest of the Spanish invaders, many tribes & fragments of tribes fled towards the north, those nearest the scenes of the greatest atrocity pressing upon the remote, who in turn fled before the more cultivated tribes of the South. In this way many tribes who originally passed from the north along the Pacific to the Gulph of California & thence over all New Spain, were returned towards the north over the plains of Texas & the valley of the Mississippi. Among these tribes, the traditions of the Chippewas says, that their ancestors came, leaving on their way portions of their number, who have deviated from the purity of their language, the sites of their mines &

4

minerals. Hence also the reason why they suppose all mineral sub-
stances bought for, & taken from their country are to be converted
into gold or silver.

Manito Poles: Whenever an Indian falls sick, his friends set up a
sapling or pole from which the bark has been peeled, near to his lodge.
Upon this a dog, sometimes a ribband, a piece of red scarlet, or silver
band, is tied, as an offering to the manito, to propitiate his wrath, &
relieve the suffering man. These poles are often painted with red, or
other stripes. A few days after our arrival, one of the officers of the
detachment, having occasion for some poles to put up a tent, sent a
soldier to take down, one of these manito poles, which stood near by.
But it was soon observed by the Indians and reclaimed. They placed
it in the same spot which it had been.

To Our Correspondent, Leelinau[39]

The letter of our female correspondent "Leelinau," we have perused
with pleasure, and recommend to the attention of our readers. The
simplicity and artlessness of her details of Indian life and opinions, do
not constitute the exclusive attraction of her letter. It develops truths
connected with the investigation of Indian history and traditions. We
solicit further communications from the same source, and feel ex-
tremely desirous for the promised "pretty songs and stories." Her
lines under Rosa, possess chasteness in the selection of her images,
united to a pleasing versification.

Character of Aboriginal Historical Tradition

To the Editor of the Literary Voyager

Sir,

   I have learnt from a correspondent of yours, a very distant relation
of mine, your intention of publishing a Paper; the utility and true
meaning of which, has been fully explained to me by my friend. And
as you are willing to admit contributors from amongst my countrymen and women, it has induced me to take the liberty of addressing
you, and by this means I hope you will be able to form a more correct
opinion of the ideas peculiar to the Ojibways. And at the same time,

my own humble thoughts shall no longer be breathed out to the moaning of the winds through our dark forests;—sounds which have formed a lonely response to my plaints, since I became a poor Orphan.

Alas! no longer does my kind, fond mother braid up my black hair with ribbons which the good white people gave me, because, they said, I was always willing and ready in my duties to my dear father, when he returned weary and thirsty from the chase. And oh! my father, you can no longer kiss away the starting tear before it falls from my cheek; nor kindly ask, What grieves your little girl! But ye, my parents, are now both gone to the pleasant land of spirits! Still your poor child feels as though you were near, nor will she ever forget the good advice you have taught her!

I hope Sir, you will forgive this digression. If you had known my parents personally, I am sure you would have loved them. My father was descended from one of the most ancient and respected leaders of the Ojibway bands—long before the white people had it in their power to distinguish an Indian by placing a piece of silver, in the shape of a medal on his breast. However, my father had one of those marks of distinction given him; but he only estimated it as being a visible proof of amity between his nation and that of the whites, and thought himself bound by it, to observe a strict attention to the duties of friendship; taking care that it should not be his fault, if it did not continue to be reciprocal. That medal my father used to wear, and it is the only relic I still retain in memory of him, who first taught me how to esteem and appreciate white people. He often told me that you had a right knowledge of every thing, and that you knew the truth, because you had things past and present written down in books, and were able to relate, from them, the great and noble actions of your forefathers, without variation.

Now, the stories I have heard related by old persons in my nation, cannot be so true, because they sometimes forget certain parts, and then thinking themselves obliged to fill up the vacancy by their own sensible remarks and experience, but it seems to me, much oftener by their fertile flights of imagination and if one person retains the truth, they have deviated, and so the history of my country has become almost wholly fabulous?

O Sir, if I could write myself, (and not trouble my generous relation as I now do) I think I should strive to make you acquainted with all our ancient traditions and customs without deceiving you in the least—just as I heard them from my father. Tell me sir, if it is true, that our great father (The President) is going to cause a house to be built, and a man in black to come and instruct us poor Indians, and if we are to dwell in that house. My heart danced with joy, and my eyes filled with tears of gratitude, when I first heard what is before us.

I have often wished to know the reason and source of many things, which have come immediately under my own observation, and not knowing how to account for such curious circumstances, I have said, "it must be a Manito." But you white people say that there is but one true, great, and good God; then I feel a deep sense of regret that I do not know more of that good Spirit, and what I ought to do to please him. But when the man in black comes to teach us poor young ignorant people the right way, I shall know better; and when I can write, I shall not forget to send you all the pretty songs and stories my mother used to teach me—to be put in your paper. Until that time shall arrive Sir, I must wish you health.

TRANCE

Suspended respiration, or apparent death, is not common among the Chippewa Indians. Some cases have however happened.

Wauwaunishkum or Gitshee Gausinee of Montreal river, after being sick a short time, died, or it turned out, fell into a trance. He was a good hunter, & among other things left a gun. His widow still flattered herself he was not dead, & thought by feeling his head she felt some signs of life. After four days had elapsed he came to life, & lived many years afterwards—He related the following story to his companions—That after his death he traveled on towards the pleasant country, which is the Indian heaven, but having no gun could get nothing to eat, & he at last determined to go back for his gun—On his way back, he met many Indians, men & women, who were heavy laden with skins & meat, one of these men gave him a gun, a squaw gave him a small kettle, still he kept on, determined to go back for his own gun which had not been buried with him. When he came to the place, where he had died he could see nothing but a great fire, which spread in every direction. He knew not what to do, but at last determined to jump through it, thinking big forests were on the other side.

7

And in this effort he awoke, & found himself alive.—Formerly it had been customary to bury many articles with the dead including all his effects, clothing etc & even presents of food etc from friends wishing them well. After this the practice was discontinued.

By an *Ojibway Female* Pen
To Sisters on a Walk In the Garden, After a Shower

Come, sisters come! the shower's past,
The garden walks are drying fast,
The Sun's bright beams are seen again,
And nought within, can now detain.
The rain drops tremble on the leaves,
Or drip expiring, from the eaves:
But soon the cool and balmy air,
Shall dry the gems that sparkle there,
With whisp'ring breath shake ev'ry spray,
And scatter every cloud away.

Thus sisters! shall the breeze of hope,
Through sorrows clouds a vista ope;
Thus, shall affliction's surly blast,
By faith's bright calm be still'd at last;
Thus, pain and care,—the tear and sigh,
Be chased from every dewy eye;
And life's mix'd scene itself, but cease,
To show us realms of light and peace.

Rosa[40]

Ancient Ojibway Custom
Diana Disrobed

It was a custom formerly prevalent among the Chippewas of the Lake to observe the following ceremony. After they had finished planting their corn & it began to shoot up into stalks, the wife chose an evening for walking around the field, past at dusk, dragging behind her, her petticoat, being completely naked. After making the circuit of the field, she came again to the lodge from which she started. This was thought to insure a fruitful & abundant crop.—and to preserve the corn from the ravages of worms & vermin.

No. 1. December 1826

Ancient Chippewa Capitol

I have heard much of La Pointe, as the French called, or Chegoimegon in lake Superior, situated near its west end, or head. The Chippewa, & their friends, the old traders & *Boisbrules,* & Canadians, are never tired of telling of it. All their great men of old times, are located there. It was there, that their Mudjekewis, or chief Ruler lived, & as some relate, that an eternal fire, was kept. There lived, in comparatively modern time, Waub Ojeeg, & Andaigweos, and there still lives one of their descendants in Gitchee Waishkee, the Great First-born, or as he is familiarly called Pezhickee, or the Buffalo—a chief decorated with British insignia. His band is estimated, at 118 souls, of whom 34 are adult males, 41 females, & 43 children. Mizi, the Catfish, one of the heads of families of his band, who had figured about here, this summer, is not a chief, but a speaker, which gives him some eclat. He is a sort of petty trader too, being credited with little adventures of goods by a dealer on the opposite, or British shores.

Do the Indians Refuse to Eat Certain Animals?

There are few animals which the Indians reject as food. On this subject they literally fulfil, in part, the declaration of Paul "that every creature of God is food; & nothing to be refused;" but I fear, the poor creatures in these straits, do anything but show the true spirit of "thanksgiving" in which this admonition is given. The truth is the calls of hunger are often so pressing, to these northern Indians, that anything in the shape of animal life, that will keep soul and body together, is eaten in times of their greatest wants. A striking instance of this kind, has just occurred, in the case of a horse killed in the public service. The animal had, to use the teamster's phrase, been snagged, & was obliged to be shot. To prevent unpleasant effects in hot summer weather, the carcass was buried in the sand; but as soon as the numerous bands of Indians, who are encamped here, learned the fact, they dug up the animal, which was however, no wise diseased, & took it to their camps for food.

Soangagezhick

A tragic occurrence took place last night, at the head of the portage, resulting in the death of a Chippewa, which is believed to be wholly

9

attributable to the use of ardent spirits, in the Indian camps. As soon as I heard the facts, and not knowing to what lengths the spirit of retaliation might go, I requested of Col. Brady a few men with a non-commissioned officer, & proceeded, taking my interpreter along, to the spot. The portage road winds along about a mile near the rapids, & all the way, within the full sound of the roaring water, when it opens on a green, which is the ancient camping ground, at the head of the falls. A foot path leads still higher, by clumps of bushes & copsewood, to the borders, of a shallow bay, where in a small opening, I abruptly came to the body of the murdered man. He was a Chippewa from the interior called Soan-ga-ge-zhick, or the Strong Sky. He had been laid out, by his relatives, & dressed in his best apparel, with a kind of cap of blue cloth and a fillet round his head. His lodge, occupied by his widow and three small children, stood near. On examination, he had been stabbed in several places, deeply in both thighs. These wounds might not have proved fatal; but there was a subsequent blow, with a small tomahawk, upon his forehead, above the left eye. He was entirely dead, and had been found so, on searching for him at night, by his wife. It appeared that he had been drinking during the evening and night, with an Indian half-breed of the Chippewa River, of the name of Gaulthier. This fellow, finding he had killed him, had taken his canoe and fled. Both had been intoxicated. I directed the body to be interred, at the public charge, on the ancient burial hill of the Chippewas, near the cantonment. The usual shroud, on such occasions, is a new blanket; a grave was dug, and the body very carefully dressed, laid in the coffin, beside the grave. Before the lid was fastened, an aged Indian came forward, and pronounced a funeral oration. He recited the traits of his character. He addressed the dead man direct. He told him that he had reached the end of his journey first, that they should all follow him soon to the land of the dead, and again meet. He gave him directions for his journey. He offered a brief admonition of dangers. He bid him adieu. The brother of the deceased then stept forward, and, having removed the head-dress of the slain man, pulled out some locks of hair as a memento. The head-dress was then carefully replaced, the lid of the coffin fastened, and the corpse let down into the ground. Two stout poles were then laid over the open grave. The brother approached the widow and stood still. The orator then addressed a few words to both, telling the survivor to perform a brother's part by the widow. He then took her by the hand, and led her carefully across the open grave, over the two poles. This closed the ceremony, and the grave was then filled, and the crowd of white and red men dispersed. At night a small flickering fire was built by the Indian relatives of the murdered man, at the head of the grave.[41]

STANDARD OF VALUE

In 1821 a reward of $30 was offered by the commanding officer at Chicago for the apprehension of a deserter. The Pottowattomies of that post brought him in, and claimed the reward. They received a certificate from the proper officer for the amount. Thirty dollars was a sum that brought no definite idea to their minds. There were five claimants, and they immediately sat down, & divided the amount and brought it, into raccoons skins. It was not until this had been done that each one could *appreciate* his reward.

CATHERINE BROWN

This daughter of the Cherokees, was one of the most remarkable females which the missionary spirit & enterprize of the American church of Christ, has brought to light in the Aboriginal race. Born in 1800 in a beautiful part of the proverbially beautiful Cherokee country, she was brought up by her parents, with more than the customary attention & care, till arriving at the threshold of womanhood. Possessing an attractive person & gentle manner, she was early noticed, by strangers visiting the country, and had even learned to speak the English language. She had also learned from Moravian missionaries, who came there as early as 1800, the elements of spelling, & a little reading. This, was the only advantage she had gained, in education, when in 1816, the American Board [for Foreign Missions] planted a regular mission & boarding school, in the Cherokee country. Catherine was one of these first pupils, and soon became the first convert to Christianity in that tribe. Readily the elements of English literature, she pressed the principles of the bible, zealously, on her kinspeople. She was the means of her father's & mother's, and two brothers conversion; and became in truth the means of the awakening & reformation of the Cherokee nation.

Her moral character was ever, irreproachable. She had the clearest views of bible truth, and had the faculty of translating into the

Cherokee tongue, with an inestimable grace. No heady denunciation proceeded from her lips, but she was ever, a produced example of truth, she taught to others. She was entrusted with the school established at Creek Path. She had a beautiful hand & conversed in a spirited style. At least six years, she remained the light of the mission. Her company was eagerly sought at the different stations & villages. But she developed consumptive symptoms. Finding the necessary attention could not be secured in the Cherokee country, she was removed, by a skillful physician to his home at Huntsville, Alabama. But the disease was too deeply seated for human skills, she lingered a time, in lasting Christian perfection, at every phase, and finally sank to her rest, in the month of July, 1824, with her mother & relatives around her, by whom her remains were taken to her native village for interring.

> On Catherine's grave when spring returns
> The natives wild wood flowers shall place,
> With odours sweet & colors fair,
> Fair emblems of that moral glow,
> That marked her life & character,
> And shall virtues e'er in—own.
>
> And oft the pious step shall go
> To seek the spot where Catherine lies
> And hopes, from her example, show
> To lend her people to the skies.
>
> Here, faith & hope, shall renew her breath,
> Here, confidence, her lamp relume,
> Here, resignation, smile at death,
> And beauty triumph at the truth.
>
> She led the way, with modest air
> Rejoicing, she this day should see,
> That op'ed a path, to worlds so fair,
> For her loved tribe, the Tsallakee.

Mr. Anderson, her biographer says,[42] "They (the Cherokees) possess a language that is said to be more precise and powerful, than any, into which learning has poured richness of thought, or genius breathed the enchantments of fancy and eloquence" (p. 14). In another place (p. 156) he observes—"The Indian languages are said to have no word that signifies *spirit,* nor the pagan Indians any idea of a spiritual existence." The difficulty, it is apprehended, is not that they have no term for spiritual existence, but that these spirits are destitute of holiness. Their name for God, or the *great being above,* is, Ga-lun-lah-ti-a-hi, and he is represented by the common interpreters, falsely, it is thought, instead of appearing on earth in material form.

Her brother, David Brown in one of his letters (p. 67) terms the Cherokee "the sweet language of Tsallakee." We are without the etymology of this word. Adair says, Cher, means fire, but leaves out that term. The word Tsallakee, reminds us of Hakewelder's, Tsalla-servi.

Theories of converting Indians, requires caution. "The position" continues the biographer of Catherine Brown, "that civilization must precede christianity, is so unsupported by facts—is so opposed to all experience, that one would think it could hardly be advanced by enlightened philosophers, or received by rational christians. What is civilization?" We believe christianity & civilization, act, as one together, as cause or effect. One cannot exist without the other.

Civilization is a system of restraints, by which old habits and opinions are put off, and new ones taken up. To enter the private dwelling, or mission school; to put on the clothing of civilized man; to take meals, retire, rise, wash the hands and face, attend stated duties or labors, every day at fixed hours; or to become familiarized to the dwellings, fields, and ordinary economy of civil life, are among the essential elements of civilization. An Indian, cannot long be subjected to these restraints, without being influenced by them.

Without some previous discipline of this kind, no Indian youth taken from the forest, is likely to become civilized, and we are free to declare our opinion that little success will attend the preaching of christianity to uncivilized savage men. Yet civilization without christianity may be a failure. The lessons of experience on this subject ought not to be forgotten. No sects were ever animated with more zeal, in this pious work, than the Jesuit fathers. They followed the Indians in their hunting excursions, and attended them in their seasons of feasting and fasting, want and warfare, enduring perils and hardships,

which prove a total abstraction from all selfish, or personal con-
siderations. But they effected no radical change in the vital moral
habits or customs of the Indians. They imposed but few restraints;
they taught no new methods of economy, and in fact, notwithstanding
their own reports, they made few real conversions to christianity.
They left the Indian, where they found him a savage in the forest;
and after the lapse of a century, a vague tradition among some of the
tribes, where they laboured, and here and there, a crucifix, worn
chiefly, as an ornament, and not as a symbol, is all that often remains
in modern times, to attest their labors.

> Ask for St. Mary's, or for St. Ignace,
> The *name* is all the traveier can trace.

EXPERIMENT ON THE CAUSE OF TEMPERANCE WITH THE INDIANS OF NORTH AMERICA

Every effort to restrain the use or introduction of ardent spirits among
the Indians, is commendable. It is useless to lament the existence of
evils, if we do not set ourselves about remedying them. Every person,
who has paid the least attention to this subject, must be aware, how
difficult it is to enforce, either corporate or congressional laws, against
practices which custom sanctions and convenience dictates. Custom is
often more powerful than law, even in a land of law, and the axioms
of reason and right, are in vain urged in opposition to pecuniary interest. This is emphatically true on the frontiers, and it is of the
frontiers I purpose speaking. Popular errors demand popular correc-
tives, but it requires time to introduce them, and time to enable them
to operate. Rash and hasty measures would only involve public officers in difficulties, which are easier excited than quelled. Where much
remains to be accomplished, it is better to do a little that is practi-
cable, than to attempt much which cannot be effected. Such at least,
were the views, which have been acted on, in a public assembly of the
Indian tribes, at Prairie du Chien in 1825.

Individual examples operate with great force upon the minds of the
Indian. Every good man, whether in place, or out of place, has it in
his power to do much to correct the prevalent practice of selling
liquor to this unfortunate portion of the human race. Indians as they
are, their condition would be much improved, if, in our intercourse

with them, our citizens could be induced uniformly to think like philanthropists, to feel like Christians, or to act like men.

At the conclusion of the treaty just held, at which, the principal tribes on the Upper Mississippi were assembled, a public feast was given, by the United States Commissioners to the whole collected body of the tribes, who had assisted in the proceedings. By addressing the appetites of men under such circumstances, the good feeling which they had displayed in the settlement of their territorial boundaries, was sought to be confirmed, and to be left associated in their minds with pleasing recollections. Such feasts, in which each is invited "to take his portion," and rejoice in his labor, are not uncommon on like occasions. But this, particularly commends itself to our notice, by its being a feast enjoyed without *ardent spirits*.

To prove to the Indians the truth of what has often been asserted, that it is not the *value* of the liquor to our government that prevents its being liberally distributed on public occasions, but solely, the dread of its injurious consequences to them, an ample quantity of whiskey was also brought into the centre of the bower under which the tribes were peacefully partaking of meat and bread. The weather being very warm, they were supplied, during the repast, with a beverage consisting of sugar and water. After the repast was finished, every one of the red guests appeared anxious for the arrival of the moment, when, as they expected, the whiskey also, would be distributed. While all eyes were intent, on the movement, a party of employees came, bearing a considerable number of large, new capacious tin kettles, such as are used in the trade, filled to the brim with high wines, setting them down carefully, in a row. At this moment the Commissioners came forward, and one of them addressed them, in a few brief and pertinent remarks, on the bad effects of drinking; the baneful influence it had already exerted upon their character as nations, and as individuals; and the still worse effects that must be expected to ensue, if so pernicious a habit was persevered in. When their attention had been fully called to the subject, and every eye was directed to the speaker, the vessels of whiskey, standing in front of them, were overturned and spilled out upon the grass. The liquid might be seen filling the inequalities in its surface, forming pools or passing off beneath the rustic benches.

But the Indian is a stolid man. He sat moveless. He did understand the lesson taught. Wonder, astonishment, and disappointment might be seen depicted in the fixed countenances of the multitude, as they sat beholding this novel and unexpected & unaccountable proceeding. Some may doubt the wisdom of this kind of teaching. Its good effects, however, cannot, it is believed, but be felt. Many will reflect upon it, perhaps when they return to their villages, and the deeper they reflect the more sensible must they become of the considerate and benevolent motives which could lead to such a step. Precepts are feeble, where nothing but precepts are employed. And would all who have the power, exert it, to present to the observation of this people, examples of disinterestedness, justice, and magnanimity; or lessons of virtue and temperance, we should witness improvements in their moral and physical condition, which are, by many deemed impracticable. The drawback is, that the Indian is not a man of moral sensibilities.

Prairie du Chien. 1825   Abieca[43]

FRIENDLY SPEECH OF SHINGABOWOSSIN TO HIS BAND[44]

I have told you your great father, is powerful and kind. If you look around, you will see that within a very few years he has sent his soldiers to build forts at Green Bay, at Tipisagee, St. Peter's, & Council Hills on the Missouri, where he feeds & clothes a great many people. It is not a year since he established this last post, & one at Sagana.—Is not this an evidence of his strength?

When the British King, wishes any of your lands, he puts his foot upon them, and says it is mine! He holds no treaty with you to buy it, nor does he pay you for it.

But when your American father wants your lands, he sends some of his civil chiefs to buy it, and to agree with you on the price of it. Is not this an evidence of his justice?—

Look at your brothers the Saganaws, the Ottoways, the Pottowattomies, the Menomonies & the Foxes! Do they not every year receive large sums of money from him? This is for the lands they have sold.

Whenever your American father has sent soldiers, he has sent an Agent to see to your wants, to feed you when you are hungry; to clothe you when you are naked, and to give you drink when you are thirsty. Is this not an evidence of his kind big heart?

Look among your brothers, who are under the American government. Have they not plenty? You go sometimes to visit them. Have
you not seen that they have horses, & cattle, guns & traps, fine
blankets and clothes, and every thing else to make them happy?
Where do they get these things? From the Americans. You have also
begun to feel the benefit of Abieca,[45] a young friend, coming here. Is
there one person among you who can get up & say that he has ever
turned a deaf ear to you? Has he ever sent any of you hungry from
his door?
April 1823—

ANNAMEA GEEZHITOUD[46]
LITERARY MEN SHOULD RESPECT THE SABBATH

The following may be advanced as proof of the influence of the Sabbath on the intellectual character of man. It had been proclaimed by
a periodical opposed to the administration of Sir Robt. Peel, that his
excessive labors were impairing his health. This insinuation is replied
to in these words by the Editor of the Standard. "Sir Robt. does not
work 7 days in a week which to me is full assurance that his work
will not impair his health." Then he adds these memorable words—
our experience may be taken for something—for a newspaper editor's
life is no time of idleness; we hold it to be an incontravertible fact
that no man ever suffered in his health, by the hardest conscientious
labor during six days of the week—But we will add for the instruction of the young & studious to whom we particularly address this
remark, that during many years observation of *intellectual laborers,*
we never knew a man to work 7 days in the week, who did not kill
himself & his mind.

LINES, ON COMING TO RESIDE AT SAULT STE. MARIE

Remote from all the world—away—away.
Where lone St. Mary's waters foam and play
And broad Superior's mountains, rising high
In pictured forms, imprint the northern sky;
Far, far from every haunt the heart holds dear,
What can engage the contemplative, *here.*
Long mazes past, where lakes and streams resound

17

I seem to stand at earth's remotest bound.
I turn me round to ask if such scenes bless,
Such wilds, such wastes; and Truth replies yes! yes!
Man on himself can turn, and he shall find,
Food for the noblest gifts of heart and mind.

If cities, towns, and men, be absent
Its very loneliness and woods are dear.
The wild magnificence that marks the zone,
Gives to the mind new vigor, power and tone
Above, the clouds, with light and fleecy bound,
Deck the bright arch, & scatter gems around,
Below, the winding waters devious play,
Superior's self proud trembling on its way
In crystal torrents, that with fretful roar,
With murmur's speed along St. Mary's shore;
By day I hear these falls their tale recite,
And on my ear, they murmur all the night,
It is the diapason deep whose organ forms,
Are lightnings, thunders, winds, tornadoes, storms.

Above, around expressive vastness reigns,
And nature stalks a giant o'er the plains;
Gems glitter from the heavens, a starry road,
Where spreads the typic footprints of a God.
To view this sight, the painted Indian stands,
And tells how giants big, once filled the lands,
And oft of heroes speaks, once killed in wars,
By necromancers were transformed to stars.
Or demi-gods, who hold divided bound,
With Monedo himself, & deals thunders round.
A poor philosopher is he, on Newton's plan,
He reasons just of what he knows of man
And nature; and e'er kindly takes
God on his side, and deems that He partakes
In all his wigwam lore & care & fondly deems
His grim old priest oft speaks his will in dreams.
Talk to this man,—a Turk or a Chinese,
Are not more erudite in Heaven's decrees.

No. 1. December 1826

Or how the world began, and why & when
Kind Heaven made beasts, & birds, the world and men.

Turn we from nature to her forest child,
What see we, but the human form run wild
A man of dreams and fancies,—to his hopes,
Thoughts, signs, beliefs, a world wide vistas opes.
Why burns the grave light, on yon burial height,
At midnight,—it is to give his wandering spirit light.
Why dance, the auroral vapors in the skies,
They are the ghosts of his own paradise,
Who joy in realms of compensating bliss
For miseries endured, through life, in this.

On civic toils he looks as something sore
Which white-men have brought over to the shore,
And letters, and all that,—but for himself his fears,
Are but for want of beavers, elks and bears;
Ah, wanderer of the woods!—if far thy steps have trod
Far from all social light & letters, truth and God,
In the lone region where thou now dost stray,
With ocean-lakes to mark the ample way.
Yet is there hope for thee, in noble cares,
That point, with heavenly faith, above the stars.
There is a sympathy that ever burns,
For the lone step that from its error turns.
Heaven is not, in its fiats to be blamed,
Nor made the Indian simply to be damned.
If far thou art, O savage of the plain
Where arts and light & truth & letters reign,
Yet in that very want, a cause may seem,
That makest thou thyself, an ample theme,
Despite the lonesomeness of place and line,
And much I err, or else thou shall be mine.

Ekiega

The Vine and Oak[47]

A vine was growing beside a thrifty oak, and had just reached that
height at which it requires support. "Oak," said the vine, "bend your

19

trunk so that you may be a support to me." "My support," replied
the oak, "is naturally yours, and you may rely on my strength to
bear you up, but I am too large and too solid to bend. Put your arms
around me, my pretty vine, and I will manfully support and cherish
you, if you have an ambition to climb, even as high as the clouds.
While I thus hold you up, you will ornament my rough trunk with
your pretty green leaves and shining scarlet berries. They will be as
frontlets to my head, and I shall stand in the forest like a glorious
warrior, with all his plumes. We were made by the Master of Life to
grow together, that by our union the weak should be made strong,
and the strong render aid to the weak."

"But I wish to grow *independently*," said the vine, "why cannot
you twine around me, and let me grow up straight, and not be a mere
dependant upon *you*." "Nature," answered the oak, "did not *so* design it. It is impossible that you should grow to any height *alone*, and
if you try it, the winds and rain, if not your own weight, will bring
you to the ground. Neither is it proper for you to run your arms
hither and yon, among the trees. The trees will begin to say—"It is
not my vine—it is a stranger—get thee gone, I will not cherish thee."
By this time thou wilt be so entangled among the different branches,
that thou cantst not get back to the oak; and nobody will *then* admire thee, or pity thee."

"Ah me," said the vine, "let me escape from such a destiny;" and
with this, she twined herself around the oak, and they both grew and
flourished happily together.

THE RAINBOW
A CHIPPEWA ALLEGORY

A prophet lived near the falls of St. Mary's, for many years. He was now an old man, and he was regarded, as one who ever lived in close communion with the Great Spirit. He could read the clouds. He could understand every mystic sound. There was no hard question put to him, which he could not answer. He was a wise man. He had made mysteries his study, till all mysteries were plain to him. He possessed a small stature, & a thin body, legs & arms. Some thought his bones were hollow, like a bird's, he was so light. But his eyes were black and sparkling & his voice had a peculiar intonation. His hair was long, and as white as snow and the older he became, the longer and whiter it grew.

He had been married, when young, and had a daughter named Olla, whom he tenderly loved and cherished, and to whom he had taught some of his songs & arts. Olla was the pride of her village, modest kind and respectful, she became an example and pattern for the village maidens. But she was taken very ill one day, in her father's lodge & died, before any relief could be given, while, it was observed, that a rainbow from the Falls, rested on the top of her father's lodge. Whether it was this incident, or some early dream, that had given the name of the Rainbow, or Hair of the Sun, is not known. Many thought that the girl had been miraculously transferred to the skies, & he sided with this opinion, for he had often seen her sitting & gazing intently at the sky.

He had a little drum, the rim of which, was covered with heiroglyphics, and a curious stick, upon the end of which, was tied a string of a deer's hoofs, which made a sharp noise at every stroke, and he sang with a solemn tone:

> Hear my drum, ye spirit high,
> Earth & water, air and sky
> Ye, to me, are common ground,

> Spirits, listen to my sound
> Walking, creeping, running, flying,
> Near or distant, living, dying,
> Ye, are but the powers I sway,
> Hearken, to my solemn lay
> I compel you, hither—come,
> Hear my rattle—hear my drum
> From your highest circles come.

The bark rolls of his lodge had been lifted up, while he uttered this incantation, & the gorgeous red and green rays of the rainbow, rested directly on his hair. They seemed to be mingled with his long hair, and when he put up his hands, to disentangle it, he found himself rising by a strong attraction, and he rose up to the skies, by this light & silky filaments.

Very long & bright silver ledges, & open green plains, were the first things that presented themselves. And he saw that smoke which issued from this in large sheets of blue & pink & white, from the clouds surrounded by the globe. He was kindly received at the chief's lodge, where a wide circle of red chairs were occupied by chiefs who sat smoking their pipes. He saw, that at every exhalation of the smoke there were bright little flames, and this is the cause of what we call *annung*, or the stars.

Very soon his daughter stood before him, in a beautiful robe of pale green. "Father," said she, "I have expected you a long time. I told those tall & majestic chiefs yonder, that if they would untie, & let down the silken threads of the long sashes, which bind their robes, you could come up. But father, it is not here, as with you. We do not want. We do not hunger; we do not die. There are no marriages here; there are no births. We are all spirits. Our senses are high. We can hear the slightest whisper from below; & see the smallest thing. It seems the distance is not broader than my hand. Your drum & rattles sound plainly & the words of your songs are instantly understood."

"There is no war, or bloodshed here. There is no hunting. The animals come out of the woods unhunted. The sharp rocks are only shadows. We can walk through them. Everything is pleasing, & we are happy here. The Great Spirit, only visits us by angels. He dwells in yonder region, surrounded by bright stars."

"I see you have brought along, your drum & rattles. Sit down on yonder green bank, by the crystal waters & play a while. I go to report your coming, to a higher power." The music he made was of unusual sweetness, & when he looked, the instruments had changed into silver. He had played but a little while then came on the waters, stately white swans, & birds of bright plumage, & when he looked around him, he saw droves of deer & antelopes & elks, in peaceful gambols.

Where he took his seat, he remained sitting; and this is the reason of that bright planet, called the Evening & the Morning Star. It is only one of the little ornaments which surround the Great Spirit, & when it rains, in heaven, you behold those bright lights, we call Dancing Ghosts, by white men, aurora borealis, & blazing stars.

Listener, wouldst thou be instructed behold the deaths of the aged prophet Miscogandic-a-ub, & his daughter Olla, and their translation to the abodes of the Great Spirit.

WAUB OJEEG OR

THE TRADITION OF THE OUTAGAMI AND

CHIPPEWA HISTORY NO. 1

The following tradition is related by Oshaguscodawaqua,[48] a female of Chegoimegon on lake Superior, the ancient capitol of the Chippewa nation. A grand daughter of the reigning chief of that place,—possessing a high opinion of the origin, bravery and position of her tribe, with every means of learning their traditions, full credence appears to be due, to the general incidents of her narrative. Having at sixteen become the wife of a gentleman of information, polite manners, and warm susceptibility, she was removed, at this early age to the comforts and conveniences of a civilized dwelling—a change of life which gives the narrative a striking similarity to that of Pochahontas. But, although raising a family of children, by this union, she remained firmly attached to the traditions of her people, and continued to speak only the Indian language.

Chippewa tradition affirms, that their ancient council fire—and capitol was on the island of Chegoimegon in lake Superior. They were governed by a chief officer, called Mujekiwis, who was, always, the eldest son of the reigning OGIMAU, or Chief. At this place, they maintained their ancient mode of worshipping the Great Spirit, whom they propitiated by hymns, prayers, and sacrifices, offered especially to the Sun.

The chieftain's wife had long been settled in the line of the **Totem** of the Reindeer, and the mark of this animal was the authoritative sign of the ruler, wherever it was placed. Waub Ojeeg succeeded by birth to this authority about the middle of the seventeenth century. But his father, Ma Mongazida, did not die and give up the entire rule, till a later period. The French supremacy had then been long established, and rumors only began to be heard, of the coming of the Saganooks—the Algonquin name for the British. The latter were at first distasteful to the Indians, who passionately loved the French rule, & the French manners. Braddock's defeat in 1755, and the various triumphs by which the French & Indians had kept back the British colonies, were events heard by the lake Indians, with pleasure.

The fall of Quebec in 1759, of Montreal in 1760, and of all Canada, in a short time following, was dreadful news to the Indians. They did not believe, what they did not like, and determined not to give up the country without a struggle. Pontiac placed himself at the head of their effort, and made most vigorous & bloody efforts, to repel the Saxon race. But these efforts proved vain, & the year 1763, saw the whole nation power prostrate, & the British flag triumphant.

Ma Mongazida, did not die, & give up his authority at Chegoimegon till about 1790. This event, left Waub Ojeeg the sole rulership, a right to which he lent claim by his vigors and skill as a huntsman, & his bravery & diplomatic talents as a warrior.

The same period saw a young gentleman from the north of Ireland, come to the capitol of British North America, to recruit the rental of an exhausted estate, by engaging in the half Quixotic and chivalrous enterprize of the Fur Trade. The tale is simply told. A few years saw the ardent son of Erin at the death bed of Ma Mongazida, and the fast friend of his brave and talented son, Waub Ojeeg.

Centuries have elapsed since hostilities commenced between the Chippewas and Sioux. They lived on terms of amity, so long as the abundance of game rendered precise limits an object of little consequence, and while their leaders saw no cause to apprehend that they were, at a future day, to become rivals; and earn the hated name of *Nadowasieu*, or Rattlesnake in the grass.

The Sioux felt little uneasiness at the inroads made by the Chip-

pewas into those remote and woody borders of their extensive hunting grounds, which stretch around the head of lake Superior. They
had few inducements to penetrate far towards the north, while the
fertility and mildness of the Mississippi plains, and the facility of
procuring food operated to confine their villages to the banks of that
river. But when their new neighbors, on that quarter, began to sally
from their inhospitable woods into the plains, in quest of the larger
animals, which at certain seasons, quit the forests altogether, and
when their numbers and power began to make them formidable; it is
reasonable to conclude that a strong jealousy was created.

Hostilities once begun, there is nothing in the institutions of Indian
society, that would induce them to preserve any connected details of
its impelling causes. Nor should we feel surprized that these original
causes of enmity have been nearly forgotten, when we reflect, that
every season has been supplying fresh fuel to the flame.

Tradition represents that the Chippewa bands who first settled
themselves at Shogwoinecan,[49] or *LaPointe,* on lake Superior, had the
lands bestowed upon them by the Outagamis,[50] who were temporarily
fixed there; but had resolved on migrating further west. A greater
proof of the perfect amity existing between these two tribes could not,
perhaps, be given. They were, in fact, descended from a common
ethnological stock, spoke dialects of the same language, and practised
the same general customs. They were brother-tribes. Whenever, they
met, they lived together as one and the same people, and mutually
sympathized in each other's reverses, or well-being.[51]

Between the Outagamis and Sioux, a good understanding existed,
which had been matured, till, it seems, mutual aid was expected to be
given to each other, in cases of emergency. Through this alliance, the
Chippewas were well received on their first arrival at LaPointe, and
for many years afterwards the Sioux regarded them as friends. Offices
of civility were exchanged, and visits and intermarriages took place;
and they tacitly acceded to the arrangement made by the Outagamis,
respecting the lands.

In process of time the intimacy, which had bound together the
Outagamis and Chippewas, during their weak and migratory state,
cooled; they no longer looked upon each other as friends, and they
soon quarrelled for the possession of a country, which they had, at
first, shared in amity.

The Outagamis, who had retired from the lake to the table lands intermediate between the Mississippi, lake Michigan, and lake Superior, envying the increasing power and strength of the Chippewa settlement at LaPointe, commenced inroads into their best hunting grounds, depriving them of means of subsistence which had become, more important, as their numbers were augmented.

Before resenting this conduct, the Chippewa chiefs held a council, and determined on demanding an explanation. When the messengers employed on this mission entered the camp of the Outagamis, they found them in council, and immediately proclaimed their errand.

They asked the Outagamis, what wrong, or injustice they had ever done them; they declared that the lands they occupied had been freely given their fathers by the Outagamis; and that they had made no encroachments. They concluded by saying, that they had always regarded each other as brothers; that they were so in reality, they would be very sorry to shed their blood on the graves of their forefathers, who had been so generous towards them. But, that if they did not put a stop to their young men's depredations, they were determined to defend themselves, as several of their young hunters had already been decoyed and slain.

The Outagamis answered; that they (the Chippewas) were the aggressors; that they had wrongfully wrested the lands from their forefathers; and that far from stopping the attempts which had been already made, they would encourage their young men in every effort to drive them off the land. The council broke up with this threat, and the messengers, with difficulty, returned to their town.

Open hostilities soon commenced on either side, and although the Sioux sided with the Outagamis, and united with them in battle, yet the Chippewas totally defeated them in several bloody recontres; they broke up their villages at the Flambeau and Ottowa lakes, and compelled the remnant of the tribe to quit the sources of the Wisconsin, Chippewa, and Bad rivers, and ultimately to seek shelter behind their allies, the Sioux.

In this war the Chippewas were first brought into contact with the Sioux, and from that period they have scarcely ever enjoyed a moment's peace.[52]

RESIGNATION

How hard to teach the heart, opprest with grief,
Amid gay, worldly scenes, to find relief;

And the long cherish'd bliss we had in view,
To banish from the mind where first it grew!
But Faith, in time, can sweetly soothe the soul,
And Resignation hold a mild control;
The mind may then resume a proper tone,
And calmly think on hopes forever flown.

Rosa.

CUSTOMS OF DISTANT NATIONS

Herodotus says, of the ancient Thracians, that "the most honorable life with them, is a life of indolence; the most contemptible, that of a husbandman. Their supreme delight is war and plunder."

The same remark may be made of some dozen tribes of our North American Indians; but what is the conclusion to be drawn? Surely no reasonable man will hence infer, that the American Indians were originally Thracians. Yet one half of the deductions of zealous theorists rest on no better foundations.

Coincidences have been observed in the manners and customs of barbarous nations, situated in distant parts of the world, and living in eras not less distant; between whom, however, there is not the least probability that there ever existed any connection by the ties of blood, or commerce.

Such coincidences must in fact, be deemed purely accidental; and ought to be regarded only, as evidences of the identity of the human species.

TYPE OF MEXICAN CIVILIZATION

Nothing is more manifest on reading the "Conquest of Mexico,"[53] than that the character and attainments of the Mexicans are exalted far above the reality, to enhance the fame of Cortez, and give an air of splendor to the conquest. Exact observation was not a characteristic of that age, and dense as was the population of the Mexican provinces, the numbers were undoubtedly over-rated. In the same spirit, every stone cottage, or log dwelling was a palace, and every petty independent chief of a band of hunters, a prince in jewelled robes. That the Mexicans had made considerable advances towards civilization, is unquestionably true; but that these advances were totally

27

over-rated by Cortez and his interested followers and retainers, appears to us equally undeniable.

The cacique of Tempoala, being the first dignitary who paid his respects personally to Cortez, is described as wearing a robe of cotton flung over his naked body, enriched with various jewels and pendants, which were also observed upon his person. In plain parlance, he wore a cotton blanket, with ear bobs.

"Canoes" and "periogues of wood," were their usual means of conveyance by water. The "books" mentioned at page 100, were deer skins, well dressed and folded up accurately, after having been painted with hieroglyphics; and were probably very little different from the paintings upon buffalo robes, made by the Pawnees, Osages, and other south-western tribes of the present day.

The Mexicans, he says, at p. 93 "had rings in their ears and lips," which, though they were of gold, were a deformity instead of an ornament.

By the nearest route from St. Juan de Ulua to Mexico was 180 leagues. The journey was performed by Montezuma's runners, or scouts, within seven days, to and from, being 25 to 26 leagues per day. This excited the wonder and incredulity of the sluggish Spaniards, who were credulous enough on other occasions. But would certainly be considered an ordinary day's journey by our northern tribes, and by no means a proper effort for such an extraordinary emergency.

Distance they counted by time, like our Indians. "A Sun, was a day's journey."

"One of the points, continues De Solis, of his (Cortez) embassy, and the principal motive which the king (Charles V.) had to offer his friendship to Montezuma, was the obligation Christian princes lay under, to oppose the errors of idolatry; and the desire he had to instruct him in the knowledge of the truth, and to help him to get rid of the slavery of the devil."

The first presents sent to Cortez by Montezuma, were cotton cloths, plumes, bows, arrows, and targets, precious stones, collars of gold, representations of birds and beasts of the same metal, a plate of gold resembling the sun, and another of similar dimensions resembling the moon. It was the fatal error of this unfortunate monarch to exhibit his wealth to the Spaniards. It was precisely what they were in search of, and the arrival of these rich presents may be seized upon, as the date from which Cortez resolved upon the conquest.

No. 2. December 1826

ANIMOOSE

Pork I love, but drinks I hate
Oh, what joy to lick a plate.

Sir,

Oh, master, why did you whip me! I cannot help thinking that you have done me injustice in the punishment inflicted, for my having chawed up your literary papers. I confess I did not know the value of these papers. Dog, as I am, and subject to lie at your feet, in your office, I did not know that these papers embraced your conjugations of Indian verbs. Besides, you know my youth and indiscretion. When I saw you lock your door, and go to dinner, my gnawing teeth, impelled me to try their use, and I seized the papers, and chewed and tore them up, without any idea of my indiscretion, and without knowing what trouble it would put you to, to procure other examples. Remember how easy it will be for you to set your big red nosed interpreter, Yarns,[54] to furnish other data; and if he cannot do it, correctly or acceptably, as I suspect, you know the favor with which we both, are regarded at the Erin Hall,[55] where the subject of the Indian languages can be so profitably discussed. I beg you, therefore to excuse my ignorance, and for the future I promise you on the word of a pretty little Pointer, not to meddle with your literary papers, of any sort. I was originally named after the great Pontiac, and it shall ever be my aim to imitate his noble deeds, and to bite and snarl only at the oppressive and unjust.[56]

Ponti

SHINGABA WOSSIN

This dignified & majestic man, is a son of Naidosagee of the reigning Crane Totem.[57] He is First chief of the band of St. Mary's, and is one of the most respected and influential men in the Chippewa nation. He is some six feet three inches in height and well proportioned, erect in his carriage, and of a commanding and dignified aspect. Of a turn of mind deliberate and thoughtful, he is at once respectful and respected. He knows how to be cheerful without descending to frivolity. A man of policy, as well as bravery, he was early sensible that the prosperity of his nation depended upon peace, and an assiduous attention to their ordinary occupations. He gave up much of his time, in late years in attending the public councils convened under the authority of government to secure a permanent peace, with the tribes with whom the Chippewas are at variance. While quite a youth, he joined several war parties against the Sioux, although living upwards of 400 miles from the lines. And he fought & conquered under Waub Ojeeg, at the great battle at the Falls of the St. Croix,[58] which terminated the feud forever between the Chippewas and Foxes & Sauks.

His father Naidosagee was at once the chief and the legendary chronicler of his tribe. And with him died much of their most reliable traditionary information. Naidosagee, was also noted for the imaginary legends, allegories, tales and fables, which he related for the amusement of the young, some traces of which will appear in these sketches. With shrewdness enough to manage the concerns of the band, he was a voluptuary. He married four wives, three of whom were sisters, by whom collectively he had twenty children. Each of the male children, in time deemed himself, a legitimate ruling chief, and attached to himself some followers. The harmony of the band was thus, impaired & in a measure, destroyed, and the ancient village weakened, by migrations to new regions and its once heavy population scattered along the waters of the basin of lake Superior & the river St. Mary.

Shingaba Wossin gradually drew upon himself the principal notice, and was at last looked up to, and universally acknowledged as the first man—a distinction he well merited by the qualities both of his head and heart. His good sense enabled him to point out the proper course to be pursued by his band, in their emergencies. And his kindness, and benevolence rendered him beloved. He was always the organ of expressing the wants of his band, and the medium through which they received advice and aid from the officers of government.

Shingaba Wossin attended and signed the great *treaty of limits* at Prairie du Chien in 1825, and it was at his suggestion that the Commissioners inserted a provision for calling together the body of the Chippewa nation at Fond du Lac, at the head of lake Superior in 1826, in order formally and fully to explain the important stipulations of the treaty, and procure their assent to them. In this step, he acted like a prudent ruler, who, was sensible of the true interests of his tribe, and at the same time, moral boldness of conduct. In attending the treaty at the head of lake Superior he sought to make provision for the half breed relatives, of the nation by granting each a section of land. This measure originated entirely with him, and it was urged on the ground, that this class of people, were in reality their best and most constant friends, and gave them aid and succor in time of need & necessity. He also advised his people to set apart the thousand dollar annuity—the only annuity they receive—for the purpose of a school for their children to be located at St. Mary's river. He was not a strong advocate for school knowledge in his own family, but remarked that some of the Chippewas might wish it, and it would, in the end, do good. He also went to the council at Butte de Morts in 1827,[59] and thus by his presence and aid, completed the settlement of the Chippewa and Indian boundaries with the Sioux, Menomenees, Winnebagoes & Wabnokies.[60]

OJIBWAY TRADITIONS

The following replies to the historical inquiries issued by Gov. Cass in 1822, are from the pen of John Johnston Esqr. It is to be regretted, from his long residence in the country and intimate knowledge of Indian history, that he had proceeded no farther, in his proposed task. 1. What is the original name of the Tribe? Ans. Ojibway. 2. What is the present name? The same. 3. What is the meaning of the name in English? The origin of the name lost in antiquity. 4th they are related to the Ottaways, who were the agricultural branch of the Tribe —the Ojibways and Miamies were the warrior classes. 5th This quest can be no otherwise answered, than that they all came from one country to the Southard and Westard of this: That a part of the nation yet called Otagahmeg, or in English Otagama, who were there precursors, are still settled near the sources of the Mississippi. 6th Their earliest tradition is of their wars with the Otagamies, whose country they in part possessed themselves of, and retain to this day. 7th They came from Southward, progressed to the country they now occupy. 8th This question is answered in reply to Quest. 6 & 7.[61]

ALGIC LANGUAGE

There is, among the generic native languages in this part of America, one, for which its peculiar idiom provides the above epithet, although the more popular and *limited* one, of Algonquin is generally prefixed to it. This language appears to be the parent of most of the Indian dialects east of the Mississippi, obscured as these dialects are, by various appellations, and corrupted by tribal peculiarities of sound and sense. It abounds with open vowel sounds; is very copious; and has a measured nervous flow, something inclining to pompous, but rather pleasing and agreeable from the frequent recurrence of liquids and vowels. In its grammatical forms it ranks with the class of languages, which writers on universal grammar have denominated transpositive, from the frequency of its transformations, and the variety of its inflections. Its substantives and verbs are wonderfully rich in these transpositive forms, and embrace, in the course of their grammatical evolutions, & inserted syllables, the powers and properties of all the other parts of speech, which, like the filling upon a loom, serve to make up the complex texture of their synthetical forms. Nevertheless it possesses adjectives, pronouns, adverbs, prepositions, articles, and conjunctions, which are not only used (*to preserve our figure*) as *filling* to the verbs and substantives, but are also employed in their disjunctive and elementary forms.

Considered in all its accidents, and reciprocal changes, and they are certainly very numerous, it is a language which would not seem to have been involved or invented by any of the numerous nations by which it is now spoken. Neither the state of society in which they live, or have ever lived, so far as history extends, nor their physical wants or moral habits, seem to demand a language so varied in its pronominal range & combinations, and so complex in its syntax. The greatest defect which it discloses, is the want of gender to its pronouns, which are merely animate, and inanimates. He, & she, are the same. I, and you, are visiological. Standing like an unfinished edifice amidst barbaric wastes, there appears sufficient before the eye, to show that it is abnormal and has never been reformed, & reduced to regular rules of science but it wants the polish, proportions & chiselling. That the language is susceptible of this polish, and capable of bold and energetic combinations, through which philosophy might pour the richness of thought, and genius breathe the enchantments of poesy and eloquence, is the opinion of some, who have directed their study, to the unravelling of its grammatical involutions, and the comprehension of its recondite principles.

There are orientalisms—probably Asiatic-isms. It seems literally buried under the grammatical rubbish of accumulativeness. Where such a people should have received such a language, is the most inexplicable consideration which the subject presents. Can it be traced among the fixed, or erratic hordes of northern Asia? It is useless to look to the harsh consonantal dialects of Greenland, or to the gutteral and impoverished tongue of the frigid Esquimaux, in which love has no range for the expression of its emotions, or hatred for the modified utterance of its dislike.

Hermes

TO THE BRAVE,
WHO FELL IN THE WAR OF 1812

On Niagara's banks, they sleep,
And in Erie's stormy deep;
Where the rapid Wabash glides,
On Ontario's warlike sides;
By the deep where Lawrence fell,
Or in lone Moravian dell;
On the field where Pike was slain,
At Sandusky—at Champlain;
There the bones of heroes rest,
Honor'd, loved, lamented, blest.

Lake Dunmore 1815.[62]

CONUNDRUMS

What letters of the alphabet, form the name of a river in South Carolina? Ans. P.D. Peedee.

What generals of Greece & the American Revolutionary army, by a union of these names, constitute the name of an Indian tribe? Ans. Leonidas. Oneida.

When did a wagon crush the western Indians? Ans. When Gen. Wayne drove over them at Maumee.

THE BIRCHEN CANOE

In the region of lakes where the blue waters sleep
  My beautiful fabric was built;
Light cedars supported its weight on the deep,
  And its sides with the sunbeams are gilt.

33

The bright leafy bark of the betula[63] tree,
    A flexible sheathing provides;
And the fir's thready roots drew the parts to agree,
    And bound down its high swelling sides.

No compass or gavel was used in the bark,
    No art but the simplest degree;
But the structure was finished and trim to remark,
    And as light as a sylph's could be.

Its rim was with tender young roots woven round,
    Like a pattern of wicker-work rare;
And it pressed on the waves with as lightsome a bound,
    As a basket suspended in air.

The heavens in their brightness and glory below,
    Were reflected quite plain to the view;
And it moved like a swan—with as graceful a show,
    My beautiful birchen canoe.

The trees on the shore as I glided along,
    Seemed rushing a contrary way;
And my voyagers lightened their toil with a song,
    That caused every heart to be gay.

And still as I floated by rock and by shell
    My bark raised a murmur aloud;
And it danced on the waves as they rose and they fell,
    Like a fay on a bright summer cloud.

I thought as I pass'd o'er the liquid expanse,
    With the landscape in smiling array;
How blest I should be, if my life should advance,
    Thus tranquil and sweetly away.

The skies were serene, not a cloud was in sight,
    Not an angry surge beat on the shore,
And I gazed on the waters and then on the light,
    Till my vision could bear it no more.

No. 2. December 1826

Oh! long shall I think of those silver bright lakes,
   And the scenes they exposed to my view;
My friends—and the wishes I formed for their sakes
   And my bright yellow birchen canoe.
Novr. 12th 1825

The Literary Voyager

No. 3.   Sault Ste. Marie   January 1827

THE MEDA SOCIETY

The association of men in the Chippewa nation, calling themselves Medas, has enlisted my inquiry, and the result has led to some developments, which it is the object of this communication to mention. My attention was first especially called to this class of men, by seeing, in the hands of one of them, a thin quadrangular tubular piece of wood, covered with hieroglyphics, cut in the surface, and painted in strong colors of red, black, green and other colors. Finding that there were notations of songs, sung in this society, I requested the possesser to explain the device to me; but this, he intimated he could not do, to any other than a member of the Meda society. I then proposed myself as a member of that society agreed to observe all its requisites, having in my service a good interpreter of the language, requested that he might be permitted to attend, to explain the ceremonies. I at the same time, offered my office to be used, on the contemplated evening, for the initiation.

The evening having arrived, and the Indian Medas, being assembled, with their musicians, and sacred pouches under their arms, the door was carefully locked, and the window curtains closely put down. The master of ceremonies, Shingwauk, came forward and seated himself near me, laying his inscribed music-board, on my table, and commenced his songs, agreeably to the order of the notation, figure by figure. As these songs proceeded, he went through with the necromantic tricks, alluded to, by the words of the song. Thus small shells &c. were swallowed and re-gorged &c. and various transformations of legerdemain attempted. This series of operations, was sometimes adroitly performed, but generally, it required no little amount of endurance and patience to sit through the initiation honors. I was minute, however, in noting down the original words and translations of each song, with its pictographic signs. There was a flow in the song, which sometimes, reminded me of the poetic-prose of Gessner;[64] but however this was varied, the choruses, appeared to be permanent and regular, and the recurrence of certain syllables, supposed to have a sacred or hieratic meaning, was very remarkable. The first address to a spiritual being was made to the Deity or Great Spirit; all the others, to supposed spiritual mirage existences hovering around. It is purposed, in some future number to give you a detailed description of these nocturnal ceremonies.

Abieca.

THE ORIGIN OF THE ROBIN
AN ORAL ALLEGORY[65]

Spiritual gifts, are sought by the Chippewas through fasting. An old man had an only son, a fine promising lad, who had come to that age which is thought by the Chippewas to be most proper to make the long and final fast, that is to secure through life a guardian spirit, on whom future prosperity or adversity is to depend, and who forms and establishes the character of the faster to great or ignoble deeds.

This old man was ambitious that his son should surpass all others in whatever was deemed most wise and great amongst his tribe. And to fulfil his wishes, he thought it necessary that his son must fast a much longer time than any of those persons known for their great power or wisdom, whose fame he envied.

He therefore directed his son to prepare with great ceremony, for the important event. After he had been in the sweating lodge and bath several times, he ordered him to lie down upon a clean mat, in the little lodge expressly prepared for him, telling him, at the same time to bear himself like a man, and that at the expiration of *twelve* days, he should receive food, and the blessing of his father.

The lad carefully observed this injunction, laying with his face covered with perfect composure, awaiting those happy visitations which were to seal his good or ill fortune. His father visited him every morning regularly to encourage him to perseverance, expatiating at full length on the renown and honor that would attend him through life, if he accomplished the full term prescribed. To these admonitions the boy never answered, but lay without the least sign of unwillingness till the ninth day, when he addressed his father—"My father, my dreams are ominous of evil! May I break my fast now, and at a more propitious time, make a new fast?" The father answered—"My son, you know not what you ask! If you get up now,

37

all your glory will depart. Wait patiently a little longer. You have but three days yet to accomplish what I desire. You know, it is for your own good."

The son assented, and covering himself closer, he lay till the eleventh day, when he repeated his request to his father. The same answer was given him, by the old man, adding, that the next day he would himself prepare his first meal, and bring it to him. The boy remained silent, but lay like a skeleton. No one would have known he was living but by the gentle heaving of his breast.

The next morning the father, elated at having gained his end, prepared a repast for his son, and hastened to set it before him. On coming to the door, he was surprized to hear his son talking to himself. He stooped to listen, and looking through a small aperture, was more astonished when he beheld his son painted with vermillion on his breast, and in the act of finishing his work by laying on the paint as far as his hand could reach on his shoulders, saying at the same time:—"My father has ruined me, as a man; he would not listen to my request; he will now be the loser. I shall be forever happy in my new state, for I have been obedient to my parent; he alone will be the sufferer; for the Spirit is a just one, though not propitious to me. He has shown me pity, and now I must go."

At that moment the old man broke in, exclaiming, "My son! my son! do not leave me!" But his son with the quickness of a bird had flown up to the top of the lodge, and perched on the highest pole, a beautiful robin red-breast. He looked down on his father with pity beaming in his eyes, and told him, that he should always love to be near men's dwellings, that he should always be seen happy and contented by the constant cheerfulness and pleasure he would display, that he would still cheer his father by his songs, which would be some consolation to him for the loss of the glory he had expected; and that, although no longer a man, he should ever be the harbinger of peace and joy to the human race.

Leelinau

In the foregoing story, we recognize the pen of a female correspondent, to whom we have before been indebted. A descendant herself, by European parentage, and of the race whose manners and customs, she depicts, in these legends, they derive additional interest from her familiar knowledge of the Indian legendary mind, and the position she occupies between the European and aboriginal races. The tale, she observes illustrates the Indian custom of fasting to procure a personal spirit. The moral to be drawn from it, is perhaps the danger of ambition. We should not seek for unreasonable honors, nor take unusual means to attain them.

The spirit fasted for, by the young man, proving averse to him, he requests his father to exempt him from further fasting; and on being denied, gives a proof of filial obedience, by persevering in abstinence. In reward for this, the spirit, though unfavorable, partly relents, and instead of compelling the son to pass a miserable life in the human form, changes him to a bird, who will take a peculiar delight in lingering around the habitations of men.

WAUB OJEEG

OR

THE TRADITION OF THE OUTAGAMI AND CHIPPEWA HISTORY
No. 2

A short time before the breaking out of the Outagami war, and while the Sioux and Chippewas were on friendly terms, a Chippewa girl was demanded in marriage by a Sioux chief of some distinction in his nation, and she accordingly, became his wife, and bore two sons—the eldest of whom became the father of the celebrated Sioux chief, Wabasha. These boys were in their infancy, when hostilities began. These Outagamis and Sioux who had intermarried with Chippewas and lived with them, precipitately retired to their respective countries. Some of the Chippewa women went with their husbands, others remained.

Among the latter, was the wife of the Sioux chief; and the chief himself remained, for a short time; but animosity displaying itself in more daring acts every day, it was deemed best that a separation should take place.

In this step the parents of the wife concurred, and even urged the execution of it. As they did not think their child safe in the country of the Sioux, neither did they think their son-in-law safe in their own;—for if once he should incur the ill-will of the Chippewas, no authority could restrain them from murdering him. The two little boys were thought equally unsafe in the mother's hands, as the blood of the Sioux flowed in their veins. It was therefore determined they

39

should accompany the father. The relatives conducted them on their way till they were out of danger.

The young woman remained a long time inconsolable for the loss of her husband and children; and it was not till the lapse of several years, that she consented to become the wife of a Chippewa of Shogwaimican [Chequamegon], of the Totem of the Reindeer, being of the family who had borne sway at that place from the earliest times.

Her first child by this second marriage was Ma Mongazida, otherwise called Mashickeeoshe, who became a man of considerable note, and was the principal chief in authority at that place, when the Canadas fell into the possession of the English—an event that was distinctly remembered, from the part which the Indians of that quarter took in the wars which led to it.

'Mongazida was therefore a half-brother of the elder Sioux chief, the father of Wabasha; and in this manner the family became related to the Sioux; but 'Mongazida was not himself a Sioux, as has been erroneously asserted.

'Mongazida was strongly attached to the French, who were the first Europeans that ventured with goods into lake Superior. As a proof of this attachment, and at the same time, of the influence which they had acquired over the minds of the Indians, it deserves to be mentioned that he took a decided part in the warfare which was carried on against the English colonies, and was at Quebec with a party of warriors, when that place surrendered to the army under Gen. Wolfe. (Oct. 18, 1759)

He carried a short speech from Montcalm to his band, said to have been dictated by that general after receiving his mortal wound. At Quebec he first shook hands with the English, and he afterwards visited Sir William Johnson at Niagara, by whom he was well received and presented with a yellow gorget, and a broad belt of blue wampum with white figures.

The occasion of this visit formed an era in the affairs of LaPointe, which its inhabitants had cause to remember. For two years after the taking of old Mackinac by the Indians, no traders had visited that place. The convenience of this traffic was, even at that day, too highly estimated, not to make the Indians severely feel and regret the temporary loss of it. And it was to solicit that the English would send them traders, as the French had done, that 'Mongazida visited the Super-intendent General of Indian Affairs.

The belt and gorget were a long time preserved in the family. Waub Ojeeg took from the former, the wampum he employed to muster his war parties, till only a narrow strip remained. On his death, this strip and the gorget went to his younger brother Camudwa, who being overtaken by famine near the mouth of the Broulé river, was, with all his family, except a little girl, starved to death. With him these testimonies were lost.

Waub Ojeeg was the second son of 'Mongazida. An incident which occurred in his childhood is related as presaging his future eminence as a warrior. 'Mongazida generally went to make his fall hunts on the middle grounds towards the Sioux territory, taking with him all his near relatives, amounting usually to 20 persons, exclusive of children. Early one morning, while the young men were preparing for the chase, they were startled by the report of several shots, directed towards the lodge. As they had thought themselves in security, the first emotion was that of surprize, but they had scarcely time to fly to their arms when another volley was fired. This second volley wounded one man in the thigh, and killed a dog. 'Mongazida immediately sallied out, with his young men, and pronounced his name aloud in Sioux. He de-manded, if Wabasha or his brother were among the assailants. The firing instantly ceased—a pause ensued, when a tall figure in a war dress, with a profusion of feathers on his head, stepped forward and presented his hand. It was his half-brother. The Sioux peaceably followed their leader into the lodge, upon which they had the moment before directed their shots. At the moment the Sioux chief entered, where, it was necessary to stoop a little, he received a blow from a club wielded by a small boy who had placed himself near the door for that purpose. It was the young Waub Ojeeg. Wabasha, pleased with this early indication of courage, took the little lad in his arms, caressed him, and pronounced that he would become a brave man, and prove an inveterate enemy of the Sioux. These words were re-garded as prophetic.

The border warfare in which his father was constantly engaged, early initiated him in the arts and preparatory ceremonies, which pertain to the character of the warrior. While quite a youth he joined these war parties, and gave convincing proofs of his courage. Possessing a tall and commanding person, and evincing sense, shrewdness, and a dauntless behavior, he soon became a leader, and by his success fixed the eyes of the Chippewa bands upon himself, as the person destined to protect their frontiers against the inroads of a powerful enemy. He was seven times a leader against the Outagamis [sic] and Sioux. The eighth war party he mustered, went no farther than the environs of Ottowa lake, where he was met by a deputation of old men from that village, who advised him to return, saying, they wished repose. With this request he complied.[66]

Some Singular Customs of the Chippewas

The manners and customs of this people, have been a constant theme of observation, since our landing here [Sault Ste. Marie], with a military detachment, on the 6th of July '22. Having paid a good deal of my attention to this subject, a few of these traits may be mentioned.[67]

There seems to be little in the animate creation, which they will not eat, when impelled by hunger. While the cantonement was being erected, a horse of the quarter master was wounded, and died, and was immediately interred. Burial of meats in light arenacious soil, appears for a brief space, rather to retain the freshness, than to accelerate its decay. However this may be, the Indians dug it up, and used it as food.

One of the early labors of the military was to erect a road sixty feet wide from the fort to the noted eminence in the rear called Wudjoowung, or Hill—place by the Indians. In the progress of this work, they cut down, or destroyed the locality, of a large species of the sorbus Americana, or mountain ash. This tree is invested by the Indians, with magical virtues. It is one of the species, from which their priests make their oracular lodges.

The tree which occupied this spot, had become hollow, which gave it further claims on their superstitions, for when the winds blew, they fancied sounds to issue from it. When the trunk fell, by its natural decay, they threw a branch on the site, in passing, and this pile had much increased, at the period noted. Its destruction by the road making party, was the innocent cause of interference with one of their superstitions.

When sickness visits a lodge, a sacrifice is hung up, on the top of a long pole, in front of it. This sacrifice is, commonly a white dog, with bits of ribbon or scarlet above it. The soldiers having occasion for tent poles, a few days after their arrival, took one of these lodge sacrificial or Manito poles. It was soon observed by the Indians and reclaimed.

The superstitions of this tribe respecting mines are remarkable. It is deemed offensive to the spirits whom they worship to disclose the sites of mines to white men. Whether they have ever encountered unfavorable results from such disclosures to foreigners in former ages, or not, is not known. Individuals have brought to me specimens of the sulphuret and carbonate of copper, and small pieces of native copper, but have been very careful to conceal the particular localities.

Tacitus[68]

The White Fish[69]

Of ven'son let Goldsmith so wittingly sing,
A very fine haunch is a very fine thing
And Burns in his tuneful and exquisite way
The charms of a smoking Scots haggis display
But 'tis often much harder to eat than discard
And a poet may praise what a poet may want,
Less doubt there shall be 'twixt my muse and my dish,
Whilst her power I invoke, in the praise of white fish.
All friends to good living by turene or dish,
Concur in extolling this prince of a fish
So fine on a platter, so tempting a fry
So rich in *agrille,* and so sweet in a pie
That even before it, the red trout must fail
And that mighty *bonne-bouche* of the land, beavers tail.

This fish is a subject, so dainty and white,
To show in a lecture, to eat or to write
That equal's my joy, I declare on my life
To raise up my voice, or to raise up my knife
'Tis a morsel alike for the gourmand or faster
White-white as a tablet of pure alabaster
Its beauty and flavor no person can doubt,
If seen in the water, or tasted without
And all the dispute that opinion e'er makes,
Of this King of lake fishes—this deer of the lakes,[70]

Regards not its choiceness, to ponder or sup
But the best mode of dressing and serving it up.

   Now this is a point, where good livers may differ,
As tastes become fixed, or opinions are stiffer,
Some men prefer roasted—some doat on a fry
Or extol the sweet savor of *poisson blanc* pie;
The nice *petit pate,* this palate excites
While that, on a boiled dish & *bouillon* delights
Some smoked & some salted, some fresh & some dried,
Prefer to all fish in our waters beside
And 'tis thought the main question if epicures look
Respects not the method so much as the cook
For, like some moral dishes that furnish a zest
Whatever is best served up, is still thought the best.

   There are, in gastronomy, sages who think,
'Tis not only the prime of good victuals, but drink
That all sauces spoil it, the richer the quicker
And make it insipid except its own liquor
These move in a wild epigastric mirage
Preferring the dish *a la mode de sauvage*
By which it quells hunger & thirstiness both,
First eating the fish, & then drinking the broth
We leave this unsettled for palates or pens,
Who glean out of hundreds their critical tens
While drawn to the board where full many a dish,
Is slighted to taste this American fish.

   The planter, who whirls through the region by stream,
The Creole who sings as he lashes his team
The merchant, the lawyer, the cit & the beau
The proud & gustative, the poor and the low,
The gay *habitant*—the inquisitive tourist,
The chemic physician, the dinner-crast jurist
And even the ladies, the pride of the grove
Unite to extol it, and eat to approve
Full oft the sweet morsel, while poised on the knife,

No. 3. January 1827

Excites a bland smile in the blooming young wife
Nor deems she a sea fish, one moment compares,
But is thinking the while, not of fish, but of heirs.

To these, it is often a casual sweet
To dine by appointment, or taste as a treat
Not so, or in mental or physical joy
Comes the sight of this fish to the *courier de bois*
That wild troubadour & his joy-loving crew
Who sings as he paddles his birchen canoe
And thinks all the hardships that fall to his lot,
Are richly made up at the platter and pot
To him there's a charm neither feeble nor vague
In the mighty repast of the *grand Ticamey*
And oft, as he starves amid Canada snows,
On dry leather lichens & *bouton de rose*
He cheers up his spirits to think he shall still
Of *poisson blanc bouillon* once more have his fill
"Oh choice of all fishes," he sings as he goes
"Thou art sweeter to me than the Normandy rose
"And the ven'son that's stolen from the parks of the king,
"Is never by half, as delicious a thing.[71]

The muse might appeal to the science of books
To picture its ichthyological looks
Show what is its family likeness or odds,
Compared to its cousins the salmons and cods
Tell where it approximates, point where it fails
By counting its fins, or dissecting its scales
Or prove by plain reasons, such proofs can be had,
'Tis not toothless salmon but rather lake shad
Here too, might a fancy to descant inclined
Contemplate the lore that pertains to its kind
And bring up tradition, in fanciful strains
To prove its creation from feminine brains.
Here point out its habits, migrations & changes,
The mode of its capture, its cycles and ranges

45

But let me forbear—'tis the fault of a song
A tale or a book if too learned or long.

Thus ends my discussion. More would you, I pray,
Ask Mitchell, or Harlan, Lesieur or De Hay.

July 21, 1824

THE INDIAN LANGUAGES

Contrary to assertions of our earlier inquirers, into the principles of the Indian languages, their vocabularies appear to be based on monosyllabic roots. This is, at least, the case, with the Chippewa language, in which we see the primary syllables of both nouns and verbs, constituting a nucleus on which the pronominal adjuncts, are, as it were, deposited. Thus the particle *ow*, in this tongue means, a human body. Aub, the eye, nik the arm &c. &c The pronominal accidents are denoted by inseparable prefixes of fragments of the pronouns. Thus the vocabulary immediately becomes acretive. The operation of this rule is shown by the following list of forms.

Radix		My	Thy	His or her	ob. inf.
		plu	*plu*		
Ow	Body	Neow	Keow	Ow	
Aub	Eye	Neaub	Keaub	Aub	
Tshaus	Nose	Netshaus	Ketshaus	Otshaus- un	
Dön	Mouth	Nedoan	Kedoan	Odoan- un	
Beed	Tooth	Nebeed	Kebeed	Obeed- un	
Nik	Arm	Nenik	Kenik	Onik- un	
Nindj	Finger [Hand]	Nenindj	Kenindj	Onindj- un	
Kaud	Leg	Nekaut	Kecaut	Okaud	
Zid	Foot	Nezid	Kezid	Ozid	
Kun	Bone	Nekun	Kekun	Okun	
Pun	Lights	Nepun	Kepun	Opun	
Koon	Liver	Nekoon	Kekoon	Okoon	
Dai	Heart	Nindai	Kedai	Odai	
Dis	Navel	Nedis	Kedis	**Odis**	
Kut	Forehead	Nekut-ig	Kekut-ig	Okut-ig	

No. 3. January 1827

Here the root, in each case, is a monosyllable, and the first, second and third persons singular, a dyssyllable. When the object is plural, the word becomes trysyllable.

Abieca

An Etymological Lucubration

The subject of Indian etymologies, has occupied some of the brightest minds in the land. I cannot aspire to be very bright, but at the same time, think it may not be uninteresting to advance something on the subject. Writers and travellers have puzzled their ingenuity to learn the true meaning of this word. Some write it, with an O, as if it were a tribe of O'Neil's, or O'Donnels. Some put the letter y, to the final a, while all the modern writers insist that the true orthography is Ojibway. This may be food for the learned, who are often wrong, and dine their fancies on very slender food. To me, it is a gratification to find, that this tribe has not felt above drawing some of its names from our own noble English language. Thus it is easy enough to perceive that the first syllable *Chip*, is a plain derivative from our vocabulary, as if they had been thought as light as chips. By adding the term *away* to this, this idea is still further strenthened as if their lives, were at all times to be thrown away like chips. The moralist & etymologist must coincide in this conclusion at any rate, I am truly yours

William Word Catcher.[72]

The Literary Voyager

No. 4.   Sault Ste. Marie   January 12th 1827

FALSE ALARM

Our village was yesterday (11th.) thrown into commotion by the thrilling cry of the "Express"! The mistake, however, was soon corrected, with no other injury, that we can learn, but a twing of severe mental disappointment to the lovers of newspapers, and the expectants of letters. But e'n a false alarm, some good ordains. It stirs the stagnant hope within our veins. Order was soon restored, the sick who had hobbled to their windows to feast their eyes on the mail bag, quietly returned to their chairs, the pedestrians soon recovered from the slight fatigue of a walk to meet the fancied expressman; and those whom such experience in matters of this sort had tempered in some degree, to the privations of the post, made strong exertions to regain that state of *intellectual quiescence,* which is recommended as the best antidote to the pains of expectancy. It is feared, however, that the *shock* has been too violent, to permit a perfect recomposure under several days.[73]

NATIVE COMITY

Sir,

I am an Indian, and although I do not pretend to the knowledge of politeness, I mean that sort which regards domestic manners, yet I believe there is a native politeness existing, in some measure, in every human breast; and that an Indian feels it, and exercises it, as well as the most refined and civilized amongst the whites. For instance, amongst my people, no one would ever think of snatching anything out of another's hand, unless he were angry. But we take care, at social meetings and feasts, &c. never to appear angry, even if we do feel so.

I believe, as far as my knowledge of your customs go, you likewise consider such conduct vulgarity and rudeness. Now sir, I beg you will give me your opinion, and tell me if I am right or wrong, & by so doing you will greatly oblige

R. A Native[74]

THE CHOICE[75]
ADDRESSED TO MISS J. J.

A sweet retiring simple, modest mein
Not shunning & not seeking to be seen
A taste in dress & each domestic care
Neat but not gaudy, pleasing without glare
Such have I often wished "heavens last best gift," should be,
Such have I oft, with joy, remarked in thee.

An even temper, mild, endearing kind,
A sound discreet and regulated mind
Improved by reading, by reflection formed
By reason guided, by religion warmed
This have I often prayed "heavens last best gift" to be
This have I oft, with joy, remarked in thee.

Benevolent to all, to soothe or cure
But a firm friend to all the neighboring poor
The poor in worldly goods, or *bon ton* merit
The sunk in sickness & the bow'd in spirit
This have I often hoped "heavens last best gift" to be
This have I oft, with joy, remarked in thee.

Possessing spirit, yet a gentle creature,
Lover of quiet & the charms of nature
With no vain rage to simper, glare or roam
Pleas'd if abroad, but mostly pleased at home,
This have I fondly hoped "heavens last best gift" to be
This have I oft, admired, sweet maid, in thee.

In person comely, rather than renowned,
In books conversant, rather than profound,
With too much sense to slight domestic duty
Or sigh to shine a wit, or flaunt a beauty
This have I fondly wished, "heavens last best gift" to be
Such have I seen thee oft, &, often hope to see.

In virtue principled, in love sincere,
In manners guarded, in expression clear
Kind to all others in a just degree
But fixed, devoted, loving only me
This have I ever hoped "heavens last best gift" would be
This have I sought, and heaven blest found in thee.

Thee, in whose gentle manners, polished mind,
Grace, sweetness, taste, benevolence are joined
Sense to engage, a *naivette* to admire
Candor to please, & love itself to fire
Thee, have I fondly hoped, "heavens last best gift" to me
And all my hopes of bliss are hopes of thee.

(1823)

ACROSTIC ON

Cunning, active, full of bravery,
Hating av'rice, toil, and slavery,
Iron-hearted in their daring,
Prizing valor, and way-faring,
Prone to give, in cot or waste,
Ever happy at the feast,
Who shall say, they lack the merit,
All may seek—but few inherit.

WAUB OJEEG
AND
THE TRADITION OF THE OUTAGAMI
AND CHIPPEWA WAR
No. 3

He had received three wounds in battle. One, in his thigh, another in his right shoulder, and a third in his side and breast, being a glancing shot. His war parties consisted of volunteers, raised in the different villages on the shores of the lake, to each of which he sent tobacco and wampum. His first war party consisted of 40 men, and his largest mustered three hundred.

This war party was made up of warriors from Shogwoimican, Fond du Lac, Ontonagan, Keweena bay, Grand Island, and Sault Ste. Marie. They assembled at LaPointe, and danced the war dance on the shores of the lake between LaPointe and Bad river. They went up Bad river, and crossed a portage to a tributary of the St. Croix, called Namacagon. From the time they struck this river until they discovered the enemy, they passed six nights.

They went but a short distance each day, moving with great caution, and had always scouts ahead. On the evening of the seventh day the scouts discovered a large body of Outagamis and Sioux. They were encamped at the lower end of a portage around a fall, or rapid. The four Chippewa scouts who had made this discovery, did not however get off undiscovered themselves. The Foxes being on the alert, fired on them. A skirmish ensued. The White Fisher arrived with his whole force in season, and a bloody battle was fought, in which the allied Foxes and Sioux were defeated with the loss of nearly every man. They fought however with bravery against superior numbers; but the Chippewas had extended themselves in a circle across the small peninsula of the portage, and escape was next to impossible.[76]

This great battle decided the long struggle between the Chippewas and Outagamis; and the latter have never ventured to renew the contest. It also had the effect to raise the fame of Waub Ojeeg, to its climax, and he was from this time regarded as the head of the nation. His war songs were repeated in every village, and some of them are yet remembered. The lofty sentiments and the unconquerable spirit which they breathed, have seldom been surpassed. The following beautiful versification of one of these songs, from the pen of Mr. [John] Johnston, preserves the prominent ideas operating upon the mind of the warrior under circumstances of a temporary discomfiture.

WAR SONG[77]

I.

On that day when our heroes lay low—lay low,
  On that day when our heroes lay low;
I fought by their side, and thought ere I died,
Just vengeance to take on the foe—the foe,
  Just vengeance to take on the foe.

51

II.

On that day when our Chieftains lay dead—lay dead,
   On that day when our chieftains lay dead,
I fought hand to hand, at the head of my band,
And here on my breast have I bled—have I bled,
   And here on my breast have I bled.

III.

Our chiefs shall return no more—no more,
   Our chiefs shall return no more,
Nor their brothers of war, who can show scar for scar,
Like women their fates shall deplore—deplore,
   Like women their fates shall deplore.

IV.

Five winters in hunting we'll spend—we'll spend,
   Five winters in hunting we'll spend,
Till our youth grown to men, we'll to war lead again,
And our days like our fathers we'll end—we'll end,
   And our days like our fathers we'll end.

The carrying on of the Sioux war, did not withdraw the attention of the White Fisher, from the chase. His war excursions were generally made in the leisure of spring and summer. His followers were hastily assembled, and the whole expedition was generally terminated in a few weeks.

Large bodies of Indians can seldom be kept long together. Were it possible for the Indians to submit to the necessary restraints for a great length of time, the difficulty of subsistence must always have opposed the most serious obstacle to long campaigns. In fact, they generally lived upon very little, submitted to fatigues and privations of every kind without a murmur, and when success had crowned their efforts, they eagerly sought refreshment and repose in the security of their villages. Then, as now, the whole efficacy of a war party, consisted as much in the expedition with which it could be mustered, marched and dispersed, as in the valor they displayed before the enemy.

After the leaves have begun to fall, and during the whole winter and early part of spring, seasons the most valuable for hunting, no war party was ever conducted. The severity of the climate, and the facility with which scouting parties may track each other on the snow, forbid all attempts of the kind. And hence it is, that the care and business of war, scarcely, ever interrupted the pursuits of the chase. Waub Ojeeg was, in fact as much noted for his skill as a hunter, as for his prowess and daring as a warrior.

His hunting grounds extended along the shores of lake Superior, from the Montreal river to the Broule of Fond du Lac—a district abounding in moose, bear, beaver, marten and muskrat. Besides these, the mink, lynx, and smaller furs were also taken, and the woodlands stretching east of the Mississippi plains afforded the Virginia deer, during certain seasons. A more favorable position for the employment of hunting could hardly have been selected; and nothing equal to it, existed along the entire borders of the lake. In addition to this, the climate was favorable, that curve of the lake including Fond du Lac extending farthest south and west, and approaching nearest to the skirts of the Mississippi valley. The LaPointe Indians were able to raise corn, beans and pumpkins, articles which were annually culti-vated in their gardens. The waters of that part of the lake also pro-duced fish of various kinds, particularly white fish, trout and sturgeon.

Superadded to these advantages, the entrance of three principal rivers into the lake near that point, together with numerous smaller ones, presented so many avenues, which like radii, penetrated the interior, and opened channels of approach, enjoyed by no other spot on the southern coast of the lake. That the original settlement of the Chippewas at that place, had been determined by observing these advantages can not be doubted, and it may be regarded as the prin-cipal cause of its soon becoming one of the most flourishing and populous parts of the Chippewa territories. For we find, that so late as 1790, this was the great mart of the Indian trade on the southern shores of lake Superior, where the Mackinac traders annually resorted to exchange their goods for the valuable furs of those shores.

A consideration of the causes which have led to the dispersion of the LaPointe Indians into the department of lac de Flambeau, Folle Avoine &c. and the consequent decline of the parent settlement, would carry us into portions of history connected with the lives of cotempo-rary chiefs, and lead to the development of principles which have operated in all parts of the Indian country.

The amount of furs and skins usually taken by Waub Ojeeg during the year, fell little short of four Indian packs, averaging probably, sixty pounds each. Of this quantity, about one pack and a half consisted of beaver, one of bear, the remainder otter, marten, muskrat, and other small furs; worth, estimating within bounds, $360. With this sum he amply clothed himself and family, purchased arms, ammunition, traps, axes and knives, and had usually a sum left, which he appropriated to silver ornaments, vermillion and other extra, and ornamental articles.

As a hunter he was expert, and diligent, guarding with jealousy his rights to hunt in certain parts of the country, and esteeming the intrusion of others a trespass which he on one occasion in particular, punished in an exemplary manner. In his sales he evinced method and prudence.

He had attained nearly the heighth of his reputation before he married, which was not till he had reached nearly the age of thirty; and he then married a widow, with whom, however, he lived but two years, and had a son. He then married a girl of fourteen of the Totem of the Bear, by whom he had six children.

In his domestic habits he was affectionate and forbearing. When the hunting season was over, he could never bear to be idle, and employed those moments in adding to the comforts and conveniences of his lodge; thus uniting qualities of mind, which have been supposed incompatible with the hunter state. His industry proceeded from forecast, added to a strong sense of obligation to his family. His views, were enlightened, compared with the mass of Indians who surrounded him. He saw the true situation, not only of his relatives, but of the whole nation; and he resolved to use all his influence to rouse them to a true sense of it. With this view he admonished them to be active and diligent. To hunt well, and to fight well, were the cardinal maxims of his life, upon which he believed the happiness and independence of the nation to depend.

He possessed respectable powers as an orator, and he frequently addressed his people during those short seasons of leisure and festivity, which always succeed the close of the hunting seasons. To a ready flow of words, he united the all-powerful persuasive of personal fame. He possessed a stature of 6 feet 6 inches in height, with a keen searching black eye, and a countenance and bearing commanding high respect. His movements were lofty and dignified; he swayed as much by his air and manner as by his words. Custom had rendered his decisions a law; and although all the government exercised by Chippewa chiefs, is that of mere opinion, he ruled his village with a power almost absolute.

Such is the effect of great personal prowess, and a reputation for bravery and sagacity, among savage nations. The whole power and destiny of such nations hinges upon the private character of a few great men, who start up, at long intervals, rouse and direct the energies of their followers to a few favorite points, and when they have succeeded in moulding them to purposes of activity and combined action and feeling, die, and leave them to fall back into their former state of apathy and indolence. Where nothing is written, nothing is long remembered with accuracy; and hence, in a few years, their very history is lost, or involved in the inextricable labyrinth of fiction.

Waub Ojeeg had fixed his residence permanently at LaPointe, upon the main. His lodge was of an oblong shape, about 60 feet long, formed of posts fixed in the ground, and covered with the rind of the betula. From the centre, rose a stout post, reaching above the roof some feet—on the top of which was the carved figure of an owl, so placed as to turn with the wind, and serve the purposes of a weathercock. When he went to his wintering ground, this lodge was shut up, and re-occupied again on his return. During the short excursions, made in spring and summer, the family retained possession of the lodge.

In one of these excursions, he had a most singular contest with a moose. He went out early one morning, to make marten traps; and had set about forty, and was returning, when he encountered a large animal of this species in his path, who evinced a disposition to attack him. As he was armed with only a small hatchet and knife, he tried to avoid him. But the moose came towards him in a furious manner. He took shelter behind a tree, shifting his place from tree to tree, as the enraged animal pressed upon him. At length as he fled, he picked up a pole, and quickly untying his moccasin strings, tied his knife to the end of it. He then placed himself in a favorable position behind a tree, and when the moose came up, stabbed him several times in the throat and breast. At length the animal fell. He then cut out the tongue as a trophy of victory, and returning to his lodge, related, to his family, the singular encounter he had had, and *where* they would find the animal. When they came to the spot, they found the snow trampled down in a wide circle, sprinkled with blood, and resembling a field of battle. The animal proved to be one of uncommon size.[78]

A frame slender in proportion to his extraordinary height, together with great exposure of his person in his numerous war excursions, brought on a premature decay. He lingered several years with a pulmonary complaint, attended with spitting of blood. He lived long enough to see his eldest daughter and child united to Mr. Johnston, and died in 1793—aged about 45 years.

Moowis

THE INDIAN COQUETTE[79]

A CHIPPEWA LEGEND

There was a village full of Indians, and a noted belle or *muh-muh daw go qua* was living there. A noted beau or *muh muh daw go, ninnie* was there also. He and another young man went to court this young woman, and laid down beside her, when she scratched the face of the handsome beau. He went home and would not rise till the family prepared to depart, and he would not then arise. They then left him, as he felt ashamed to be seen even by his own relations. It was winter, and the young man, his rival, who was his cousin, tried all he could to persuade him to go with the family, for it was now winter, but to no purpose, till the whole village had decamped and had gone away. He then rose and gathered all the bits of clothing, and ornaments of beads and other things, that had been left. He then made a coat and leggins of the same, nicely trimmed with the beads, and the suit was fine and complete. After making a pair of moccasins, nicely trimmed, he also made a bow and arrows. He then collected the dirt of the village, and filled the garments he had made, so as to appear as a man, and put the bow and arrows in its hands, and it came to life. He then desired the dirt image to follow him to the camp of those who had left him, who thinking him dead by this time, were surprized to see him. One of the neighbors took in the dirt-man and entertained him. The belle saw them come and immediately fell in love with him. The family that took him in made a large fire to warm him, as it was winter. The image said to one of the children, "sit between me and the fire, it is too hot," and the child did so, but all smelt the dirt. Some said, "some one has trod on, and brought in dirt." The master of the family said to the child sitting in front of the guest, "get away from before our guest, you keep the heat from him." The boy answered saying, "he told me to sit between him and the fire." In the meantime, the belle wished the stranger would visit her. The image went to his master, and they went out to different lodges, the image going as directed to the belle's. Towards morning, the image said to the young woman (as he had succeeded) "I must now go away," but she said, "I will go with you." He said "it is too far." She answered, "it is not so far but that I can go with you." He first went to the lodge where he was entertained, and then to his master, and told him of all that had happened, and that he was going off with her. The young man thought it a pity she had treated him so, and how sadly she would be punished. They went off, she following behind. He left her a great way behind, but she continued to follow him. When the sun rose high, she found one of his mittens and picked it up, but to her astonishment, found it full of dirt. She, however took it and wiped it, and going on further, she found the other mitten in the same condition. She thought, "fie!! why does he do so," thinking he dirtied in them. She kept finding different articles of his dress, on the way all day, in the same condition. He kept ahead of her till towards evening, when the snow was like water, having melted by the heat of the day. No signs of her husband appearing, after having collected all the cloths that held him together, she began to cry, not knowing where to go, as their track was lost, on account of the snow's melting. She kept crying *Moowis* has led me astray, and she kept singing and crying Moowis nin ge won e win ig, ne won e win ig.

Leelinau

Gov. Cass' Repose of Character

Physical peril does not appear to affect this gentleman. I saw him once exposed to imminent peril, in a canoe in the middle of lake Erie. I was sitting beside him. We had left the Detroit river, with a brisk breeze. It was on the 4th July 1821. The wind rose almost imperceptibly, to a gale, before which we were driven some thirty miles. It was impossible to make the shore, from the impossibility of turning the vessel, without swamping it. The waves rolled behind us in glorious swells, whose bright and pearly crests broke behind us, and around us, with a murmuring noise, falling like showers of scattered crystals. We were literally driven on "the wings of the wind." At length the crowning wave of one of those long series, which had been chasing us, broke high above our heads and poured in torrents over us, and rolled down our breasts, filling the canoe. I thought all was over, and that we were inevitably destined for the green weeds and smooth pebbles at the bottom of the lake. I looked at Gen. Cass. His eye and countenance denoted a sense of danger, without the slightest disturbance. Not a word was uttered by him or me.[80] I had myself a trustful spirit, and saw him with quite as much. His was a repose that spoke volumes. The next series of waves lifted us on, on our perilous way, as if by giant jerks, the men busying themselves in bailing, as if all they had to do, must be done quickly; and before another royal series of the angry element, gathered up its strength, to finish us, as if with the stroke of a whale in the Pacific, we passed into the sheltering jaws of the outer capes of Maumee bay, and were safe.

Amicus[81]

ACROSTIC
TO HIS EXCELLENCY

L.over of letters—mild and able,
E.ver zealous, prompt and stable,
W.ithout pomp, or vain parade,
I.n the camp, the court, the shade,
S.tudious, cautious, penetrating,
C.andid, courteous, wit-creating,
A.ctive, quick, by word or brow,
S.ure to plan, defend, avow,
S.uch was Hampden, such art Thou.

Clio

WONDERS OF ANCIENT ART

We are informed in Bailey's Dictionary,[82] that glass was first invented in Sidon. The first maker of it in Rome, was in the reign of

Tiberius. An artist of this time, having made vessels of such a temper, that being cast on the ground, they did not break, but only bruise. These indentations, the maker smoothed with a hammer, and straightened before the Emperor; but this ruler, is said to have put him to death, for fear of glass should detract from the use of gold or silver. This relation has amused, for nearly eighteen centuries. That some fictitious production was exhibited to Tiberius, which was called Vitrum or glass, is probable. That it was glass, in a proper sense, that is, fused silex and alkali, in a transparent form, is contradicted by all the principles of chemistry. Malleability is one of the characteristics of metals, and the utmost we can grant is, that some ancient artist had found the secret of taking away the opacity of metal. This can be readily done, by fusing its oxides with silex, but the result is, a brittle body.

The same authority tells us, that in 1610, the Sophy emperor of Persia, sent the King of Spain, six glasses that were made malleable. In the year 1662, glass was first brought into England, by Renault, a foreign monk or bishop. Dr. Johnson adopts this chronology, in the end of his dictionary.

A Vitreologist[83]

A Defect in Making Indian Treaties

The cession of lands from Indians, should invariably be made by a map drawn by them & appended to the original treaty. Countries are sometimes bartered by a wave of the hand. A bad or careless interpreter, who in explaining a written treaty, points his finger wrong in defining a boundary, leads a tribe to suppose they have not ceded, accessory to this wave of the hand. Millions of acres are thus, sometimes, put in dispute. Treaties are made to explain treaties, & purchases to cover purchases. All resulting from a bad interpreter, or the want of a ms. or sketch map.

Glory

Say, what is glory? Glory to Nimiad's eye,
Was to up-rear a tower to the sky.
The son of Phillip, placed it in renowns,
Of slaughtering armies, To returning towns
To Ceasar, twas the glitter, & the bloom,

That smote the giant commonwealth of Rome.
Nor judged on one just empereal Charlemagne
Who placed it, in a despot's power to reign.
Was Charles' rule, a rule of softer guise?
On Frederick's, who made red the Pougcas skies
Nay—had Napoleon, pure hopes and fears?
In rattling kingdoms about Europe's care.

Pagwabecaega

The Literary Voyager

No. 5.   Sault Ste. Marie   January 1827

NEWS, AT HOME & ABROAD

The express reached us on the evening of the 19th instant, bringing Detroit papers to Dec. 5th, New York to Novr. 17th and Washington to Novr. 21st. Presuming our male readers have taken care to supply themselves with the current news, we shall briefly enumerate the leading topics of intelligence for the benefit of the ladies.

The only item of much interest in the Detroit papers, is the speech of His Excellency Governor Cass, to the legislative council—a sound, practical address, suited to the situation and prospects of the territory.[84] In New York, Gov. [DeWitt] Clinton is reelected by a small majority; but the anti-Clintonian party has triumphed in the election of Gen. [Nathaniel] Pitcher as Lieutenant Governor, and in securing a majority in the Senate and Assembly. From Washington we learn, that the (then) approaching session of Congress was anticipated with the same intense interest, that has marked the last half dozen sessions of that body.

Casting our eyes beyond the Atlantic, we see the farce of the "Holy Alliance," playing off very much in the old way. In this farce, certain monarchs have undertaken to act the part of public performers. The people, who have been all along hoodwinked, are expected to dance, so long as the monarchs play, and to pay the piper into the bargain. If any are bold enough to pull off the bandage, to express a dislike to the tune, or to stop dancing, they are knocked on the head with the fiddlestick.

John Bull, who was never a good dancer, sat down some years ago; although he continued to pay the piper for others, who danced in his place. Portugal lately imitated John's example, as Spain had unsuccessfully done twice before. But this step has thrown the whole orchestra into discord. Nothing but jarring and confusion is heard. It is feared if this obstinacy on the part of Portugal goes unpunished, the entire "troupe" will follow the example.

What adds to the embarrassment, is the sudden incursion of certain

Turkish and Persian performers, who threaten to dance a *saraband* of their own; and that too, on the very borders of Europe. It is supposed this last occurrence, will bring out the best players on the continent, and lead to a denouement of the Piece. The emperor of Austria, it is thought, will try to restore harmony by a few airs on the German flute; Charles Xth. will give divers flourishes on the French horn; while Nicholas, makes the air resound with the terrible knout. But it is shrewdly suspected that John Bull will insist on adding the music of the drum and fife.

Seriously, we believe posterity will wonder, how long state tricks are capable of arresting the march of the human intellect; and blinding nations to the rights and enjoyments which the Creator has spread before them.

> Dance nations now, & if ye miss the tread,
> *Nomporte,* Napoleon the Great is Dead.

LANGUAGE

Language is the tell tale of history. I have been a humble inquirer after the principles of the Chippewa language and offer some remarks, which I think, deserve notice. It was observed, of the Carib language, when first noticed, that it exhibited a sexual feature, that is, that it contained a set of masculine and feminine nouns, verbs and expressions, limited to the sexes. Something of this sort exists in a limited degree, in the Chippewa. This characteristic vocabulary may be judged of, by the following examples.

	nouns male		nouns female	
My friend.	Nejee.		Nendongwa.	
My uncle.	Ni mi sho mai.by the f. side.		Nezhisa by the m. side	
My aunt.	Nizigus	″	Neenwisha	″
Behold.	Tyau!		Nyau!	

Consonantal peculiarities. Some of the consonants which the Chippewas do not ordinarily employ, in their vocabulary, acquire a magical value in the mouths of story tellers, medas, and jossakeeds. The letter l. and the combination of wh. fall under this denomination. Examples of both occur in the hieratic chorus, *wha-lá-lé-áa.* In the magical legend of Mishosha, the term *Pol,* uttered after that of canoe, is an imperative charm commanding the canoe to assume its magical powers, by rushing, without paddles, through the water.

The letters B. and P. are often interchangeable, and often denote idiomatic precision. Thus *Poz* is the word to embark; *Boz he,* or she embarks. *Poziwug,* they embark.

Ba-zhick, signifies one; but the duplication of the first syllable, changing, at the same time, b to p, renders the sense, united, solid, unseparated. Thus the horse is called the animal with solid, or unsplit hoofs.

Maja is simply the indicative of the verb to go, but by its duplication with stress of voice and accent, the term thus formed (maja-maja) is equivalent to may good luck attend you, or adieu.

The termination *ego* distinguishes the passive, from the active voice.

The duplication of an adjective, before a noun, gives it a superlative, or highly intensified sense. Thus gitchi-gitchi is, superlatively great. *Ish,* signifies man, in the term un- ish- in- a- ba; but *ish* appears to be used to call attention to something about to be said, and is perhaps analogous to the terms Sir, man or Mister.

The fact mentioned by our correspondent "A native," is worthy of attention. There are, clearly degrees of purity in the spoken language, according to the degree of refinement of living and manners of the people. The chief orators pride themselves on using the best language; they never violate the class of nouns; and their example becomes a standard to the young, while those families, in which there is a mixture of European blood, pique themselves on their superior knowledge of both the vocabulary and grammar.

The Chippewa has the peculiarity of making every inanimate object at the will of the speaker, animate. By this process, trees, rocks, in short every feature of the country is invested with hearing, sight and animation. Wilds and forests no longer remain desolate and lonesome, when every object, around, above and below, is a person.

Abieca

INCLUSIVENESS OF INDIAN TRADITIONS

No historical value can be found on many tribal traditions of more than three centuries standing. The Indian tribes constituting one of the language variants of mankind, have a tradition of the creation &

a general deluge. These are generally expressed under symbolic forms, or clothed with allegories. From the period of the world's origin, they drop down through centuries, to the events of yesterday. To reach integrals, & show the development of tribes, from names, we must appeal to language, physical traits, the remains of art, and natal peculiarities.

MISHOSHA,

OR THE MAGICIAN AND HIS DAUGHTERS

A CHIPPEWA TALE OR LEGEND[85]

In an early age of the world, when there were fewer inhabitants in the earth than there now are, there lived an Indian, who had a wife and two children, in a remote situation. Buried in the solitude of the forest, it was not often that he saw any one, out of the circle of his own family. Such a situation seemed favorable for his pursuits; and his life passed on in uninterrupted happiness, till he discovered a wanton disposition in his wife.

This woman secretly cherished a passion for a young man whom she accidentally met in the woods, and she lost no opportunity of courting his approaches. She even planned the death of her husband, who, she justly concluded, would put her to death, should he discover her infidelity. But this design was frustrated by the alertness of the husband, who having cause to suspect her, determined to watch narrowly, to ascertain the truth, before he should come to a determination how to act. He followed her silently one day, at a distance, and hid himself behind a tree. He soon beheld a tall, handsome man approach his wife, and lead her away.

He was now convinced of her crime, and thought of killing her, the moment she returned. In the meantime he went home, and pondered on his situation. At last he came to the determination of leaving her forever, thinking that her own conscience would in the end, punish her sufficiently; and relying on her maternal feelings, to take care of the two boys, whom he determined to leave behind.

When the wife returned, she was disappointed in not finding her husband, having concerted a plan to dispatch him. When she saw that day after day passed, and he did not return she at last guessed the true cause of his absence. She then returned to her paramour, leaving

64

the two helpless boys behind, telling them that she was going a short distance, and would return; but determined never to see them more.

The children thus abandoned, soon made way with the food that was left in the lodge, and were compelled to quit it, in search of more. The eldest boy possessed much intrepidity, as well as great tenderness for his little brother, frequently carrying him when he became weary, and gathering all the wild fruit he saw. Thus they went deeper into the forest, soon losing all traces of their former habitation, till they were completely lost in the labyrinths of the wilderness.

The elder boy fortunately had a knife, with which he made a bow and arrows, and was thus enabled to kill a few birds for himself and brother. In this way they lived some time, still pressing on, they knew not whither. At last they saw an opening through the woods, and were shortly after delighted to find themselves on the borders of a broad lake. Here the elder boy busied himself in picking the seed pods of the wild rose. In the meanwhile the younger, amused himself by shooting some arrows into the sand, one of which, happened to fall into the lake. The elder brother, not willing to lose his time in making another, waded into the water to reach it. Just as he was about to grasp the arrow, a canoe passed by him with the rapidity of lightning. An old man, sitting in the centre, seized the affrighted youth, and placed him in the canoe. In vain the boy addressed him. "My grandfather" (a term of respect for old people) "pray take my little brother also. Alone, I cannot go with you; he will starve if I leave him." The old magician (for such was his real character) laughed at him. Then giving his canoe a slap, and commanding it to go, it glided through the water with inconceivable swiftness. In a few minutes they reached the habitation of Mishosha, standing on an island in the centre of the lake. Here he lived, with his two daughters, the terror of all the surrounding country.

Leading the young man up to the lodge "Here my eldest daughter," said he, "I have brought a young man who shall become your husband." The youth saw surprize depicted in the countenance of the daughter, but she made no reply, seeming thereby to acquiesce in the commands of her father. In the evening he overheard the daughters in conversation. "There again!" said the elder daughter, "our father has brought another victim, under the pretence of giving me a husband. When will his enmity to the human race cease; or when shall

65

we be spared witnessing such scenes of vice and wickedness, as we are daily compelled to behold."

When the old magician was asleep, the youth told the elder daughter, how he had been carried off, and compelled to leave his helpless brother on the shore. She told him to get up and take her father's canoe, and using the charm he had observed, it would carry him quickly to his brother. That he could carry him food, prepare a lodge for him, and return by morning. He did in every thing as he had been directed, and after providing for the subsistence of his brother, told him that in a short time he should come for him. Then returning to the enchanted island, resumed his place in the lodge before the magician awoke. Once during the night Mishosha awoke, and not seeing his son in law, asked his eldest daughter what had become of him. She replied that he had merely stepped out, and would be back soon. This satisfied him. In the morning, finding the young man in the lodge, his suspicions were completely lulled. "I see, my daughter, you have told me the truth."

As soon as the sun rose, Mishosha thus addressed the young man. "Come, my son, I have a mind to gather gulls eggs. I am acquainted with an island where there are great quantities; and I wish your aid in gathering them." The young man, saw no reasonable excuse, and getting into the canoe, the magician gave it a slap, and bidding it go, in an instant they were at the island. They found the shore covered with gulls eggs, and the island surrounded with birds of this kind. "Go, my son," said the old man, "and gather them, while I remain in the canoe." But the young man was no sooner ashore than Mishosha pushed his canoe a little from land and exclaimed: "Listen ye gulls! you have long expected something from me. I now give you an offering. Fly down, and devour him." Then striking his canoe, left the young man to his fate.

The birds immediately came in clouds around their victim, darkening all the air with their numbers. But the youth, seizing the first that came near him, and drawing his knife, cut off its head, and immediately skinning the bird, hung the feathers as a trophy on his breast. "Thus," he exclaimed, "will I treat every one of you who approaches me. Forbear, therefore, and listen to my words. It is not for you to eat human food. You have been given by the Great Spirit as food for man. Neither is it in the power of that old magician to do you any good. Take me on your beaks and carry me to his lodge, and you shall see that I am not ungrateful."

The gulls obeyed, collecting in a cloud for him to rest upon, and quickly flew to the lodge, where they arrived before the magician. The daughters were surprized at his return, but Mishosha conducted as if nothing extraordinary had taken place.

On the following day he again addressed the youth. "Come, my son," said he, "I will take you to an island covered with the most beautiful pebbles, looking like silver. I wish you to assist me in gathering some of them. They will make handsome ornaments, and are possessed of great virtues." Entering the canoe, the magician made use of his charm, and they were carried, in a few moments, to a solitary bay in an island, where there was a smooth sandy beach. The young man went ashore as usual. "A little further, a little further," cried the old man, "upon that rock you will get some finer ones." Then pushing his canoe from land, "Come thou great king of fishes," cried he, "you have long expected an offering from me. Come, and eat the stranger I have put ashore on your island." So saying, he commanded his canoe to return, and was soon out of sight. Immediately a monstrous fish shoved his long snout from the water, moving partially on the beach, and opening wide his jaws to receive his victim.

"When" exclaimed the young man, drawing his knife, and placing himself in a threatening attitude, "when did you ever taste human food. Have a care of yourself. You were given by the Great Spirit to man, and if you, or any of your tribes, taste human flesh, you will fall sick and die. Listen not to the words of that wicked old man, but carry me back to his island, in return for which, I shall present you a piece of red cloth."

The fish complied, raising his back out of water to allow the young man to get on. Then taking his way through the lake, landed his charge safely at the island, before the return of the magician.

The daughters were still more surprised to see him thus escaped a second time, from the arts of their father. But the old man maintained his taciturnity. He could not, however, help saying to himself, "What manner of boy is this, who ever escapes from my power. His spirit shall not however save him. I will entrap him tomorrow. Ha! ha! ha!"[86]

[Next day the magician addressed the young man as follows:

"Come, my son," said he, "you must go with me to procure some young eagles. I wish to tame them. I have discovered an island where they are in great abundance." When they had reached the island, Mishosha led him inland until they came to the foot of a tall pine, upon which the nests were. "Now, my son," said he, "climb up this tree and bring down the birds." The young man obeyed. When he had with great difficulty got near the nest, "Now," exclaimed the magician, addressing the tree, "stretch yourself up and be very tall." The tree rose up at the command. "Listen, ye eagles," continued the old man, "you have long expected a gift from me. I now present you this boy, who has had the presumption to molest your young. Stretch forth your claws and sieze him." So saying he left the young man to his fate, and returned.

But the intrepid youth drawing his knife, and cutting off the head of the first eagle that menaced him, raised his voice and exclaimed, "Thus will I deal with all who come near me. What right have you, ye ravenous birds, who were made to feed on beasts, to eat human flesh? Is it because that cowardly old canoe-man has bid you do so? He is an old woman. He can neither do you good nor harm. See, I have already slain one of your number. Respect my bravery, and carry me back that I may show you how I shall treat you."

The eagles, pleased with his spirit, assented, and clustering thick around him formed a seat with their backs, and flew toward the enchanted island. As they crossed the water they passed over the magician, lying half asleep in his canoe.

The return of the young man was hailed with joy by the daughters, who now plainly saw that he was under the guidance of a strong spirit. But the ire of the old man was excited, although he kept his temper under subjection. He taxed his wits for some new mode of ridding himself of the youth, who had so successfully baffled his skill. He next invited him to go a hunting.

Taking his canoe, they proceeded to an island and built a lodge to shelter themselves during the night. In the mean while the magician caused a deep fall of snow, with a storm of wind and severe cold. According to custom, the young man pulled off his moccasins and leggings and hung them before the fire to dry. After he had gone to sleep the magician, watching his opportunity, got up, and taking one moccasin and one legging, threw them into the fire. He then went to sleep. In the morning, stretching himself as he arose and uttering an exclamation of surprise, "My son," said he, "what has become of your moccasin and legging? I believe this is the moon in which fire attracts, and I fear they have been drawn in." The young man suspected the true cause of his loss, and rightly attributed it to a design of the magician to freeze him to death on the march. But he maintained the strictest silence, and drawing his conaus over his head thus communed with himself: "I have full faith in the Manito who has preserved me thus far, I do not fear that he will forsake me in this cruel emergency. Great is his power, and I invoke it now that he may enable me to prevail over this wicked enemy of mankind."

He then drew on the remaining moccasin and legging, and taking a dead coal from the fireplace, invoked his spirit to give it efficacy, and blackened his foot and leg as far as the lost garment usually reached. He then got up and announced himself ready for the march. In vain Mishosha led him through snows and over morasses, hoping to see the lad sink at every moment. But in this he was disappointed, and for the first time they returned home together.

Taking courage from this success, the young man now determined to try his own power, having previously consulted with the daughters. They all agreed that the life the old man led was detestable, and that whoever would rid the world of him, would entitle himself to the thanks of the human race.

On the following day the young man thus addressed his hoary captor. "My grandfather, I have often gone with you on perilous excursions and never murmured. I must now request that you will accompany me. I wish to visit my little brother, and to bring him home with me." They accordingly went on a visit to the main land, and found the little lad in the spot where he had been left. After taking him into the canoe, the young man again addressed the magician: "My grandfather, will you go and cut me a few of those red willows on the bank, I wish to prepare some smoking mixture." "Certainly, my son," replied the old man, "what you wish is not very hard. Ha, ha, ha! do you think me too old to get up there?" No sooner was Mishosha ashore, than the young man, placing himself in the proper position struck the canoe with his hand, and pronouncing the charm, N'CHIMAUN POLL, the canoe immediately flew through the water on its return to the island. It was evening when the two brothers arrived, and carried the canoe ashore. But the elder daughter informed the young man that unless he sat up and watched the canoe, and kept his hand upon it, such was the power of their father, it would slip off and return to him. Panigwun watched faithfully till near the dawn of day, when he could no longer resist the drowsiness which oppressed him, and fell into a short doze. In the meantime the canoe slipped off and sought its master, who soon returned in high glee. "Ha, ha, ha! my son," said he; "you thought to play me a trick. It was very clever. But you see I am too old for you."

A short time after, the young again addressed the magician. "My grandfather, I wish to try my skill in hunting. It is said there is plenty of game on an island not far off, and I have to request that you will take me there in your canoe." They accordingly went to the island and spent the day in hunting. Night coming on they put up a temporary lodge. When the magician had sunk into a profound sleep, the young man got up, and taking one of Mishosha's leggings and moccasins from the place where they hung, threw them into the fire, thus retaliating the artifice before played upon himself. He had discovered that the foot and leg were the only vulnerable parts on the magician's body. Having committed these articles to the fire, he besought his Manito that he would raise a great storm of snow, wind, and hail, and then laid himself down beside the old man. Consternation was depicted on the countenance of the latter, when he awoke in the morning and found his moccasin and legging missing. "I believe, my grandfather," said the young man, "that this is the moon in which fire attracts, and I fear your foot and leg garments have been drawn in." Then rising and bidding the old man follow him, he began the morning's hunt, frequently turning to see how Mishosha kept up. He saw him faltering at every step, and almost benumbed with cold, but encouraged him to follow, saying, we shall soon get through and reach the shore; although he took pains, at the same time, to lead him in round-about ways, so as to let the frost take complete effect. At length the old man reached the brink of the island where the woods are succeeded by a border of smooth sand. But he could go no farther; his legs became stiff and refused motion, and he found himself fixed to the spot. But he still kept stretching out his arms and swinging his body to and fro. Every moment he found the numbness creeping higher. He felt his legs growing downward like roots, the feathers of his head turned to leaves, and in a few seconds he stood a tall and stiff sycamore, leaning toward the water.

Panigwun leaped into the canoe, and pronounced the charm, was soon transported to the island, where he related his victory to the daughters. They applauded the deed, agreed to put on mortal shapes, become wives to the two young men, and for ever quit the enchanted island. And passing immediately over to the main land, they lived lives of happiness and peace.]

Bame-wa-wa-ge-zhik-a-quay[87]

LINES
TO A FRIEND ASLEEP

Awake my friend! the morning's fine,
Waste not in sleep the day divine,
Nature is clad in best array,
The woods, the fields, the flowers are gay;—
The sun is up, and speeds his march,
O'er heaven's high aerial arch,
His golden beams with lustre fall,
On lake and river, cot and hall;—
The dews are sparkling on each spray,
The birds are chirping sweet and gay,
The violet shows its beauteous head,
Within its narrow, figured bed;—
The air is pure, the earth bedight,
With trees and flowers, life and light,
All—all inspires a joyful gleam,
More pleasing than a fairy dream.
Awake! the sweet refreshing scene,
Invites us forth to tread the green,
With joyful hearts, and pious lays,
To join the glorious Maker's praise,
The wond'rous works—the paschal lamb,
The holy, high, and just I Am.

Rosa[88]

ORNITHOLOGY

Mr. Ozhabeigde,[89]

I have been an observer of the natural history of this vicinity, from the first establishment of the post, and the object has given increased interest to my little excursions. In one of these excursions, to observe the Indian method of making sugar from the sap of the acer sacharinum, or rock maple, in the month of March, I observed a species of grosbeck, which is, manifestly, a sojourner here, for a period, from more northerly latitudes. The natives call it, paush-cun-da-mo.—a name which appears to refer to its power of breaking, or penetrating the surface of what it feeds on. An Indian boy brought me a specimen, which he had killed with his bow and arrow. Using the *beekut,* or blunt-headed arrow, the species was not at all injured, which enabled me to stuff and prepare for the New York Lyceum of Natural History. It was there, determined to be a new specimen of the grosbeck, and received the name of vespertina, from an impression of Major Delafield, who had seen the species in the North West of lake Superior, that it sings at evening.

Pennant

An Essay on the Origin of the Indian Tribes

'Twere hard by reason, or prophetic date,
To tell the Indian's utter end and fate,
But this may seem to human view more clear,
God formed the man, & led his footsteps here,
Albeit God formed him, his own word is plain,
Who formed all flesh & nothing formed in vain.

Adam and Noah, are the links that bind,
Two nether worlds and one creative kind
But food and climate, passion and disease,
Fulfilled minuter changes and decrees
Imprinting hues, in all their terrene track,
From paradiseal white, to ebon black
'Twas still the same created creature-man!
Run out, in kinds, through all th' eternal plan.
If red the Indian, be it understood,
'Tis of that work divine, pronounced all good.

I quote no learned lore, to tell you why,
God gave a blue, a brown or hazle eye,
A rosy, sallow, or high-pointed cheek,

72

No. 5. January 1827

A spirit ruthless, headlong, bland or meek,
Prowess to raise a tower, or sack a town,
Or fleetness to attain the victor's crown.
These, are but gifts bestowed in part or whole,
His *moral* image stampt he on the soul,
And if the Indian bears it, or can bear,
'Tis plain he is as much a son and heir,
As He,[90] who bore the temporary call,
Till Shiloh came to let in light to all.

The Red man, whom Columbus first espied,
Was naked—but a man of stoic pride
Fond of his country—much to pomp inclined
Grave, formal, shy, and taciturn of mind
A lover of light fancies—beads and bells,
Bands, feathers, mantles, painting, gold & shells.
Seen farther north, the man was much the same,
But warmer clad, & more robust of frame
Experter proved he, with the bow and spear,
In words more eloquent—fight more severe
But still the same kind, idle, stately child,
The climax of the human race run wild.

View him as Drake or Raleigh found the man,
Stretching along the shores of Powhatan
A subtil warrior, quick in every thing
A hunter, or a suppliant, or a king
Assuming here, and there declining power,
Now prompt, and now neglectful of the hour
Just as occasion swayed him,—never still,
Fixed to one rule of action, thought or will,
But shaping his expedients thin & spare,
O'er so much space, as oft to leave half bare,
And under guise of many a simple art,
Hiding the darkest purpose of the heart.

Go, scan his acts a thousand miles away,
Some lighter shades may o'er the surface play
Denoting purpose, forecast, power of thought,

73

And brow with amor patriae deeply wrought
But all as flashes, or ennobling gleams,
Leaving the mind a prey to wild extremes
Like him of old, by love supernal spurned,
And word prophetic deemed—"a cake unturned,"[91]
Whether in speech or action, taste or touch,
Too hot, too cold, too little, or too much
Sad wrecks and glimmerings of an unformed mind,
Erst ample in its feelings, powers & kind
But lured away by hate, rebellion, pride,
By glory maddened, or by rage defied
Step after step pursued its downward road
Till far away from virtue, and from God.

'Twere vague to seize, as the generic type,
For such a race, the war club or the pipe,
Or any mere external art or sign,
Which fancy might adopt, or whim resign
Unless a firmer basis we can find,
In language, rites, opinions, cast of mind
Habits in life or death—historic charts,
Letters, or signs, or monumental arts.

Small are the lights we from tradition drain
Yet, what is hardly gained, we truly gain,
As in some labors of the flinty ore,
Though few the grains, their value is the more.
If such the truths, we make our proof & test
Then prest the Indians first from east to west,
Or, if from Nilus or Euphrate's shores
Niger or Indus, or the old Azores,
Seas, islands, gulfs o'er past by will or lot,
We only name as something once forgot
But let us look a long lost people in the face
And scan the manners to denote the race.

Start where they may—the purpose once exprest,
In weal or woe the tribes fierce onward prest,

74

No. 5. January 1827

Band urging band, as some vast herd in flight,
On Rio Roxo's plains display their might
Till faltering in their course of heady zeal,
Or braved in front, the broken columns wheel
And spreading wildly, their disordered train.
Halt where kind woods or greener fields detain,
There freely breathe, and paw the verdant ground,
Till hunger gnaw, or fear inflicts a sound.
So when the first primeval hunters strayed,
From orient climes, obeyed or disobeyed,
Thence in their ire, they passed from shore to shore,
The tribes behind, impelling tribes before
Till spreading over Asia's wide domain,
They trod the boundaries of her utmost plain,
There prest by cares, oblivion blots in night,
In dread and fear began their western flight.

Some wander up, some down the orient coast,
Or to the torrid south, or land of frost,
Some hug the main, some seize the ready one,
And isle, on isle, and coast on coast explore.
Some, by a sudden gale, at random cast,
Fly like a feather on the driving blast,
But heaven sustained, within the fragile bark
Here reach an island, there a broader mark
Till wafted, by new gales, or conquest planned,
They reach at last the continental land,
One calls himself a king—the tale spreads soon,
This tumbled from the Sun, and that the Moon,
At least one trait of orient climes they bring,
Hyperbole to match the vainest king.

But most, by heaven's supernal finger shown,
Wind to the sea coasted broad Atlantic zone,
That geologic way, in love designed,
To spread the race, and all the grazing kind.
Doubtest thou the Greek?[92] Then tell me sapient seer,
How came the sloth and armadillo here?

The patient lama, or the heavy bos.
Did these in boats, or frozen oceans cross?
Or did the sunny race of tropic tone
Erst burrow in the bleak and frigid zone?
Or must thou, by some skeptic phantom bid,
Belie all Moses wrote, all Noah did?

   I go not with them. Deep volcanic fires,
Wide o'er the globe have pushed their granite spires,
Or plunged wide plains beneath the deepest tide,
Where once the banner waved in all its pride
And temples stood;—the everlasting sea
Hath warred upon its borders wide and free.
And beat down continents of shelly coast
Enlarging her own empire. Means so vast
In elder times, ere letters had a name
Divided tribes, and thus the Indian came.
Better philosophy do thou devise!
Like Kant and Voltaire built on doubts & lies.
Fear to believe a miracle, with Hume
Lest truth o'er heavens bright Oracle should bloom,
With Milman[93] grope lest God should work by rule,
Or shifting Buckland[94] brand thee as a fool
Or with the poor blind Indian date his birth,
And say his grandsires crept from out the earth.

                                           Clio[95]

SOME ACCOUNT OF THE CELEBRATED MR I

Mr I, was the brother of the noted Mr. YOU, HE, and SHE, whose children were we, us, and ours, ye, they and them, his cousins were himself and themselves, and he was by far, the most distinguished of that eminent family. He was at once the most talented, the wisest, and the best. He was the bravest in battle, the swiftest in a race, and the most expert in a struggle. When it came to writing, he was the most ready, and fluent, the most gifted, most profound, and wise. He was an orator, a historian, and a poet. It would be difficult, indeed, to tell when and where it was, that this noted individual, did not come off first in every triumph, or attainment. He was, a Samson in strength, an oracle in wisdom, a very Solomon in knowledge. Yet, though his attainments were thus varied, we shall attempt, in a future number to let the reader see, the steps by which he rose to eminence. Other men have done nobly, but he exceeded them all. In short, all the wars, woes, and tribulations of the world, were owing to this same Mr I. He wrote the most splendid poems & histories, & fought the most celebrated battles.

EKEDO[96]

The Literary Voyager

No. 7.[97]   *Sault Ste. Marie*   *February 1827*

TRAITS OF PERSONAL ATTACHMENTS AMONG THE OJIBWAYS

Some years back I was brought to notice some of the characteristic traits, of the natives of our forests and the rarity of such circumstances. Even in polished societies, as that to which I was an eye witness induces me to state the particulars. The occurance which I shall relate, took place at what may be called the farthest, at least it was then so considered, and which few of the enterprising Eastern adventurers had as yet reached at that period. The Individuals whom I will bring to the notice of my readers, were pure natives, as I believe although they may have had some of the blood of the white man. When I saw them, and became acquainted with their history, Rosalie, the young woman had attained her eighteenth year. Her native name was, Waub Onng Aqua or the Morning Star. She was nature's pure child, and the impulses of her bosom had always flamed in the same channel, up to the present time, and they were such as what the white man would call very moral, although unacquainted with the standard by which civilized moralists are guided. Free from flattery and deceit, she belonged to a class whose manner of life differed essentially from refined society. Pure in mind & simple in appearance, she was exempt from evil, and feelings which she had formed in early life were lasting. All the arts and inducements of some could not overthrow them. As to her appearance she was tall and very fair, remarkably so for one who could or would claim but little of the white man's blood, her head was covered with black flowing hair, which fell over her shoulders, and which was kept smooth by a head comb, over the edge of her high forehead she wore a black ribbon, which showed that to advantage.

Her teeth were white as pearl, her features were exact, her appearance at first sight was engaging and modest and in all her movements very graceful, she was adept in all the simple accomplishments of her sex, she looked handsome in her garnished mockesins, & her neat plain blue mantle, which induced others to copy her neatness. There was a peculiar pleasantness in her looks, and her dark beaming eyes gave a finish to the whole.

Glade, the young man was about twenty years old, little over six feet strait and well proportioned, well skilled in the arts of a hunter and fisher, bold & brave in the sport or Dance or in the use of fusee[98] & arrow. He was the pride of all. Such were the individuals, who had formed a friendship in infancy, and which grew with their growth, till they found that the tie was impossible to break. Circumstances had rendered it necessary for the young man, whose Indian name was Wawabegwonabec (or the Waving Plume) to leave his birthplace for a year at least. Others were busy in their preparations for a voyage to the Upper Mississippi. And it was at this period that I first became acquainted with him. The interest I took in him, caused him to place confidence in me, and he related to me his situation and prospects. I told him I would aid him as much as lay in my power, and when inquiry was made, if they could take Rosalie along, the answer was, that it was utterly impossible, and having given his word that he would go on the voyage, and impelled by other motives, he concluded that sooner than break his promise, that he would go, and leave her behind for a year, one whom he thought to have taken as his betrothed wife, and in whom his whole affections were centered.

The voyagers to the Mississippi, were to leave by the earliest dawn, and the party had already encamped about one mile from the village.[99] He requested me to accompany him, to bid farewell to the friend of his childhood, and the loved object of his youth. We reached the lodge a little before sunset, which was situated on a high point of land, which overlooked the rapids, and beyond the foot of the falls. The view extended a mile or two over the smooth gliding waters of the river, and the place was shaded by tall and majestic elms and maples, which cast a melancholy shade over the whole, and where often her plaintive notes were heard, as she watched or expected her lover to arrive in his light and buoyant bark canoe. We found her seated on a rock, listening to the passing bubbling stream, and gazing on the smooth surface of the river, as it glided along a short distance below, and which the declining rays of the sun, gave a golden appearance, and those rays cast their mellow shades over the beautiful scenery around. As we approached, her eyes beamed with pleasure, and the young man took a seat near her. It was some time before he could tell her, that it was impossible for her to accompany him and that he had come to bid her farewell. With great exertion he told her the sad news, and he rose, and stood before her. She gazed at him with a look of vacancy, and extended her arms, and said, "will you thus leave me," and both clasped each other in their arms. When she was again seated, I used all the encouraging language I could to relieve their feelings. I told them to hope for future happiness, and brighter prospects. I then took the young man by the arm, and led him from the painful scene. The young woman cast a wild look after us, and then dropped her head on her bosom, and we turned an angle of the road or path, and she and all the village was lost to our view.

The next day saw us on the blue waters of the Lake; days passed, but what a change in the young man. I tried to console him, and his eye at moments would beam with joy, but it was only momentary, but his looks were sad and melancholy, and he would never join in the sport and boisterous laugh of the young men who composed the party. His only relief appeared to be, to come to me, and mention those fears and hopes, which hung nearest his heart, and after receiving all the soothing consolation which I could give, appeared to retire with some relief. And it was not, till some time after we had entered the hazardous incidents of an overland journey to the Mississippi, that he appeared to get over his sadness. A long winter succeeded. Days and months wore away. At last Spring came, with it, partially his flow of spirits returned, as we rapidly descended the streams which took us to the lake, and when we once more viewed the wide blue waters of it, which would lead us home, he ran and jumped with joy, on the fine white sand, and his countenance once more beamed with joy.

We will turn for a few moments to the young woman, who as anxiously as himself expects his return. We left her seated on a rock, and the intensity of her feelings were such, that no tears came to relieve her in this painful situation, and it was not till late in the evening, that she entered the lodge. She did not upbraid her fate, although the young man she knew would have to undergo perils. Her sorrow was still and melancholy, and she never mentioned any thing connected with it to any one. Only days afterwards, could she shed tears, which were balm to her bosom, and she looked more serene and happy, and when that name was mentioned, her eyes would beam with inward pleasure. She never would join her friends in their innocent amuse-

ments, but preferred remaining at home, and passed her time in antici-
pating the wishes of her parents, brothers and sisters. She loved to
walk under the shades of those trees alone, and take her seat near the
brink of the rapid and foaming stream, and there pour out her feelings, in that low plaintive and melancholy strain which is so peculiar
to the Indian women, and which only those who understand it, can
appreciate. Time passed, and she had to undergo trials. Numbers of
her own rank in life showed her all the attention they possibly could.
Offers were made, and those whose pecuniary means could have made
her happy were among the number. Arts were used and high inducements held out to her, but she turned from them with eyes moist with
tears and mildly refused all their offers. Spring came on, with its accustomed loveliness, and their lodge was once more situated on that
beautiful spot which we have mentioned before, and it was in the
latter part of May, the ground was covered with wild flowers, the
weather mild and exhilarating, and she was seated on the same rock
which we have mentioned before, it overlooked a village of lodges
below, all were enjoying the pleasant afternoon. All appeared to be
happy but herself. When word was brought to her that the boats from
the lake were in sight, she hastily threw on her blue mantle and went
up to the accustomed landing place. When she reached it, the Boat
was just nearing the land, and before it touched they clasped each
other in their arms; I never witnessed a more affecting meeting. Some
of the baggage was landed, in order that the boats might descend the
rapids with safety. She said she would accompany him, and when all
was landed at the village, I went to visit those in whom nature had
implanted such strong feelings of virtue, and those females who are
gifted with such virtues, devotedness & constancy; they are indeed
ornaments to their sexes, and a blessing to man, and may all such
realize the joys which this world can give. I witnessed the ceremony
which connected their hearts for life, & they were happy in the circle
of their friends. A pleasant period after I bid adieu to them and the
interesting scenes of the West.[100]

TRADITION
RESPECTING POINT IROQUOIS

Oshawushcodawaqua[101] relates, that the Chippewas, when settled at
Garden river,[102] lived in continual dread of the Iroquois; war parties
of whom were often on their borders, and carried off stragglers. One

day, a man with his wife and two children, went down the river, fishing. While thus employed, they were surprized and taken by a party of Iroquois in four large canoes. The latter held on their way up the river, to the falls, taking the west channel, by which they escaped notice. The friends of the captured family, fearing that some accident had befallen them, sent a scout to ascertain. This man, learning the fact of their capture, and the route the enemy had pursued, lost no time in reporting it, to the Garden river band. A council was immediately held. It was determined to collect their forces, and give pursuit. But as a preparatory step, several scouts were sent up the river to make discoveries. When they came to St. Mary's, they landed on the Canada shore, near the head of Sugar island, and following cautiously through woods and grass till they came opposite the village of St. Mary, described the Iroquois encamped upon the hill. They had boiled the Chippewa captive, and were dancing round the kettle, each warrior holding his spear-club before him, and occasionally thrusting it into the kettle and taking out bits of the flesh— then shouting with one voice. The most fearless defiance marked their whole conduct.

The Chippewa scouts having returned and given information of what they had observed, a war party was soon mustered, and started in the pursuit. They were joined on the way by others, making the total number of warriors about one hundred.

When this party reached the old village of St. Mary's, they found the Iroquois had passed on, directing their course into lake Superior, but so recently, that their drums could still be heard as they advanced up the river. When the enemy reached Point aux Pins,[103] the wind was ahead, and they were detained there two days. On the third day, they attempted the passage at a late hour, the waves still running high. It was almost dark when they reached the cape of land, since called Point Iroquois;[104] where they encamped in six lodges. They had time before dark, to fix their camp, peel some bark, &c. The weather was threatening.

The Chippewas had narrowly watched all their movements, and kept at a distance behind. They were led by four chiefs, one of whom was a prophet. They reached Point aux Pins a short time after the Iroquois left it, and were in great doubt about following them that evening. The prophet had recourse to his art, and announced that if a dark cloud arose, and appeared to pursue an irregular waving course through the air, their enterprize would be crowned with success. What had been easily foretold, in so unsettled a day, happened, and the whole band inspirited by this favorable omen embarked in two divisions—one holding on into the lake with a view to strike the shore beyond Point Iroquois, the other keeping more directly across the strait to make the land on this side. Both parties reached the shore in the dark and undiscovered. They united and formed a circle around the camp of the Iroquois. They then sent scouts to observe narrowly the situation of the enemies camps. They found them still up, singing their war songs, and beating their drums in the same fearless manner which they had carried at St. Mary's. They seemed wholly unsuspicious of any approaching enemy.

This being reported, the Chippewa leaders determined to wait, till they should go to sleep. The prophet predicted that it would rain towards day-break. It was arranged in their evening council, that each tent should be surrounded at the same moment, the poles lifted and the tent thus precipitated upon the sleepers. And that they should then use their clubs in putting to death each one, as he arose, and struggled to get free. Their bows and arrows were of no use.

The plan succeeded according to their most sanguine expectations. They entered the camp during a shower of rain, near day light. Not a soul was awake to give the alarm; and every Iroquois was put to death except two. There were about fifty in all.

The two saved, tradition adds, were furnished with canoe, and told to go and inform their relatives of the result, and to tell them never again to venture into the Chippewa country.

Thus far the tradition. On comparing it with Alexander Henry (*vide his Travels*[105]) important variations will be found. He says 1000 Iroquois were killed. Carver had previously stated that the Chippewas were aided by the *Foxes,* or Outagamis, and that the battle was fought, partly in *canoes.* We adhere to the account above given, deeming it much more rational and consistent. We doubt whether the Chippewas were ever in sufficient force, in this quarter, to defeat and *kill* a thousand Iroquois. We have also great doubts whether the Foxes, at that period, the enveterate enemies of the Chippewas, ever had the magnanimity, as related by Henry, to lay aside their animosity, and assist their enemies.

The Literary Voyager

The rule which we have adopted, with regard to communications, does not require that we should express an opinion of their merit, in any more definite manner than is to be inferred from their insertion.

Our acknowledgements are due to our esteemed correspondents Hibernicus[106] and Rosa,[107] for their poetic contributions. The former has placed in our hands many of the effusions of his younger years, with permission to extract *ad libitum*. We have derived pleasure from their perusal; and we hope, through the future numbers of our paper, to be the medium of communicating the same pleasure to our readers.

The best test of good poetry is the pleasure derived from its perusal, and we take it for granted that no poetry can please without some share of the ardor of genius, and the charms of harmony. Critics may give a thousand rules for constructing good verses, but poets are guided solely by nature. To express strongly, what they feel deeply, and in a way the most natural and brief, is the height of their art.

The opinion we expressed, in our first number, of the poetical accomplishments of "Rosa," we have seen no reason to retract. There is a naivetté in her productions which is often the concomitant of taste and genius. The chastness of her images, the lively strain of piety and confiding hope in the dispensations of Providence, and the pensive serenity which marks her favorite morning and evening landscapes, are so many traits which arrest our admiration. When to these positive recommendations of her poetic attempts, we add the limited opportunities of her early life, and the scenes of seclusion which so much of her time had been passed, we think there is still greater cause to appreciate and admire. We think the "Lines written under affliction," in the present number highly beautiful, possessing at once both energy and consonance. We solicit a continuation of her efforts.

LINES WRITTEN UNDER AFFLICTION

Ah! who, with a sensative mind possest,
   Recalls the swift years that are gone,
Without mingled emotions—both bitter & blest,
   At the good & the ill he has known.

Or, how could a beautiful landscape please,
   If it showed us no feature but light?

'Tis the dark shades alone that give pleasure & ease,
'Tis the union of sombre and bright.

So wisely has God in his mercy ordain'd,
    That the bitterest cup he has cast,
Is mixed with a sweetness, which still is retain'd,
    To be drank and enjoyed at the last.

Thus feelings are chasten'd, & life is refin'd,
    By pangs that misfortunes convey,
To minds that have faith, & to bosoms resign'd,
    To bear—to forbear, and obey.

And tho' for a while, he condemns us in strife,
    To languish, and suffer, and die;
Yet the sunshine of promise—of hope & of life,
    Allures us to bliss in the sky.

                Rosa

MUSHKOWEGEECHIS, STRONG OR ANGRY SKY

This young man with his wife and two children from the upper part of lake Superior, appeared among the visitors at the new post, and agency established here in 1822. On the night of the 26th July, he was murdered in a drinking affray at an Indian camp at the head of the portage. The murderer was a half breed called Gaulthier from the Lac du Flambeau region, with whom he had been carousing during the night. Gaulthier and his savage companions fled, leaving his victim stretched out, lifeless on the grass. As soon as the affair was reported, the agent proceeded to the spot. Meantime, his widow and the brother of the deceased had dressed the corpse in his best apparel, and a new blanket, putting a cap and feathers on his head. He had been killed by a heavy blow with a pipe tomahawk, just above his right eye brow. The agent caused the body to be removed to the ancient Indian burial ground, near fort Brady, and decently interred. The Indian ceremonies, preparatory to this, were impressive. The coffin was brought and laid beside the open grave, and the lid removed. An Indian orator then pronounced a eulogy, in which his acts and character were recited. The brother then removed his cap, and pulled out some locks of his hair, when the cap was replaced, and the lid tied (not nailed) down. Two sticks of wood were now laid across the open grave. The brother then took the hand of the widow, and led her across the grave, he, taking one, and leaving her the other stick to walk on. The earth was then cast in, and the grave rounded up, and a cedar post put at its head, marked with hieroglyphics.

Marquette[108]

CONCHOLOGY

I recently observed an Indian pouch garnished with beads, interspersed with a species of small elongated univalve sea shell. The nacre of this shell was very white and smooth. The specimen itself tapers to a point. A string of leather passed through each shell, which enabled the wearer to fasten it, in a transverse direction, on the ornamental parts of the pouch. It was evidently regarded, by the native owner, as possessing a magic virtue, which is generally attributed to shells from the ocean. From close inspection, it proved to be the Dentalium eliphanticum, with the lip removed. It had been originally derived, from Indians at the mouth of the Columbia river, and passed from hand to hand, and transmitted in their traffic with each other, to this distant point.

Abieca

WORSHIP OF THE SUN

Tacitus informs us, Vol. 3, p 242. Oblations and public thanksgivings were decreed, at Rome, to the Sun, who was installed among the multifarious gods of that empire.

Shingwauk a Meday of the Chippewas, and one of the chiefs of the St Mary's band, informs me, that the Sun was formerly worshipped by the northern Indians. They regarded it, as a symbol of the deity— not as the deity himself, and by the divergence of its rays, it was deemed to diffuse intelligence, as well as light, through the world.

In examining some pictured scrolls, of this nation, the sun is depicted, in several places, to represent the Great Spirit. The pictograph is uniformly drawn as a human head, with heavy rays, surrounding it, resembling a rude halo.

ALGONAC, A CHIPPEWA LAMENT
ON HEARING THE REVELLIE AT THE POST OF ST. MARY'S

From dreams short and broken, prophetic and high,
I wake in my cabin to ponder and sigh!
I think on the days, when transcendently blest,
My forefathers revelled, the Lords of the West,
And fired by ambition, or valor severe
They wing'd the dread arrow, or brandish'd the spear—
I think how their wisdom their valor, their might,
Prevailed in the council, the chase, and the fight,
And I sigh to reflect, all deprest and o'ercast,
Those ages have vanish'd—those glories are past!
But hark! from yon battlements bristled with steel,
What sounds o'er these woodlands so heavily peal?
Now rolling—redoubling, concussive and clear,
'Tis the signal of day for the soldier. To him,
There's a joy in the music no tears ever dim,
It speaks to his feelings—his habits—his pride,
More keenly than all human language beside:—
But me—far, far diff'rent sensations oppress
It strikes on my ear like the note of distress
Ah! how can those sounds please my kindred or me,
Which remind us, our nation no longer is free!
My fancy reverts to the moments so bland,
When my own native music prevail'd in the land;
And my fathers danced blithe, on the oak-covered hill,
Remote from the White-man, and all his proud skill.

Day breaks in the east! but its glimmer no more,
Lights hope in our bosoms, or joy on our shore;—
Ah! why should its beams more illumine the cot,
Where the war song is mute, and the war dance forgot,
Where the bow & the arrow, the spear and the mace,
Gleam no more in the battle, or ring in the chase!
Ah! why should not heaven, kind heaven, resume,
Its primitive darkness, &, shroud me in gloom?
Oh fly! ye bright streaks that bedapple the morn,
Nor shine on a mortal so sunk and forlorn!

The Literary Voyager

The beauty of day, I no longer can see,
Night-midnight, alone is congenial to me.
Ye birds cease your warblings! my heart cannot bear,
The joys that, so thrill'd it, when fortune was fair,
And roud'd by the combat, or led by the chase,
I rov'd, unconfined, thro' the regions of space,
Track'd the deer from his covert, the wolf from his den,
Or rush'd to the charge with the noblest of men.
Oh teach me! ye wise men, who broadly survey,
The causes that hasten my nation's decay,
Come! teach me, to smile on the beauties that lie,
In the bright vernal landscape, the red evening sky,
While pining in want,—by misfortune opprest,
The scorpion, slavery, is gnawing my breast.

Wabishkizzy[109] may smile, Wabishkizzy may say,
I will teach you to read, I will teach you to pray,
But say, when our arts, manners, customs are lost,
What, then shall we cherish, what then shall we boast.
When the war flag is struck, &, the war drum is still,
And the council fire glimmers no more on the hill!
Can we feel any pride, but, our forefathers pride
To live as they lived—&, to die as they died.
They tell me, that, blessings for me, are in store,
The sage's-saint's-poet's-philosopher's lore
The comforts that, labor and science bestow,
The loom &, the compass, the sickle &, plough!
But, ah! can they tell me, where joy shall abide,
Without, national customs, or national pride!

And here my grief presses!—these ramparts so high,
White-white as the summer cloud floats in the sky,
These walls but, remind me, how cruelly cast,
My own native woods are encompassed at last,
In vain 'tis averr'd, with no hostile design,
That, in guarding their country, they tranquillize mine.
But, whenever I look on those common-pierc'd walls
A fearful sensation my bosom appals,—

No. 7. February 1827

Whenever I see, on these once-happy grounds
The sentinel pacing his limited rounds,
Or borne down the stream with the low evening hum
I hear the loud notes of the deep rolling drum,
I start from my visions—I cannot but see,
My nation, my nation! no longer is free;
That, all this long muster of cannon &, steel,
Tho' prudence may sanction, deny, or conceal,
But, gleams o'er the war-path that leads to the grave,
Their object,—to conquer, destroy, and enslave.

Thus rous'd from his slumbers, proud Algonac sung,
A wild native melody dwelt, on his tongue,
Then folding his robe, he sunk back on the plain,
And courted his dreams &, his slumbers again.

(Feb. 1)   Alalcol[110]

89

The Literary Voyager

No. 8.   *Sault Ste. Marie*   *February 13th 1827*

Every undertaking to amuse, through the medium of pen, ink and paper, implies some degree of order in the employment of time, and some moral, or literary effort, however humble. And it can be known to those only, who have made the experiment, how greatly the labor is facilitated by the aid of the press—where it is the business of others, to decypher, copy, and arrange. In fact, no inconsiderable part of the whole time we devote to this sheet, is taken up by the drudgery of transcribing.

In supplying it with matter, we did not, at the beginning, expect much assistance, out of the circle to whom it is dedicated, and we have not received much. The little we have received we are, however, very thankful for, and solicit a continuance of it. If it does not greatly swell in *bulk*, it tends to diversify and amuse. We much regret that those who are so competent to aid us, in this way, should ever want the leisure or the inclination.

THE AGE OF SCIENCE
A SATIRE
No. 1

States have advanced with Statesman, laws with crimes,
Scholars with schools, & governments with times;
Arts, science, letters, enterprize and trade,
New genius brighten'd, new discov'ries made,
Till ancient errors, fading one by one,
In the pure light of truth's all-searching sun,
No longer linger o'er the human mind,
Taught, rais'd, enlighten'd, altered and refin'd,—
Till human labor stript of half its care,
Winds, fire & water, steam and acids share—
Till power, no longer swayed by tyrant hands
Reverting to its source—hath burst its bands—
Till mind & matter's laws display'd we see,
And man, long-fetter'd man, at last is free!

No. 8. February 13th 1827

But in this change, so happy & so bright!
In this proud glare of intellectual light,
Is there no spot to soil its sunny hue!
No murky cloud to blear the flatt'ring view,
No latent folly, hov'ring o'er the times,
To dim their brilliancy, & point their crimes?
Turn and survey, you learn, cadav'rous throng!
In vain inventive, clamorously wrong,
For whom in vain, great Faustus hath essay'd,
Wits written, poets sung, & martyrs pray'd,
Whom light could ne'er illume, nor reason school,
The schemer, the empirio, and the fool.
Mark Mechanistus—plodding underground,
For novel modes of motion, light, and sound,
For principles, unknown to nature's laws,
Ends without means, effects without a cause;—
Now wrapt in golden doubts, & midnight schemes,
He hews a model, fancied once in dreams!
Or buoyed with hopes, mole-working dulness feels,
Lost in the plenitude of cranks and wheels,
He sees in thought before his sleepless eyes,
Wide o'er the land his labor'd engines rise,
And streamless wastes, & high o'er hanging hills,
Groaning with self-impelling cars or mills;—
He joys within himself, that none before,
Had found the long-sought mighty, golden power!
Ah! luckless man, with all thy hair-brain'd skill,
At lock or pulley, lever, crank, or mill,
How link'd, how like's thy nature & thy rules,
Perpetual motions and perpetual fools.

Lo! yonder night, who, sour'd by fortune's frown,
Now walks at noon-day slip-shod thro' the town,
He, lost to mirth, and foe to cleanly rooms,
Plods in lone cellars, or in attic glooms,
Buried in chips & gauzes, glues & strings,
The proud materials of human wings:
Alike to him, if Greek or Turk prevail,
So he can mould a wing, or form a tail,

91

Nay, fleets may perish, quadrupeds all die,
For what their further use? he soon will fly!
Strange! that a being formed for high pursuits,
Should covet thus the meaner pow'rs of brutes,
Turn from his proper business, sphere & use,
And sigh for the endowments of a goose!

Rhabdomus, arts more daring aims to teach,
Arts that supernal powers alone can reach!
With monkish skill & old alchemic lore
From foreign climes he seeks our happy shore;
Well skill'd is he, in many a darkling trick,
By magic rod, or prescient hazel stick,
Or quick effluvia, piercing through the ground,
His nostrils guiding, as they guide a hound.
Deep read, in nature's most occult designs,
And erudite in cabalistic signs,—
Well vers'd in many a wizard-wise conceit,
Where hidden waters run, & where they meet,
Where subterranean treasures lie forgot,
In isle or main, bed, cavity, or pot:
Nor less to him, such powers of speech belong,
As still may serve to hold the gazing throng,
And fix their wonder; they on tiptoe stand,
To catch his tale, but eye his gilded wand;
They ponder much on all that he has wrought,
Gold in each hope, a mine in every thought,
And still with dumb belief, the wonder spreads,
To hear of all he sees & knows & dreads!
They marvel much, how any mortal eye,
Light task for him! can read the fates on high,
Tell when propitious, & when adverse signs,
Shine thro' the Stars in clear prophetic lines;
Or, if beneath, he casts his piercing view,
What beds of rock his vision passes through,
What envious flint the silver store detains!
What stubborn granite hides the golden veins!
The while, he points their course & their extent,

And estimates their value—to a cent!
Thus fortified, with sight and smell canine,
To trace, predict, unravel and divine—
Thus wrapt in skill, he moves across the plain
A walking pestilence, a living bane,
Shame, dullness, and delusion in his train.
At his approach the lawn-devouring spade,
Upturns the area, mars the promenade;
The urn-cap'd wall, a venerable show,
Is doomed to fall—*a treasure lurks below!*
The box-hedg'd garden, late so choice a care,
Is next destroy'd—*a spring is flowing there!*
The dusty public way, the planted field,
Nor grain can save, nor rattling cars can shield.
The grave itself, revered for many an age,
No longer sacred, feels the mad'ning rage,
And e'en the mansion, loved more dear than well,
Curs'd by the rage, at last is doomed to fall.

And are there minds, so much by toil debas'd,
So lost to reason, truth, religion, taste,
Who, spite of all that science hath design'd,
And the broad march of letters & of mind,
Still pleas'd can stoop to fan this flagging rage,
And fix a vulgar stigma on the age?
Let Yale reply—Yale's hoary, classic shades,
And Ulster's plains, & Richmond's island-glades!

Damoetas[111]

THE FORSAKEN BROTHER
A CHIPPEWA TALE

It was a fine summer evening; the sun was scarcely an hour high,—
its departing rays beamed through the foliage of the tall, stately elms,
that skirted the little green knoll, on which a solitary Indian lodge
stood. The deep silence that reigned in this sequested and romantic
spot, seemed to most of the inmates of that lonely hut, like the long
sleep of death, that was now evidently fast sealing the eyes of the

93

head of this poor family. His low breathing was answered by the sighs of his disconsolate wife and their children. Two of the latter were almost grown up, one was yet a mere child. These were the only human beings near the dying man. The door of the lodge was thrown open to admit the refreshing breeze of the lake, on the banks of which it stood; and as the cool air fanned the head of the poor man, he felt a momentary return of strength, and raising himself a little, he thus addressed his weeping family. "I leave you—thou, who hast been my partner in life, but you will not stay long to suffer in this world. But oh! my children, my poor children! you have just commenced life, and mark me, unkindness, and ingratitude, and every wickedness is in the scene before you. I left my kindred and my tribe, because I found what I have just warned you of. I have contented myself with the company of your mother and yourselves, for many years, and you will find my motives for separating from the haunts of men, were solicitude and anxiety to preserve you from the bad examples you would inevitably have followed. But I shall die content, if you, my children promise me, to cherish each other, and on no account to forsake your youngest brother, of him I give you both particular charge." The man became exhausted, and taking a hand of each if his eldest children, he continued—"My daughter! never forsake your little brother. My son, never forsake your little brother." "Never, never!" they both exclaimed. "Never—never!" repeated the father and expired.

The poor man died happy, because he thought his commands would be obeyed. The sun sank below the trees, and left a golden sky behind, which the family were wont to admire, but no one heeded it now. The lodge that was so still an hour before, was now filled with low and unavailing lamentations. Time wore heavily away—five long moons had passed and the sixth was nearly full, when the mother also died. In her last moments she pressed the fulfilment of their promise to their departed father. They readily renewed their promise, because they were yet free from any selfish motive. The winter passed away, and the beauties of spring cheered the drooping spirits of the bereft little family. The girl, being the eldest, dictated to her brothers, and seemed to feel a tender and sisterly affection for the youngest, who was rather sickly and delicate. The other boy soon showed symptoms of restlessness, and addressed the sister as follows. "My sister, are we always to live as if there were no other human beings in the world.

Must I deprive myself the pleasure of associating with my own kind?
I shall seek the villages of men; I have determined, and you cannot
prevent me." The girl replied, "My brother, I do not say no, to what
you desire. We were not prohibited, the society of our fellow mortals,
but we were told to cherish each other, and that we should no [do]
nothing independent of each other—that neither pleasure nor pain
ought ever to separate us, particularly from our helpless brother. If
we follow our separate gratifications, it will surely make us forget
him whom we are alike bound to support." The young man made no
answer, but taking his bow and arrows left the lodge, and never
returned.

Many moons had come and gone, after the young man's departure,
and still the girl administered to the wants of her younger brother. At
length, however, she began to be weary of her solitude, and of her
charge. Years, which added to her strength and capability of directing
the affairs of the household, also brought with them the desire of
society, and made her solitude irksome. But in meditating a change
of life, she thought only for herself, and cruelly sought to abandon
her little brother, as her elder brother had done before.

One day after she had collected all the provisions she had set apart
for emergencies, and brought a quantity of wood to the door, she said
to her brother. "My brother, you must not stray far from the lodge.
I am going to seek our brother: I shall soon be back." Then taking
her bundle, she set off, in search of habitations. She soon found them,
and was so much taken up with the pleasures and amusements of
society, that all affection for her brother was obliterated. She accepted
a proposal of marriage, and after that, never more thought of the
helpless relative she had abandoned.

In the meantime the elder brother had also married, and settled on
the shores of the same lake, which contained the bones of his parents,
and the abode of his forsaken brother.

As soon as the little boy had eaten all the food left by his sister, he
was obliged to pick berries and dig up roots. Winter came on, and the
poor child was exposed to all its rigors. He was obliged to quit the
lodge in search of food, without a shelter. Sometimes he passed the
night in the clefts of old trees, and ate the refuge meats of the wolves.
The latter soon became his only resource, and he became so fearless of
these animals, that he would sit close to them whilst they devoured
their prey, and the animals themselves seemed to pity his condition,

and would always leave something. Thus he lived, as it were, on the bounty of fierce wolves until spring. As soon as the lake was free from ice, he followed his new found friends and companions to the shore. It happened his brother was fishing in his canoe in the lake, a considerable distance out, when he thought he heard the cry of a child, and wondered how any could exist on so bleak a part of the shore. He listened again more attentively, and distinctly heard the cry repeated. He made for shore as quick as possible, and as he approached land, discovered and recognized his little brother, and heard him singing in a plaintive voice—

> *Neesya, neesya, shyegwuh gushuh!*
> *Ween ne myeengunish!*
>   *ne myeengunish!*
> My brother, my brother,
> I am now turning into a Wolf!—
> I am turning into a Wolf.

At the termination of his song, he howled like a Wolf, and the young man was still more astonished when, on getting nearer shore, he perceived his poor brother half turned into that animal. He however, leapt on shore and strove to catch him in his arms, and soothingly said—"My brother, my brother, come to me." But the boy eluded his grasp, and fled, still singing as he fled—"I am turning into a Wolf—I am turning into a wolf," and howling in the intervals.

The elder brother, conscience struck, and feeling his brotherly affection returning with redoubled force, exclaimed in great anguish, "My brother, my brother, come to me." But the nearer he approached the child, the more rapidly his transformation went on, until he changed into a perfect wolf,—still singing and howling, and naming his brother and sister alternately in his song, as he fled into the woods, until his change was complete. At last he said. "I am a wolf," and bounded out of sight.

The young man felt the bitterness of remorse all his days, and the sister, when she heard of the fate of the little boy whom she had so cruelly left, and whom both she and her brother had solemnly promised to foster and protect, wept bitterly; and never ceased to mourn until she died.

Leelinau[112]

Lines Written Under Severe Pain and Sickness

Ah! why should I at fortune's lot repine,
Or fret myself against the will divine?
All men must go to death's deform'd embrace,
When here below they've run their destin'd race;
Oh! then on Thee, my Savior, I will trust,
For thou art good, as merciful and just,—
In Thee, with my whole heart I will confide,
And hope with Thee, forever to abide.
To Thee, my God, my heart & soul I raise,
And still thy holy, holy name I'll praise!
O! deign to give me wisdom, virtue, grace,
That I thy heavenly will may ever trace;
Teach me each duty always to fulfil,
And grant me resignation to Thy will,
And when Thy goodness wills that I should die,
This dream of life I'll leave without a sigh.

Rosa

Antique Art of the Indians

It has been remarked that the North American Indians have left no monuments by the study of which, their history is to be elucidated. And in fact, they have left none, if we require any advanced state of the arts, or even phonetic signs, inscriptions, or the use of iron tools in any form, as essential to constitute monumental remains. Their sculptural attempts in bone, shell, and steatite or clay stone, their spear heads of jasper or hornstone, their lancets of fractured flint, and even their more labored efforts in the production of the Mikeen-gwun, or stone chisel for fleshing raw skins, and axes of hornblende and porphyry, and their stone pestles for pounding grain, are the works of a people in a very rude state of society, and evince neither much industry or ingenuity beyond what may be deemed essential to supply the incipient wants of a state of nature. There is probably, a greater proficiency in mechanical or manufacturing skill, evinced in the construction of their earthen cooking vessels, than in any of their rude simple monuments.

Having had a strong desire, from the frequent examination of small fragments, to procure an entire vessel, we succeeded in ascertaining that two vessels of this kind, were buried on an island. It required an effort to overcome the reluctance of the chief, who knew the locality, to discover them. He would not consent to conduct any person to the spot. He, at length, consented through the influence and politeness of T[homas] G. Anderson Esqr. of the British Indian Department to remove one of the vessels to his village. We visited his residence for the purpose of receiving it in the spring of 1826. After the customary preliminaries of such a visit, he said he had removed the vessel, and would point it out to us. We followed him into the woods a considerable distance. When he came near the spot where he had secreted it, he stopped and informed us it was at hand. He had still a reluctance to point out the precise locality, and left us to search for it. It was deposited under the body of a fallen tree. We detail these circumstances to exemplify a degree of caution and distrust which is a general trait of the Indian character.

In shape and capacity this relic is not unlike a modern iron pot, except that it is without legs. The lower part is globular, contracting at the neck, and the lip is inflected. It appears to have been used, by being placed on a bed, or earth, or ashes, in the manner of a chemical retort upon a sand bath. It is formed with general regularity, and of an equal thickness. The exterior appears to have been carefully smoothed, but has not the circularly striated appearance of common pottery turned in the lathe. The interior structure, as shows upon a fractured edge, is coarse, and the materials employed in the mixture, appear to be essentially silex and clay. Upon the interior of the rim, is a blackish carbonaceous crust.

We enquired of the chief, how long he supposed it was since his people had relinquished the use of such vessels. He replied that he was the seventh chief, in a direct line, since the first appearance of the French among them. And that the French had supplied them with copper and brass kettles, which were not so easily broken, and that the women, whose province it was, to make the earthen pots, had long since lost the art. This chief, who is still living, and whose name is Kewikonce, evinced a degree of knowledge of Indian history, and a reflective turn of mind, which it is not frequent to meet with among his countrymen, circumstances, which lead us to place more reliance upon his statements than we otherwise should.

"Elmwood" the headquarters of the Michigan Indian Agency was built on the banks of the St. Marys River, Sault Ste. Marie in 1827, the present site of the Sault Edison Plant. Courtesy of Bayliss Public Library, Sault Ste. Marie, Michigan.

The rapids of the St. Marys River, looking south. Fort Brady is on the right. Courtesy of Bayliss Public Library, Sault Ste. Marie, Michigan.

Ojibwa Medicine Lodge from Schoolcraft's *Historical and Statistical Information Respecting the History, Condition, and Prospects of the Indian Tribes of the United States* (Philadelphia: Lippencott, Grambo & Co., 1857), part VI, p. 172.

Obijwa village on the St. Marys River. Courtesy of Bayliss Public Library, Sault Ste. Marie, Michigan.

John Johnston and his Ojibwa wife, Ozha-guscoday-way-quay (the Woman of the Green Glade). Courtesy of Bayliss Public Library and Buffalo and Erie County Historical Society.

View of Water Street looking west, Sault Ste. Marie, 1870. Artist Wharton Metcalf. Courtesy Judge Steere Collection, Bayliss Public Library, Sault Ste. Marie, Michigan.

Fort Brady, built in 1822. Artist Wharton Mecalf. Courtesy Judge Steere Collection, Bayliss Public Library, Sault Ste. Marie, Michigan.

No. 8. February 13th 1827

If we assume the period of Cartier's first visit to the St. Lawrence (1534) as the era of the first intercourse of the North Western Indians with white men, and this is perhaps a few years too early, a fraction over four scriptural generations has only elapsed since the event. By the statements of Kewikonce, seven generations of Indians, being a fraction over 40 years to each generation, has passed away within the same period. This instance is too partial to admit, of a general conclusion. But may be regarded as affording proof that the Indians have not, at least since the discovery, attained the longevity of the European stock.

Antiquarius

The Yellow Isle
A Fragment

"Listen white-man! go not there!
Unseen spirits stalk the air;
Hungry birds their influence lend,
Snakes defy, and kites defend.
There, the star-ey'd panther prowls,
And the wolf in hunger howls;
There, the speckled adder breeds,
And the famish'd eagle feeds,
Spirits prompt them, fiends incite,
They are eager for the fight,
And are thirsting night and day,
On the human heart to prey;
Touch not then, the sacred lands
Of the yellow isle of sands.

European
"Tell me red-man! hunter hoar,
Dweller on 'Chigomme's shore,
Wherefore, bound by spell or wile,
Spirit-guarded is yon isle?
Is there not, embowelled there,
Many a gem of lustre rare?
Glows there not, in hidden mine,

99

Gems that sparkle, ores that shine?
Beams there not, along the strand,
Glittering mounds of golden sand?
Tell me hunter! can'st thou not,
Guide, me, to the treasur'd spot?
Arms, with Europe's skill prepar'd,
Shall the daring deed reward,
Bands shall deck thee; feathers bless!
And the skill of Albion, dress!
With Columbia's banner'd pride,
And a chieftain's plate beside.

Indian

"Listen white-man!—moons have past,
Since this earth was all a waste!
Rains had drench'd it, earthquakes rent,
Winds demolish'd, ages spent;
And the waters black and still,
Slumber'd deep o'er every hill,
And not one ling'ring beam of light,
Illum'd the vast and moonless night:
'Twas then the Spirit of the sky,
In mercy hung yon lamps on high,
Sun, moon, and stars! and by their light,
Expell'd the dread chaotic night;
Then cloth'd he, hills and vales with trees,
And slated bounds to lakes and seas,
Then sent he, birds and beasts in woods,
And fish in all our limpid floods
And creatures small, of foot and wing,
And every living, breathing thing.
Last sent he man! (a barb'rous race;
From whom my long descent I trace)
As lord o'er all; and thus benign,
Address'd the parent of our line:—
To thee, I give these smiling woods,
These lofty hills, and peopled floods
Fill'd with all needful game; and blest

No. 8. February 13th 1827

For thy convenience, peace, and rest.
I give thee bow! I give thee spear!
To dart the fish, and fell the deer
I give thee vessel, light, to sweep,
O'er the broad stream, and billowy deep
I give thee skins for thy attire,
To shade thee, leaves; to warm thee, fire!
More need'st thou not, nor covet more,
And peace shall round thee blessings pour.
But touch not gold!—the tempter fly!
Or all thy kin shall droop and die
For in that potent poison pent,
Lurk envy, pain, and discontent,
And luxury—of life the bane,
And woe with all her haggard train.
Listen white man! dreamest thou
My soul could e'er descend so low
To sell my country, life and line
For any frail rewards of thine!
By breaking heaven's supreme commands,
To tread the isle of golden sands:
My fare is scant! my roof is low!
My country cold, and deep my wo!
And every moon that climbs yon hill
Forbodes my race both want and ill;
But scantier still must be my meal,
And keener woes my bosom feel
A sharper winter chill our sky
And louder tempests rage on high
And every limb be rack'd with pain,
And grief consume, ere I complain!
Ere I comprise heaven's decree,
By touching gold, or guiding thee.

European

"Man of the woods! thy fancies seem,
Like some distemper'd midnight dream,
Wild and devoid of reason. Vain!

101

Are all thy fears of gold, or gain.
Vain every fear of Indian mood,
That white man, wills them aught but good,
By letters, skill and care,
Toil, temperance, virtue, peace and prayer,
Or seeks by truth's prophetic rod,
Aught, but to bring them back to God.

[Henry R. Schoolcraft]

Albany, Feb. 1821

INDIAN MODE OF RECORDING IDEAS

My attention had been directed to the mode of communicating ideas possessed by the North American Indians, by means of hieroglyphics, in the year 1820, while engaged as a member of the expedition organized that year, to explore the sources of the Mississippi. Separations of the exploring party, and the detachment of sub parties on separate routes became necessary, in accomplishing the object, in the region north west of lake Superior, and it was while on one of these occasions, while crossing the humid, level summit, between the waters of the St. Louis, and a contiguous branch of the Mississippi, that a very striking exhibition of this art was made, by the Indian guide, who conducted a detached party over that unfrequented table land.[113] I had previously observed limited symbolic inscriptions on the sticks or posts set up, to denote their graves, on the island of Michilimacinac; and along the shores of lake Superior; but here, was displayed, on the surface of a smooth sheet of birch bark, a pictorial detail of the circumstances of our encampment, the number, and character of the party, the order of the camp, and the number and kind of animals, or game, which had been killed. The whole was so well arranged, and the symbols so naturally expressed, that its import, even without the aid of an interpreter, was quite obvious. And it was executed so readily by our guides, as to evince their perfect familiarity with the system. Other evidences of the general acquaintance of the Indians with this art, were afterwards witnessed. They were generally found inscribed on bark of the same species, sometimes on the decorticated side of trees, and, in a few instances, painted on rocks, with native pigments.

This art, it was noticed, was not confined to the Ojibways, in whose territorial domains, specimens of it, were first observed. On descending the Mississippi, and reaching the confines of the Dacotah or Sioux country, the same hieroglyphic system was witnessed. At a point called by the fur traders La Petite Roche, above the Falls of St. Anthony, a sheet of bark inscribed with these figures was descried, suspended from a pole on the brinks of the river.[114] The Indians attached to the expedition, to whom this display created deep interest, at once, interpreted it, as a pictorial memorial of a visit of the Sioux, into the Chippewa nation, with an offer of terms of peace.

Abieca

THE WEASEL AND WOLF
A CHIPPEWA FABLE

There was once a conversation between a weasel and a wolf. Let us have a union in our families, said the weasel, for I have such feeble powers of body, that I am always obliged to get things at night and by stealth, for fear of man, and get but a scanty living after all. Wolf, you often walk abroad by day, and all men respect your courage and dexterity. True, replied the Wolf, but if I have strong courage, I have strong enemies both by night and day. A cousin of mine, told me that wolves get fine sheep in the south, but in this poor country, we are lucky if we can catch a lynx or rabbit, and I am often put to my shifts for a meal, whereas your very feebleness is your protection. Be satisfied with what you are. You can catch mice, and get grain or roots. The Creator has tempered our powers and apetites very well, and you often escape dangers, that would crush me. Man is my worst enemy, and I am told a price is set on my head. At this moment, the trap of a hunter, sprang, and the poor wolf was caught by the legs, while the weasel scampered off.

THE DESERTED INDIAN MAID

The affections of the Indian women are strong. Their love of their offspring is not surpassed in interest, or intensity by any nation. They are deeply attached to their friends, families, relatives and tribes. The following is a free version of a native song of a Chippewa girl, the original and literal translation of which, was put in our hands.

Ah, when remembrance brings to mind
The youth as brave as he was kind,
Love, hope, and joy alternate start,
And wake a transport in my heart.

And when he bid the sad adieu,
He said "my love I'll go with you."
"I'll go with you," my heart replied,
But on my tongue the answer died.

Alas what grief—what pain of mind
I felt when I was left behind.
The kiss he gave—oh grief may kill,
Brave youth! but I shall love thee still.

The Literary Voyager

No. 9.   *Sault Ste. Marie*   *February 16th 1827*

SKETCHES OF WESTERN SCENERY
No. 1
TO CHARLES G. HAINES ESQR. N.Y.[115]

July 6th 1821

Sir: I comply with your request, by sketching the outlines of a tour, which has been commenced with some little preparation on my part, and pursued under the advantages arising from a situation in the public employment, under a distinguished person[116] who has a perfect knowledge of the history of the interesting region we are to pass. Thoughts put to paper in the profoundest depths of the woods, and by the light of a campfire at night, cannot be expected to possess the grace of diction, or research which are demanded of the closet student. It is the facts alone, which are expected to sustain my narration, and even in presenting these, I shall have nothing to excite amazement, or produce wonder. If there is any wonder in the West, it is to see with what facility, forests are felled, prairies cultivated, and towns erected. The Indian has been often described, and the only wonder he excites is that he is still wedded to his savage pursuits. To travel rapidly is our aim. You will not therefore be surprized, if I do not supply deficiencies in topography, on the natural history of the region before us. The mission of the western people is to conquer a wilderness, and in this they possess no higher powers than the axe, the saw, the lever and the water wheel. The gospel is often preached in groves, which lately re-echoed the Indian yell. Churches and school houses form the second picture of western settlements.

But, although, I have wonders to describe, like all other travellers and tourists, since the days of Megesthines, and Marco Polo, I shall expect you only to see with my eyes, and to hear with my ears, yet, I must apprize you at the outset that you are not to expect all I see, or all I hear, or all that any other person placed in my situation, could, or might see, or hear, but only such particulars, obtruding themselves to a hasty notice, as I may deem worthy, or find it convenient, to allude to. With these remarks you will be enabled to follow me in the journey more understandingly, and I will only add, that I hope you will not take it ill, if my narrative becomes tiresome, when the journey was so.

From New York to Buffalo, occupied seven days. Thence to Detroit, through Lake Erie was a steamboat journey, of two days and two nights. Owing to unavoidable delay, I did not reach Detroit until the morning of the day fixed for our departure, and I embarked on the journey with no better preparations than could be made within three hours after my arrival. It was at twelve o'clock on the third of July, when we quitted the landing in front of the mansion house of Gov. Cass, where a crowd of citizens had assembled to offer us their best wishes and salutations. The wind blew directly down the straits, and impelled our buoyant canoe at the rate of eight miles per hour. We passed rapidly down the channel of the Detroit river, checquered with its fine islands and highly cultivated shores, and held our course along the southern banks of lake Erie, but we did not find it convenient to effect a landing at any place. Our steerman pointed out to us, as we passed, the prominent points of land, that jut out into the lake, with their appropriate names, and the rich alluvial tracts which border the mouth of the river Raison, celebrated as the scene of the defeat and massacre of the army of Gen. Winchester in 1813. As we approached the entrance to Maumee Bay, we could plainly see, on our left, the cluster of islands, which mark the scene of Perry's victory. The wind, which blew strongly through the straits, exposed us to a heavy swell, the moment we entered the lake, and our slender mast bent under the momently-increasing pressure of the gale, so that we were soon compelled to reef our little sail, and more than once the waves broke furiously over our heads, and drenched us to the skin. But we encouraged our men to proceed, and at eight o'clock in the evening landed at Port Lawrence, which is at the point where Swan creek discharges itself into the head of Maumee Bay, being a distance of about seventy miles from Detroit. We were literally driven like a ship before the gale. Our mode of conveyance, consists of a birch bark canoe, such as were employed upon a former occasion, on the tour to the sources of the Mississippi, paddled by six Canadian voyageurs, and provided with a square sail. And the party is made up of Governor Cass, his secretary, myself, and a cook, ten persons in all. Our canoe is one of the most beautiful and airy models, expressly prepared and fitted up for the purpose. It carries the national standard at the stern, to indicate to the Indian tribes the character of the mission, and is provided with an awning to protect ourselves from the heat of the sun, at noon, an improvement which has been adopted from the great inconveniences we suffered for the want of it, during our passage through lake Superior in 1820. Thus prepared we are to pass the Maumee and the Wabash, the Ohio, the Mississippi, and the Illinois, and finally, to dismiss our canoe, at Chicago, on lake Michigan, which is the point of our destination. Major Forsyth, having occasion to remain one day longer at Detroit, did not embark with us, but proceeded on horseback, and joined us at Fort Meigs.

Thus Sir, I have detailed to you, our mode of travelling, the number of our party, and the limits of our route. Expect me only to continue these sketches, at irregular intervals, and do not entertain the idea of an unbroken correspondence, with one whose time, is to be passed, in the language of Chateaubriand "in the depths of the wilderness, and under the huts of the American savages."

Such have been indeed, the scenes I have encountered, since leaving the sylvan shores of lake Dunmore, and the polished circles of Middlebury and its collegiate circles, where our friendship commenced. Five years have passed away since this happy period, and they have been to me five years of busy, practical experience and instruction in the realities of life on a vast frontier, where the ambitious, the enterprizing, and the unsatisfied are seeking their fortunes, far from the homes they loved. I have learned to sleep on a prairie, under the open canopy of heaven, serenaded sometimes, by howling wolves—to dine on grapes or blackberries, if they were fortunately by the way, or on acorns, if the wild turkies, or bears, had spared them. And in default of either, to take a drink of spring water to encourage hope.

Patwabincaega[117]

The Unchangeable Character
of the Indian Mind

To the traveller who visits the upper lakes for information,—to the man of business who casually passes over them in the pursuit of gain or to the christian teacher, who is activated by more exalted motives, no object presents itself so forcibly to mind, as the impoverished, feeble, and erratic native tribes. We there observe the moral problem of a race, who have existed in contact with a people differing from them in all that constitutes physical and intellectual distinction, without having embraced, in any visible degree, manners and opinions urged upon them by the precept and example of centuries, or without having lost any of the distinguishing traits, which mark them as a peculiar people. We see the lean and lynx-eyed hunter directing his stealthy footsteps along the shores of these ample waters, like some solitary and discontented ghost, wandering over the deserted plains, where mighty nations once flourished. We see the warrior, smeared with earthy pigments, and decorated with feathers, treading the mystic ring of the war dance, and panting for the only species of honorable distinction, warlike renown, known to his forefathers. We see the Indian physician, the juggler and the wabeno, practising their rites, or exercising their skill, and rivetting the attention of their credulous auditors, or more credulous patients. If we examine the Indian household, we find the consecrated gus-ki-pe-qa-gun, a medicine sack, containing charmed medicines. If we visit the dwelling of the sick, we find offerings to an invisible agency of spirits, suspended from a pole conspicuously placed. And if we go to the graves of the dead, we observe the idea of materiality throwing its grovelling fetters around the disembodied soul, in the food deposited upon the grave, and the implements buried within it. In all this, there is little to distinguish the Indian of 1827, from the Indian of 1534. They both exhibit the same patient endurance of human suffering, the same stoical indifference to pain and hunger, the same passion for warlike achievement and love of a wild forest independence, which have cost them so many battles, so many defeats, and so profuse a loss of numerical force, and territorial sovereignty.

Philanthropy cannot console itself that its efforts to meliorate their condition have produced any important changes in their mental habits—that it has led them to adopt any new trains of thought, or more refined and methodical modes of action. Religion has no cause to exult in the extent of its achievements. Nor can it be said that Industry has produced results at all corresponding to the efforts she has made. We are not aware that the Occums,[118] Hendricks,[119] Caloins, Obookaiahs,[120] and Williams'[121] whom our colleges have sent back to their native tribes, have had the influence to make their people, as a people, more temperate and moral and pious, than were their ancestors. Eliot[122] in 1640, Brainard[123] in 1740, and Kirkland[124] in 1770 did not certainly, labour in vain. But the tribes are still, "a cake unturned."

As respects the mere exterior man, we have effected, all that has been effected. We have clothed him in a robe of woolens, instead of skins, and we have put a gun into his hands, and taught him the use of an explosive mixture, infinitely more prejudicial and destructive to life, and the means of his subsistence, than the bow and the arrow. But, with every means and appliance, we have wrought far less change in the native constitution of his mind, and made far less advances in his good opinion, than it is consolatory to our pride to admit. And whenever he has been called on for opinions by which the conduct of life is regulated, or passion and prejudice governed, we have found the primeval character essentially unchanged. A single Pontiac or Tecumseh, has done more to preserve their original manners and customs and modes of thinking and acting, than all the Sagards[125] and Marquettes, or the Eliots and Brainards who have occupied the missionary field since the era of the discovery. We do not mean to underrate the labors either of our own, or foreign missionaries, or to express any opinion adverse to a work recommended by noble and exalted sentiments. We refer only to the existing state of facts, and to a principle in the Indian mind, which has enabled it to resist intellectual culture, for so long a time, and to so great an extent.

During the time they have been placed in juxtaposition to our population, they have steadily declined in numbers. They have often changed their abodes, receding as we advanced, and have passed through several degrees of longitude. But under every change of position, they have manifested a uniform reluctance to agriculture and the mechanic arts, as modes of subsistence, and a uniform preference for the chase. Perhaps the general causes of their declension, have never been placed before them, in a manner better suited to their comprehension, than they are found, in a reply of Jefferson, to a delegation of Delawares, Mohegans, and Munsees, in 1808.[126]

"The picture which you have drawn, of the increase of our numbers, and the decrease of yours, is just; the causes are very plain, and the remedy depends on yourselves alone. You have lived by hunting the deer and buffalo; as these have been driven westward, you have sold out on the seaboard, and moved westwardly in pursuit of them. As they became scarce there, your food has failed you; you have been a part of every year without food, except the roots and other unwholesome things you could find in the forests. Scanty and unwholesome food produce diseases and death among your children, and hence you have raised few, and your numbers have decreased. Frequent wars too, and the abuse of spirituous liquors, have assisted in lessening your numbers.

"The whites, on the other hand, are in the habit of cultivating the earth, of raising stocks of cattle, hogs, and other domestic animals, in much greater numbers than they could kill of deer & buffalo. Having always a plenty of food and clothing, they raise abundance of children, they double their numbers every twenty years. The new swarms are continually advancing upon the country, like flocks of pigeons, and so they will continue to do. Now, my children, if we wanted to diminish our numbers, we could give up the culture of the earth, pursue the deer and buffalo, and be always at war. This would soon reduce us, to be as few as you are; and if you wish to increase your numbers, you must give up the deer and buffalo, live in peace, and cultivate the earth. You see then, my children, that it depends on yourselves alone, to become a numerous and great people."

The frigid apathy with which they appear, thus far, to have contemplated their fate, may be denominated stoicism or philosophy. But could any of the descendants of European stocks, have been placed in a similar condition, and so long resisted the influence of industrious example,—so long put off the work of reform, and so steadily declined the task of preparing for the future, we might have found a harsher epithet to denote the indifference.

Where the pressure of white men, has yet created no demand for the extensive domain, to which they hold the title of possession, thousands of acres are held by a few isolated individuals. Populous villages in the days of the Jesuit fathers, are dwindled to a few hunters, or fishermen. And whole nations are only recognized by as many feeble and insignificant bands. Doomed to extinguishment by some inscrutable fiat, we see the race of aborigines, like the primitive inhabitants of Canaan, falling before their invaders like grain beneath the scythe, and leaving their rich inheritance "to men of other minds." Whether the question of their origin, can ever be settled, is comparatively unimportant. Learning and ingenuity have been employed in tracing them to the house of Jacob, by proofs, not always the best of which the subject admits, and by conclusions quite unsatisfactory; but which, if undisputed, ought to have very little practical bearing upon the subject. We live under a dispensation, in which the Jew and the Gentile, "the bond and the free" are alike subjects of moral and religious cultivation and improvement. That inscrutable Power, who deemed it suitable to seal the great propitiary sacrifice, by rending the vail of the temple, from that instant, recognized the whole human race as coming within the scope of the faith and promises.

We live in an age favorable to missionary and school efforts, and under a government tolerant of human rights. Whether we have acquitted ourselves of our duty towards our aboriginal population, is a question, momentous in itself, but which we are not prepared to decide. In the interim of continued experiment, while opinions are forming and renewed efforts making, it is the dictate of a humane and liberal spirit to improve every opportunity for acquiring fresh information, and eliciting new and authentic traits of their character and history.

It has been remarked that the Indians of North America are, to the inhabitants of this continent, what "the fallen arch, the broken column and the incrusted medal" are to the philosophers of Europe. But it may be further remarked, that the study of the former is enveloped in a more impenetrable mystery, for the base of the arch itself is gone, the column is shattered into a thousand fragments, and the medal is without inscription. The study of our Indian history is, indeed, rather the province of the Menologist & antiquarian than the historian, and few have probably attempted to investigate the one or the other, without discovering how little aid is to be gleaned from authentic books, or learned from the inspection of their monuments.

THE INDIAN RHAPSODIST

The following response to sentiments of "Algonac," was hastily sketched by one who admires both the thoughts and the livery in which they appeared. It is placed at the disposal of the editor of the Literary Voyager.

> The lyre the forest minstrel strung,
> In strains responsive to his grief—
> Swell'd full and soft the tide of song,
> That bore along the patr'arch chief.
>
> He sung of days forever fled,
> He prais'd his nation's prowess more,
> He struck the war-notes of the dead,
> And drew the bow—now strung no more.
>
> He wail'd no white man's happy'r state,
> Nor car'd he for the plough or loon;
> But deeply mourn'd his nation's fate,
> As such, fast gliding to the tomb.
>
> Zina Pitcher[127]

CHIPPEWYANS

We occasionally see a stray individual here, from this remote northern tribe. Mackenzie informs us that the progress of the Chippewyans is easterly, and according to their own traditions, they came from Siberia, "agreeing in dress and manners with the people now found upon the coast of Asia."[128] Their name of Chippewyan is an Algonquin word, denoting their being clothed in fishers skins. They have also a tradition among them, that they originally came from another country, inhabited by very wicked people, and had traversed a great lake, which was narrow, shallow, and full of islands, where they had suffered great misery, it being always winter, with ice and deep snow.

From individuals of this tribe, who have visited the post, the Chippewyan language is seen to be radically different from the Algonquin. Its vocabulary is however comparatively barren and uncultivated. They have, few numerals, and no comparison of nouns.

TO MRS. SCHOOLCRAFT
ON THE ANNIVERSARY OF HER BIRTH-DAY

> Muse! oh maid of tuneful tongue!
> Ever happy, fair, and young;

No. 9. February 16th 1827

Ever fond of sylvan sweets,
And the peace of still retreats—
Timid, lonely, pensive maid!
Grant me now thy wanted aid,
That a wreath I may prepare,
To adorn my plighted fair,
Such as may her brows array,
Deftly on her natal day.

Let there be no gaud or splendor,
Make it simple, modest, tender,
Unaffected, sweet, and kind,
Faithful emblem of her mind:
Gather, on the mountain's side,
Rose-tipt daisies—Flora's pride,
Modest, humble, little sweet!
Such as she herself would greet.
Cull the violet's timid head,
From the garden's cultur'd bed;
Lovely flower, of sunny ray,
Ever blooming, sweet and gay:
Bring from out the shelter'd dell,
Tender plant! the blue hare bell;
Seek around the upland close,
For the simple wilding rose:
Search the Shadow-border'd mead,
For the blush-lit, *miscodeed*,[129]
Native flower, of odor sweet,
Lover of the calm retreat.
Let the soft pine's ever green,
In the faithful braid be seen,
Emblem of a faith most true,
When the flower hath lost its hue;
When the breathing spring is past,
And on life we look the last.

Put of cypress—one small leaf,
To denote a latent grief,
For the cherub that was given,
But has flown away to heaven.

Let the sweet-grass' shining blade,
Mingle in the tender braid;
Braid it neat, and braid it fine,
Let no prickly leaf entwine,
Nought to mar the tender thread,
Or excite one thought of dread.

'Tis complete! Accept it then,
Thou, to whom this verse I bring,
Borne on love's extatic wing!
Wear it, on thy natal morn,
'Twill thy gentle brow adorn;
Wear it—as an offering pure,
Of affection ever sure,
Tribute to thy manners chaste,
Virtue, tenderness, and taste,
Without taint and without guise,
Youth's reward, and Hymen's prize.

Nenabaim[130]

Sault Ste. Marie, 1826

European Prejudice

Mr. John Halket in his *Notes on the Indians*,[131] published at London in 1820, by a studiously advocated theory in despite of fact, contrasts the American policy of Indian treatment, with that of France and England, while ruling here, and as if civilization, letters, and christianity were justly chargeable for the wildest disorder of republican institutions, & they could produce nothing else, but barbarism of manners & theories.

Were not the tribes counselled during the American revolution, and since, to the highest and best objects of civilization? Did not Kirkland in 1775 teach the Oneidas christianity, instead of war and discord? Were not Skenandoah, Cornplanter, and Farmer's brother, examples of sound teachings in arts, letters, and politics? Did not Sagatowa, or Red Jacket with his shrewdness, wit, eloquence and common sense, rise to eminence under the American conferences, councils and treaties?[132] Have the just and humane dealings, which characterize the whole policy of the American government, a proof of its superior treatment of the Race?

Shawnees

The people of this nation have a tradition, that their ancestors crossed the sea. They are the only tribe of the U.S. with which I am acquainted, who admit a foreign origin. Until lately, they kept a yearly sacrifice, for their safe arrival in this country from the South. From whence they came, or at what period they arrived in North America, they do not know. It is a prevailing opinion, among them, that Florida had once been inhabited by white people, who had the use of edge tools. Black Hoof (a chief) affirmed that he had often heard it spoken of, by old people, that stumps of trees covered with earth, were frequently found, which had been cut down by edged tools.

"It is somewhat doubtful whether the deliverance, which they celebrated, has any other reference, than to the crossing of some great river, or an arm of the sea."[133]

Tecumseh, a Cause of Indian Depopulation

Among the temporary causes of depopulation, affecting the north western Indians in modern times, none, since the ravages of the small pox in 1778, has perhaps had a greater effect, than the influence and character of Tecumseh, and his brother the Prophet. By addressing themselves to the prejudices of the Indians, they acquired an influence over them, which, sustained as it was, by the resources of a foreign government, was wielded to embody a very large force. This force could, however, never be completely controlled, nor effectively employed. A force which served to keep the frontiers in alarm, and bedizen the flanks of an army, to whose strength it undoubtedly added while the British army was operating successfully, but in the moment of defeat, like elephants trained to battle, they either threw their own ranks into confusion, or fought on the triumphant side. To provide for the support of such a description of force, poorly and partially as they were in fact supported, required no inconsiderable effort. And when reverses came, the Indians were abandoned to misery and sufferings in all their complicated shapes. It is computed by those who participated in the scenes which were witnessed upon the American frontiers in 1812-14; or immediately followed, that for one warrior who was killed in battle, ten died of the effects of exposure in bad weather without tents, from scanty or defective provisions, or from diseases induced by leaving their own healthy and elevated regions, to subsist on salt food, amidst the marshes and low grounds where they were so much employed.

The efforts made by Tecumseh and his coadjutor, were commenced as early as 1806, and to the accomplishment of his scheme, he sacrificed eight years of his life in constant and almost unremitted exertions. His views, however enlarged, were impracticable. They embraced within the plan of an Indian confederacy, the most remote, as well as contiguous tribes. Unsuccessful at first, he accomplished by perseverance, by assuming arts of popularity, and by a fortunate junction of extraneous circumstances, what he could not, otherwise have effected, a partial union, and effort at concreted action, amongst the northwestern tribes. In accomplishing this ill joined confederacy he accomplished in truth, their ruin. They have never since been able to muster the same physical force, and it is assuming, but little to add, *they never will*. The Indian power, in the U.S. expired with him.

The Literary Voyager

No. 11.   *Sault Ste. Marie*   *February 1827*

To the student of the Indian mind and history, there are materials, which could be employed to show that this race, has a peculiar mythology. Unlike the Hindoo race they do not personify the great principles of nature. They have no Vistno and Siva. Their mental inventions, represent passions & personal traits and characteristics. Thus IAGOO is the prince of story-tellers—WEENG, is the embodiment of somnolency; KWASIND of strength, and PAPUCKEWIS of tricks and harlequinism. PAUGUK, represents Death, JEBI, a ghost. PUKWIADGININI, a pigmy or fairy. WINDIGO, a giant.

There is another class of creations, which may be called astronomical, or astrological. The East is personified under the name of WAUBUN, the West, KABEAN, the South, SHAWANDASEE, and the North, KABEBOONOCCA.

For the hills and mountains, they have a class of fairies or little men, called Ininees. For the lakes and rivers, and cataracts, they have a class of water-spirits, who perform the office of Naids. And for the forests and woods, there is a very numerous class of vocal spirits and daemons.

All these are entirely distinct in their offices, and powers, from the Great Spirit, the Monedo, the Ozeaud and the Master of Life. There is, indeed, reason to conclude that spiritual life exists in these great classes. I. The Deity, residing in the upper space, or blue firmament. II. Agents who dwell in the air. III. Terrestrial spirits, who occupy the surface of the earth.

PAPUCKEWIS

There are usually, two storms, of wind and drifting snow, which the Indians distinctly notice in the month of March—about the time of the vernal equinox. Sometimes the latter of these storms does not take place until the beginning of April. During such weather it is common for one of the group, who are nestled in the lodge, to observe—"Ah! Papuckewis is now gathering his harvest," and this immediately puts the whole circle into the best humor, although perhaps the moment before, they were suffering from cold and hunger. This myth is founded upon the following story.

In old times, during a long and severe winter, Papuckewis and his family were upon the point of starving. Every resource seemed to have failed. He could no longer procure fish from the lake, and the severity of the season had driven the Cariboo into the remotest recesses of the interior. He was travelling along the bleak and ice-bound shores of the Great Water,[134] where the autumnal winds had piled up the ice into high pinnacles resembling castles. "I know," said he to his family, "that there are spirits of Cabebonoca (which is the North) residing in those icy castles, and I will solicit their pity." He did so, with all ceremony. His petition was not disregarded, and they told him to fill his sacks with ice and snow, and to pass on towards his cottage, without looking back, until he came to a certain hill, and there to drop his sacks and leave them until morning, when he would find them filled with fish. But they cautioned him, that he must by no means look back, altho' he would hear a great many voices crying out "Thief! Thief!" as he went along, for it was nothing but the wind sighing among the branches of the trees. He, however, strictly obeyed the injunctions of the Spirits, and was rewarded according to their promise.

It chanced that Manabozho, who is often the subject of ridicule, came to visit him, on the day that he had brought home his sacks of fish, and he was invited to partake of a feast which Papuckewis ordered to be prepared for the occasion. But while they were partaking of the feast, the guest could not resist the desire he felt to ask his entertainer, by what fortunate means he had procured such an abundance of food, at a time when they were all in a state of starvation.

Papuckewis frankly imparted to him the secret, and the precautions which were necessary to ensure success, which the other determined to profit by, as soon as he should return to his lodge. But the ever active and inquisitive disposition of Manabozho rendered his attempt vain, and brought upon him the displeasure of the spirits of Cabebonoca. As he ran along with his sacks of ice and snow, he continually heard "Thief! Thief!" vociferated in his ears. "He has stolen fish from Cabebonoca" cried one. "Catch him! catch him!"

cried another. "Muckumick! muckumick! muckumick,"[135] cried a third. In fine, his ears were so assailed by these continued cries, that he could not avoid turning his head to see who it was, that uttered these opprobrious epithets.

But the charm was dissolved, his sacks, when examined the next morning, contained nothing but ice and snow. And the spirits as a punishment for his curiosity, condemned him every year, during the month of March to run about over the hills with his bags of ice and snow upon his back, the cries of thief! thief! stop him! stop him! Muckumick! muckumick! still following him.[136]

MANNERS AND CUSTOMS OF THE CHIPPEWAS[137]
No. 2

In the feasts we have described, the company is as general, with regard to the rank, age or standing of the guests, as the most unlimited equality of rights, and the broadest principles of good feeling, can make it. All the aged, and many of the young are invited.

There is, however, another feast instituted at certain times during the season, to which young persons only, are invited, except the entertainer and his wife, and, generally, two other aged persons, who preside at the feast, and administer its rites.

The object of this juvenile feast seems to be instruction, to which the young and thoughtless are induced to listen, for the anticipated pleasure of the feast. When the meats are ready, the entertainer if he be fluent of speech, if not, some person whom he has invited for that purpose, gets up, and addresses the youth of both sexes, on the subject of their course through life. He admonishes them to be attentive and respectful to the aged, and adhere to their counsel; to obey their parents; never to scoff at the decrepit or deformed; to be modest in their conduct; to be charitable and hospitable; and to fear and love the Great Spirit, who is the giver of life, and of every good gift.

These precepts are dwelt upon at great length, and generally enforced by examples of a good man and woman, and a bad man and woman, and after drawing the latter it is customary to say—"You will be like one of these." At the end of every sentence, the listeners make a general cry of haa!

When the advice is finished, an address to the Great Spirit is made, in which he is thanked for the food before them, and for the continuance of life. The speaker then says, turning to the guests, "Thus the Great Spirit supplies us with food; let your course through life be always right, and you will ever be thus beautifully supplied." The feast then commences, and the elders relax their manner a little, and mix with the rest; but are still careful to preserve order, and a decent respectful behavior.

Let it not be supposed, however, that the Indian's life, while on his wintering grounds, is a round of feasting. Quite the contrary. His feasts are often followed by long and painful fasts, and the severity of the seasons and scarcity of game and fish often reduce him, and his family to starvation, and even death. When the failure of game, or any causes, induce the hunter to remove to a new circle of country, the labor of the removal falls upon the female part of the family. The lodge, utensils, and fixtures of every kind, are borne upon the women's backs, sustained by a leather strap around the forehead. On reaching the intended place of encampment, the snow is cleared away—the lodge set up—cedar boughs brought and spread for a floor—the moveables stowed away—wood collected—and a fire built. And then, and not until then, can the females sit down and warm their feet and dry their moccasins. If there be any provisions, a supper is cooked; if there be none, all studiously strive to conceal the exhibition of the least concern on this account; and seek to divert their thoughts by conversation quite foreign to the subject. The little children are the only part of the family who complain, and who are privileged to complain, but even they are taught at an early age to suffer and be silent. Generally, something is reserved by the mother, when food becomes scarce, to satisfy their clamors; and they are satisfied with little.

On such occasions, if the family have gone supperless to rest, the father and elder sons, rise early in search of game. If one has the luck to kill—even a partridge or squirrel, it is immediately carried to the lodge—cooked, and divided into as many parts as there are members of the family. In such emergencies, the elder ones, often make a merit of relinquishing their portion to the women and children.

If nothing rewards the search, the whole day is spent by the father upon his snow-shoes, with his gun in his hands, and he returns at night fatigued, to his couch of cedar branches, or rush mats. But he does not return to complain, either of his fatigue, or his want of success. On the following day, the same routine is observed, and days and weeks are often thus consumed, without being rewarded with food sufficient to keep the body in a vigorous or healthy state. Instances have been perfectly well authenticated where this state of wretchedness has been endured by the head of a family, until he has become so weak as to fall in his path, and freeze to death.

When all other means of sustaining life are gone, the skins the hunter has collected to pay his credits, or purchase new supplies of clothing and ammunition, are eaten. They are prepared by removing the pelt, and roasting the skin until it acquires a certain degree of crispness.

Under all this suffering, the pipe of the hunter, is his chief solace, and it is a solace very often repeated. Smoking parties are sometimes formed, when there exists a scarcity of food—the want of provisions not tending, as might be supposed, to destroy social feeling and render the temper sour. On these occasions, the person soliciting company sends a message to this effect. "My friend, come and smoke with me. I have no food, but I have tobacco; and we can pass the evening very well with this."

All acknowledge their lives to be in the hands of the Great Spirit—feel a conviction that all comes from him—that he loves them—and that although he allows them to suffer, he will again supply them. This tends to quiet their apprehensions. Fatalists as to good and ill, they submit patiently and silently to what they believe their destiny. When hunger and misery is past, it is soon forgotten; and their minds are too eagerly intent on the enjoyment of the present good, to feel any depression of spirits from the recollection of misery past, or the anticipation of misery to come. No people are more easy, or less clamorous under sufferings of the deepest dye, and none are more happy, or more prone to evince their happiness, when prosperous in their affairs.

(The foregoing facts and conclusions have been taken down, from conversations recently held with Indians with whom we are well acquainted—whose confidence we think, we have fully acquired, and whose statements we can safely credit.)

ORIGIN OF THE MISCODEED[138]
OR THE
MAID OF TAQUIMENON

The daughter of Ma Mongazida, was the pride of her parents, and their only child. Beauty sat upon her lips, and life and animation marked all her motions. Fourteen summers had witnessed the growth of her stature, and the unfolding of her charms, and each spring, as it came around, had beheld her, in her happy simplicity, revelling amid the wild flowers of her native valley. There was no valley so sweet as the valley of Taquimenon [Tahquamenon]. There, she listened to the earliest notes of the wild birds, who returned from the south, to enliven the forests after the repose of winter; and there, also, she had prepared her bower of branches, and fasted to obtain a guardian spirit, to conduct her through life, according to the belief and customs of her people. Sweet valley of the Taquimenon, thou didst bless her with the charms of thy fragrance, causing the most profound sensations of pleasure. There, she first beheld that little angel, who in the shape of a small white bird, of purest plumage, assumed to be her guardian spirit, in cot and wood, through sun and storm, for the remainder of her days. Happy were her slumbers in this delightful visitation, and happy her awakening, as she hasted back, with fawn-like fleetness, to her parents lodge, with one more charm—one more pleasing recollection—one more tie to bind her fancy and her heart to the sweet valley of the Taquimenon. Beautiful valley of soft repose! there, she had first learned to know the sweet face of nature, and seen the river leap & laugh in foam, from the rocks, and then pursue its sylvan course through the green leafed forest. Sweet enthusiast of nature! wild gazer of the woods! There, too, were the sacred graves of her forefathers, and there, she hoped, when the Great Spirit should summon her to depart, her friends would lay her simply bark-enchased body, under the shady foliage in a spot she loved.

It was early in the Strawberry Moon.[139] The white coat of winter was remembered for its having lingered on many spots, which were secluded from the sun's influence. But the flowers of the forest were now in bloom, and the birds had re-visited the valley. There was a soft and balmy air, and life and animation seemed to be newly bestowed upon the whole face of the earth. The robin and the mamaitwa came back to sing, and the murmuring of waters, in the little glens and by-vallies, rose, like pleasing music on the ear, and denoted the time for the opening of buds, and the springing of flowers. Never, had the scene appeared more attractive to her eye. "Oh," she exclaimed, "that it were ever spring! that I could ever live and revel in the wild beauties of my native valley—the sweet valley of the Taquimenon."

But while all nature rejoiced, there was a deep gloom gathering over the brows of Ma Mongazida.[140] Whispers of the sign of an enemy on the lofty shores of the Pictured Rocks, had reached his ears. He thought of the haughty air of the audacious tribe of the Outagamies, who, but a few moons before, invaded the country, and had been baffled in their design. He thought of the bitter feuds of the border bands, yet pleased himself in his own seclusion far from the war path of the enemy, where, for the space of fifteen winters, there had not a hostile footprint been seen. While he lay on his couch, pondering on these things, sleep ensued, and he fancied himself to be the leader of a hostile band, who broke from the ambush, at the earliest dawn, and carried death and desolation to a slumbering village. Shocked at the catastrophe, he awoke. The dream alarmed him. He remembered that birds of ill omen had crossed his path, the day before.

"Had it been my *enemies*, the Dacotahs," said he to his wife, "I should have feared no evil, but to dream of raising the war club against the Outagamies my own blood kindred, and with whom we have been long in peace, bodes me sure disaster. Some hostile foot is, even now, on the track. Some evil bird has flown over my lodge. I will no longer abide here. Had I sons to stand by my side, most freely would I meet the foe; but, single-handed, with no one but thee, to bury me, if I am slain, and my tender Miscodeed to witness my fall, and become their prey, it were madness to abide. And this day, even before the sun is at the zenith, will I quit the peaceful valley I love— the sweet valley of the Taquimenon."

In haste, they took their morning's meal, and made their preparations to leave a scene, so loved and cherished, but loved and cherished by none, more than the gentle and enthusiastic Miscodeed. She was indeed a precious wild flower. But while they yet sat around their lodge-fire, the instinctive sagacity of that trusty friend of the Red

Hunter, the household dog, betokened approaching evil, at first, by restlessness and low murmurs, and then breaking into a loud bark, as he flew out of the door. It was a daring war party of the treacherous Mendawakantons[141] from the Mississippi. A volley of arrows followed, piercing the thin barks, which hung, like tapestry, around the lodge, and sealing in death at the same instant, the lips of both father and mother. "Oh, bird of my dreams," cried Miscodeed, "my beautiful white wing!—my angel of promise! save me from the hands of my cruel enemies." So saying, she sunk, lifeless to the ground.

With loud yells and rapid footsteps the foe entered. Conspicuous, in front, stood the eldest son of a warrior, who had been killed by the Chippewas in the great battle of the falls of the river St. Croix. His brows were painted red, and his spear poised. But the work of death was soon finished. There lay, motionless, the husband and the wife alike beyond the influence of hope or fear, hate or harm. But no other human form appeared, and the eye of the savage leader rolled in disappointment around, as he viewed the spot where Miscodeed, his meditated victim, had sunk into the earth. A small and beautiful white bird, was seen to fly from the top of the lodge. It was the guardian spirit of Miscodeed. The knife and the tomahawk were cheated of their prey—her guardian angel had saved her from being the slave of her enemy.

But the sanguinary rites of war were quickly performed; the scalps of the hunter and his wife, were torn away, and with hurry & fear, the enemy was soon on his way to his native land. When the friends of the slaughtered family, visited the silent lodge, where welcome had so often greeted them, all they saw on the ground where the maid of Taquimenon had fallen, was a modest little white flower, bordered with pink border which was at once destined to be her emblem.

Leelinau

Indian Names

The influence of geographical names on the literary character of history, is important and abiding; and, so far as we are indebted, in this respect, to the Aborigines, the subject forms a point of curious research. We have not yet passed out of the era for ascertaining and fixing the meaning and origin of many of these names, even in the Atlantic states, while, in the great area of the West, fuller means for the prosecution of such an inquiry exists. And it may be doubted whether there be any topic of mere taste, or propriety, to which, there is one sense, so *little,* and in another, so *much* interest attached.

Connected with this subject, is the question of the bestowal of names upon new towns, countries, villages, or residences, and the avoidance, in so doing, of the further repetition of foreign names already in use. The descriptive and sonorous character of the native languages, fit them in a peculiar manner, for this use; and it is believed, that, with proper means, a system of terse and appropriate aboriginal names, could be prepared, and the geographical nomenclature of the country, could be thus improved.

There is nothing in the geography of America, which impresses the observer more than the Indian names. The word America itself, could not have been more agreeable to poetic ears; nor, if the term were restricted to the area of the United States, could we have secured a more desirable name. But the Mexicans, the Cubans and the South Americans, come in for a share of advantage. I shall hereafter, beg for some further notice of this subject in your paper.[142]

LANGUAGE LINKS MANKIND IN FAMILIES

Were English history, struck out of existence, from the landing of Julius Caesar to the present day, we could clearly and conclusively prove, that the English language, is derived from the great Indo-Germanic family—and that at certain periods, there were large infusions of Teutonic French, Latins, Scandinavians &c. Words by fixing sounds, are a kind of medals. But if language is so important, in tracing the chain of the history of civilized nations, who have the use of letters, it is also important, is it not, to trace the former connections of savage nations, who lack all letters. They still have their chartography, and hieroglyphics.

The physical characteristic of races, is inferred from their features, color, stature &c. and craniological structure and its given formulas for comparing the intellect of races. Bloomenbach, Pritchard and others, deem this as one of the most important means of comparison. But I doubt, whether the sounds of the human voice, be not more permanent and reliable, than the color of a man's skin, or the shape of his face, the length of his arms, or the prominence of his cheek bones.

Hermes

MICHIGAN

Know ye the land to the emigrant's dear,
Where the wild flower is blooming one half of the year;
Where the dark-eyed chiefs of the native race,
Still meet in the council, & pant in the chase;
Where armies have rallied by day and by night,
To strike or repel, to "surrender" or fight.
Know ye the land of the billow and breeze
That is pois'd, like an isle, & fresh water seas
Whose forests are ample, whose prairies are fine
Whose soil is productive, whose climate benign;
Remote from extremes— neither torrid nor cold,
'Tis the land of the sickle, the plough, & the fold
'Tis a region no eye e'er forgets or mistakes,
'Tis the land for improvement— the land of the lakes.

Ye statesman who mingle in Congress debates
Who give laws to new lands, & give lands to new states
Who measure state justice & curb public fires,
And fix bounds to all things— *except your own ires,*
Come view this wide region— 'tis yours to declare
The frowns it has witnessed, the smiles it shall share.
Oh who can forget the black tale of its woes
While its lands are still dyed— But a truce to our foes,
We leave them to prosper in fetters or free,
As heaven may order, or monarch's decree.

To you then I turn— and I turn without fears,
Ye hardy explorers, ye bold pioneers,
Ye vot'ries of Ceres with industry blest,
Whose hopes are still high, & whose course is still west.
Ye men of New England— ye emigrant race,
Who meditate change, & are scanning the place,
Who dig and who delve on estates not your own,
Where an acre of land is an acre of stone,
Oh quit your cold townships of granite or brakes,
And hie with delight to the land of the lakes.

No. 11. February 1827

This land is so varied, so fertile, so fair
So few can excel it, so few can compare,
That turn where we will, & object as we may
That here is too little, & there too much *clay,*
That prairies are weary to view or to toil,
And cover'd with *blue-joint* instead of *trefoil.*
That vales do not sink, & that hills do not rise,
These down to the centre, those up to the skies.
Yet tell me ye judges of prairie and hill,
What country so perfect, it wants nothing still?

Our streams are the clearest that nature supplies,
And Italy's beauties are marked in our skies
The zephyrs that blow from the balmy south west,
Fall soft as the sighs of the Indian God's[143] breast.
Our woodlands are filled with rare plants & sweet flowers,
Of exquisite beauty and exquisite powers
And the isle-spotted lakes that encircle our plains,
Are the largest & purest this planet contains.
And talk as ye may talk of countries & wealth,
This land is the country of vigor and health.
O come then, ye woodsmen, wherever ye harbor,
Our motto is *"tandem fit surcules arbor."*

July 8th 1824   D

A Fox Indian told Lt. Z. M. Pike, in 1806, that he did not believe in a future state, but that he believed they were all destined to be drowned, by water, at a future time. Pike says that this opinion was not concurred in by the Fox nation generally.[144]

The Literary Voyager

No. 12.[145]   *Sault Ste. Marie*   *March 2nd 1827*

SKETCHES OF WESTERN SCENERY
No. 3[146]
WABASH
To CHARLES G. HAINES ESQR. N. Y.

The Wabash is one of the most beautiful, fertile and noble rivers of the West. Originating in a sylvan country of hills and dales, forests and prairies, its current is swelled by numerous tributaries, on the right and left—all clear crystal streams, which, as they wind their way south, unfold districts of the country, of unsurpassed fertility and loveliness. In this manner it is joined by the Wea, the Mississini-way, the Tippecanoe, the White river, and a hundred minor streams, minor only for size, but equal attractiveness of aspect, and sylvan beauty of border. In this broad and attractive valley, dwelt the Miamies and their cognate tribes, who chased the deer and the elk on its plains; displayed their nets in its waters, and trapped the beaver and otter, whose precious skins, formed the desire of foreign merchants. In some districts, this river washes monument banks of rock, as at Merom, where elevations command extreme views of its channel. In others, green forests are still permitted to grace its sides. The swan, duck and other wild fowl, play on its broad, and still reaches. In some localities its waters invade and undermine the large mounds which stood on its sides, as at the Bone Banks. It is the only large river of the West, whose channel is not interrupted by a cataract. Even its rapids are few, and easily surmounted.

It was in the richest part of this valley, where it passes through an unsurpassed range of prairie land, that the French, at the close of the 16th century founded their earliest settlement of Vincennes. Accumulating volume, at every tributary, this broad and fertile river reaches the Ohio, at a point, which renders it questionable, whether it be not the primary stream. Hence, old maps, continue the name of Wabash, to its junction with the Mississippi. The meaning of the name is lost in the involutions of the Algonquin language. To those best acquainted with the idiom, it appears to denote a moving White Cloud, —a name, which presupposes its forest application to some forgotten Indian hero, who occupied its banks.

Pawabecaiga

LAMENT FOR THE RACE

St. Mary's falls run swift & strong, & ever as on they go,
The waves from shore to shore prolong, a hollow sound of woe.
That sound upon mine ear doth write, the note of my tribe's decay;
That, like a murmuring stream by night, is rapidly passing away.

The storm that o'er it hangs, is black, & gathering still apace,
And in its cold unpitying track, shall sweep away my race,
They sink, they pass, they fly, they go, like a vapor at morning dawn,
Or a flash of light, whose vivid glow, is seen, admir'd, & gone.

But who their martial deeds shall sing, who wake the funeral song,
Or dancing round the magic ring, each choral shout prolong;
There were— there were, but they lie low, & nevermore shall spring,
To wield the lance, or bend the bow, to revel, fight or sing.

They died; — but if a red-man bleeds, & fills the dreamless grave,
Shall none repeat his name— his deeds, nor tell that he was brave;
Tho' polish'd not, my falling line, in quiet temp'rance grew,
And glory, pity, love divine, and many a virtue knew.

And they were free, & they were bold, & they had hearts could feel,
And laugh'd at hunger, pain & cold, nor fear'd the freeman's steel
Farewell! and ye my native words, repeat this simple verse,
Waft far the strain, ye limpid floods, ye vocal shores rehearse.

Dear native groves & hills & streams, my father's land & mine,
Tho' sunk our own, there still are gleams, that on my bosom shine,
Cold as ye are, with boreal chills, where lux'ry never smiles,
More sweet to me thy fir-clad hills, than India's sunny isles.

'Tis peace that gives a nation rest, 'tis virtue keeps it free,
These still were ours, had heaven blest, or Colon sunk at sea;

130

No. 13. March 10th 1827

Oh I could tell — but it is vain, & weep — but there's a vow,
My tribe scorn'd ever to complain, & I disdain it now.[148]

THE FUR TRADE
No. 2[149]

The regions upon which this extensive commerce is spread, embraces
portions of country, in which the civil jurisdiction of our government
is complete, as well as vast portions where the Indian title is yet un-
extinguished, and where the laws regulating trade and intercourse
with the Indian tribes only operate. It will readily occur, that in a
trade which is conducted at such remote places, some salutary regulations would be requisite, as well to secure the trader from the unlaw-
ful exactions of the Indians. The former object is provided for, by
excluding the sale or gift of ardent spirits to Indians, so that they
may remain sober and exercise their native shrewdness in making
their bargains. Regularity in the trade is provided for by requiring
the whole trade to be conducted under licenses from government,
whose authority it will always be the interest of the Indians to
respect.

The attention of our government was directed at an early day to
this point, and several laws for the better government and regulation
of the trade, have been from time to time enacted, containing salutary
provisions. To this end the Indian territory had been divided into
convenient districts, and an agent is appointed to reside in each, whose
duty it is to enforce the provisions of the laws, and to scrutinize the
conduct of traders. Every trader previously to entering the Indian
country, is required to file bonds, under suitable penalties, with
sufficient surety.

But while these laudable efforts are made at Washington, the wits
of the traders on the frontiers, are stimulated to frustrate the agents.
The latter are so few that the Indian country, cannot be closely
watched. It is the interest of fifty to one to break the laws, where
there is but one to enforce it. Do what the Agents can, it is impossible to keep a strict watch, and we must content ourselves to proportion our exertions, to enforce wholesome laws in the nation that
interest, duplicity, and daring endeavor to break them.

Indian agents, in the Indian country, are very much in the condi-

131

tion of cats, in a certain place, without claws. They are expected to keep the public cellar clear of rats and mice, without that important means. If the military are referred to, they can do but little consistently with the higher duties of the "public service." If the local courts are invited to interfere, alas they are mostly, *particeps criminis*.

Jefferson

PROGRESS OF GEOGRAPHICAL DISCOVERY
No. 2

It is not our object to go into any critical examination of works, which are well known to our readers, and upon which the voice of contemporary writers has long past. Nor shall we stop to inquire into the comparative merits of Chastelloux[150] & Volney,[151] and Chateaubriand[152]—travellers of the same country with the lately reinstituted order of Jesuits, but of a different age, and different stamp. It will be sufficient for our purpose, if we show, that previous to our separation from the mother country, & even up to our own times, we have been indebted, almost exclusively to foreign sources for our information of the transmontaine regions; and that neither as colonies, nor as a separate nation, had we acquitted our duty to ourselves, by furthering the great work of useful discovery.

The public mind, either seemed satisfied with the reports of missionaries and traders, or was not roused to a proper sense of the importance of the subject, until the elevation of Mr. Jefferson to the Presidential chair in 1800. That acute observer of nature, set on foot separate expeditions for exploring the courses of the Missouri and the Oregon, the Mississippi and the Arkansas. The result of these examinations was given to the public in the expeditions of Lewis and Clark, and in those of Lieut. Pike. At the same time a partial impulse was given to private enterprize, and we are dedicated to the decade and following this era, for the "views of Louisiana," by Brackenridge,[153] and the "Historical Sketches" of Stoddard.[154]

Here the public attention again relapsed. Our citizens appeared still too busy with the great and pressing realities of commerce and politics, to permit their taking any permanent interest in the success of projects of remote or doubtful advantage. To amass wealth was one thing, and to promote discovery another, and it is inferable, from a review of the state of public feeling, that even the volumes of Lewis and Clark, were rather admired, than appreciated.

No further interest appears to have been excited towards the progress of exploration, until the termination of the late war of 1812. Various causes tended to accelerate emigration towards the west. The demand for information from that quarter was urgent throughout the whole tier of the Atlantic States, and everything in the shape of personal observations, was eagerly purchased, and eagerly read. The supply was soon adequate to the demand. But the market for books, like the market for corn, is readily glutted. A sickly growth of productions was engendered, and of the numerous "gazetteers" and "journals" and "tours" and "travels," which flowed in upon the public, we do not recollect, any, after the mention of Drake's Picture of Cincinnati,[155] and Darby's "Louisiana,"[156] which deserves to be recalled from that oblivion into which this class of productions has already sunk.

The commencement of 1818 marked a new era in the labor of discovery in our western country. During this, and the following year, the strong desire of making discoveries in the botany and mineralogy of the western country, and their kindred topics, allured several individuals to travel in those regions, upon private resources. The result of this impulse, is perhaps, sufficiently comprehended, in Nuttal's "Travels in Arkansas,"[157] and Schoolcraft's on Missouri.[158] But a more considerable effort was made. Mr. Calhoun, acting on the policy which had been introduced and sanctioned by Jefferson, ordered a detachment of troops to ascend the Missouri and take post on the Yellow Stone and on the Mississippi to St. Anthony's falls, with a view, in part, to cover the observations of the topographical engineers, and naturalists, who were dispatched to examine and report upon the natural features and productions of these imperfectly known regions. This design, although partially frustrated by the refusal of Congress to appropriate the necessary funds, were carried out, with reputation, by the military arm.[159]

Such was the state of our information, and the means taken for extending it, in 1819. In the autumn of this year Gov. Cass of Michigan, originated an expedition, under the patronage of government, for exploring the regions north and west from Detroit, extending through the Upper Lakes to the sources of the Mississippi. The results of this important exploration, extended our geographical and topographical knowledge over five degrees of north latitude, north of Detroit. By it, we received our first scientific contributions to geology, mineralogy, botany, and zoology. A vast field of agricultural and commercial riches was explored, extending from the sources of the river, as low down, as the influx of the Wisconsin. The northern lakes were entirely circumnavigated and surveyed. Public attention, was strongly called to the value of these wide and neglected lands of the public domain. No prior exploration, since Lewis and Clark had given such an impetus to the expectations of the nation, and its extension west.[160]

Viator

GITSHEE IAUBANCE

OR

THE STRONG MAN OF KEWEENA

This chief resides at Keweena bay, or as it is called by the French, *L'Ance,* in lake Superior; where his father, and grandfather lived before him. He traces his claims to the chieftainship of his band no farther back than to his great grandfather, who received a flag from the French government.

His father's name was Augussawa. He was killed by the Sioux, at the age of about 50, leaving six sons, of whom Gitshee Iaubance, was next to the youngest. He was about ten years old when his father fell. When about 18, he joined, as a volunteer, a war party against the Sioux and Outagamies. This party consisted of 300 men, from the different villages on the shores of the lake. It was headed by Waub Ojeeg, aided by Nawondego, and Wabekonjeewona. On the portage of the Great Falls of the St. Croix, they encountered the Sioux and Foxes, rather unexpectedly the latter having also set out in quest of the Chippewas. The fight continued all day, when both parties retired. Many persons were killed, and many scalps taken on both sides; but the Chippewas claimed the victory; and the Sioux have never since ventured to meet them in much force, in the woods. It also put an end to the Outagami war, being the last engagement in which that tribe appeared against the Chippewas. This battle, by far the most important event related in the modern traditions of the Chippewas, appears to have been fought in 1763.

134

No. 13. March 10th 1827

Gitshee Iaubance has been in three war parties at subsequent periods, by none of which, however, was much effected against the enemy. He has always enjoyed the reputation of being an expert hunter, and, what next to courage is most applauded by the Indians, of possessing great personal strength. There can be no doubt, from the concurrent testimony of traders and Indians, but he has been for many years, and is still decidedly the strongest man in the Chippewa Nation. It is in fact, upon his strength and prowess, that his fame and authority as a chief, is principally founded.

As a hunter few have ever surpassed him. During the winter and spring of 1806, he killed with his own hands three hundred beavers at the post of *L'Ance*. Beaver was worth in that year, from $3.50 to $4. per pound. Estimating each beaver to weigh only one pound, and taking the minimum price, his winter's hunt must have procured him goods to the value of $1,050—a sum more than amply sufficient to support himself and family in affluence.

At this time, with every exertion, he cannot take over fifty beavers during the year, and the whole amount of his hunt, including *small furs* of every description, does not exceed a pack and a half,—worth perhaps, two hundred and fifty, or three hundred dollars.[161]

Gitshee Iaubance has six sons, all men grown, neither of whom, however, promises to equal the father in activity, strength, or influence in his band. The aggregate hunt of these six sons, does not usually exceed that of the father alone. The sixth and last son, is his favorite, and gives promise of making the most active hunter, and the best man. His name is Neezakapenas, or the single bird. This son, who is frequently still addressed by his infant name of *Penasee*, is designated to inherit his father's honors.

Many instances of the personal strenth of Gitshee Iaubance, are related. In the month of February 1808, he killed a buck moose of three years old, weighing between 400 and 500 pounds. The snow, at this time, was deep, and so soft, from the effects of a partial thaw, that the snow shoe sank into it, at every step. After cutting up the animal, and draining out the blood, he wrapped the whole in its hide, and stooping down, placed himself under the load. He then rose up. Finding his strength equal to the task, he then took a litter of nine pups in a blanket upon his right arm, placed his wallet containing a blanket, etc. upon the top of the meat, and putting his gun upon the

135

left shoulder, walked off, with a firm step, sinking deep in the partially melted snow at every stride. He travelled six miles with this enormous burden. It required John Holliday, on whose authority this statement is made, and three Canadians, to carry another moose, somewhat larger, the same distance. But neither of these men, on trial, could raise the burden of Gitshee Iaubance from the ground.

The dread of his strength, and infuriated passion, led some of the *earlier* traders, to comply with his unreasonable demands for liquor, when he no longer possessed the means of purchasing it. This demand was refused by Mr. [John] Johnston in 1793, who finding nothing would satisfy the audacious savage, while he had any thing remaining, ordered his messenger from the tent. Gitshee Iaubance, irritated by the refusal, and mad from the effects of previous drinking, seized his weapons to avenge the *insult,* for in this light he was accustomed to consider every refusal of this kind. Mr. Johnston placing his sword and loaded pistols before him, threatened the life of any Indian who should enter his tent in a hostile manner. His men, being Canadians, fled and secreted themselves in the woods. In this perilous situation, while they were in the act of coming to blows, a sudden storm of rain and wind arose, attended with severe claps of thunder. The Indian was appalled. "Englishman," he exclaimed, "put tobacco in the fire! Your God is stronger than mine." "No!" replied Mr. J. "put *you*[r] tobacco in the fire. I have full confidence in *my God.* It is against *you* that his anger is excited." At such imminent risks, was this trade formerly conducted.

Born during the latter years of British supremacy in the American colonies, and continuing in habits of intercourse with the Agents of that government in the Canadas, until a recent period, his political partialities were naturally moulded that way. Since the American government has advanced a post to the foot of lake Superior, and thereby insured protection to the Indians living south and west of the national boundary, he had ceased visiting foreign Agents, and both by his professions and conduct, has evinced a uniform reliance upon, and attachment to, our government. He has been a constant visitor at the Agency of St. Mary, from its establishment in 1822, and has received from this office a chief's flag and medal of the largest class. In the summer of 1823 he surrendered a flag, formerly received from the Agents of the Indian department in the Canadas, as an evidence that his visits to them, were terminated: and on returning to his village at Keweena bay, hoisted the American ensign in its stead. This step was unpopular with the majority of his band, and caused considerable excitement. His determination once taken, was not however, to be moved, and as no Indian of that band, possessed sufficient influence openly to oppose him, a tacit acquiescence to his course, had taken place; and his influence at this moment, is as great as at any former period.

SKETCHES OF WESTERN SCENERY[162]

No. 4

TO CHARLES G. HAINES ESQR. N.Y.

The Mississippi river may be compared to the trunk of one of those gigantic trees, on the Pacific shores, or the waters of the Ganges, which have innumerable branches, some of which rival and almost surpass the parent stem. I have called your attention to the sylvan shores and forests of the Miami of the Lakes, and to the long winding and swelling evolutions of the Wabash, unparalled in length, majesty, and natural exuberance and fertility. In calling your attention to so immense a region as the Mississippi valley, bounded in a geological view, by the Appalachian and Rocky Mountain chains, I shall preserve no order of strict topographical sequence, but skip from valley to valley, as the subject occurs.

One of the most beautiful, and at the same time secluded of these auxiliary vallies is the Unican, or White River of Arkansas and Missouri. This stream, properly belongs, to the river system of the Arkansas, with which it, however, is only connected, with the anomalous channel of intercommunication of the Cutoff.

Most of the rivers which enter the Mississippi, consist of turbid or colored waters. They rush through such rich alluvial districts, that they carry along, in their impetuous course, not only large contributions of the fertile soil, through which they run, but trunks of entire trees, and other buoyant matter, while their channels push along, towards the ocean, the stones and boulders in their beds. Thus the Missouri, is so turbid that it seems like a chaos, earths, clays, sands commingling in it, till its turbidity assumes a continually varying, and streaked, or mottled appearance. The Red river and Arkansas, are both so highly charged with marl-like clays, tinged by the red oxide of iron, that often assumes the color of stagnant blood. But the Unican, presents to the eye, in all its upper portions, a stream of light. Crystal could hardly be purer, or whiter. Every pebble or other object on its bed shines through it, with perfect clearness. Owing to this extreme purity, its depth is always underrated, and sometimes leads to fatal mistakes. Tourists and travellers who suppose themselves crossing in two or three feet, often find themselves, and horses, plunging into twenty feet. Most parts of these upper shores, are overlooked by perpendicular cliffs of limestones and sandstones. Above its great north Fork, its channel is frequently interrupted by shoals and rapids, over which its ample volume, rolls in wreaths of white and sparkling foam. Such are the Buffalo and Bull shoals. The Calico Rock is one of those perpendicular walls of horizontal rocks, over which the trickling waters, clays, and oxides have spread their tracery, which gives an aspect, resembling the Pictured Rocks on lake Superior.

Some of the minor tributaries of this river, yield pebbles of agate. Galena, blende, and mountain iron ore are found in other places, and in its more south westerly territories, its quartz veins in slate, betoken gold. For a long distance, this beautiful river, runs in defiles through the great and picturesque Ozark chain. Its western sources interlock with the Osage and the Gasconade, and its northern springs with the Merrimac, the Black and the Current.

Some of the tributaries of this river, issue in full streams from orifices in the rock. Many of the limestones of this region are cavernous, and their caves yield nitric salts. It is a region alike replete with interest to the topographer, the lover of natural scenery, the mineralogist, and the geologist.

Abieca

OTAGAMIAD[163]

In northern climes there liv'd a chief of fame,
LaPointé his dwelling, and Ojeeg his name,
Who oft in war had rais'd the battle cry,
And brav'd the rigors of an Arctic sky;
Nor less in peace those daring talents shone,

No. 13. March 10th 1827

That rais'd him to his simple forest throne,
Alike endow'd with skill, such heaven's reward,
To weild the oaken sceptre, and to guard.
Now round his tent, the willing chieftain's wait,
The gathering council, and the stern debate—
Hunters, & warriors circle round the green,
Age sits sedate, & youth fills up the scene,
While careful hands, with flint & steel prepare,
The sacred fire—the type of public care.

    Warriors and friends'—the chief of chiefs oppress'd,
With rising cares, his burning thoughts express'd.
'Long have our lands been hem'd around by foes,
Whose secret ire, no check or limit knows,
Whose public faith, so often pledg'd in vain,
'Twere base for freemen e'er to trust again.
Watch'd in their tracks our trusting hunters fall,
By ambush'd arrow, or avenging ball;
Our subtil foes lie hid in every pass,
Screen'd in the thicket, shelter'd in the grass,
They pierce our forests, & they cross our lines,
No treaty binds them, & no stream confines
And every spring that clothes the leafy plain,
We mourn our brethren, or our children slain.
Delay but swells our woes, as rivers wild,
Heap on their banks the earth they first despoil'd.
Oh chieftains! listen to my warning voice,
War—war or slavery is our only choice.
No longer sit, with head & arms declin'd,
The charms of ease still ling'ring in the mind;
No longer hope, that justice will be given
If ye neglect the proper means of heaven:
Fear—and fear only, makes our foemen just
Or shun the path of conquest, rage or lust,
Nor think the lands we own, our sons shall share,
If we forget the noble rites of war.
Choose then with wisdom, nor by more delay,
Put off the great—the all important day.

Upon yourselves alone, your fate depends,
'Tis warlike acts that make a nation friends
'Tis warlike acts that prop a falling throne,
And makes peace, glory, empire, all our own.
Oh friends! think deeply on my counsel—words
I sound no peaceful cry of summer birds!
No whispering dream of bliss without allay
Or idle strain of mute, inglorious joy
Let my bold voice arouse your slumb'ring hearts,
And answer warriors—with uplifted darts,
Thick crowding arrows, bristled o'er the plain,
And joyous warriors rais'd the battle strain.

    All but Camudẃa,[164] join'd the shouting throng,
Camudẃa, fam'd for eloquence of tongue
Whose breast resolv'd the coming strife with pain,
And peace still hop'd, by peaceful arts to gain.
'Friends'—he reply'd—'our rulers words are just,
Fear breeds respect and bridles rage or lust,
But in our haste, by rude and sudden hate,
To prop our own, or crush our neighbors state
Valor itself, should not disdain the skill
By pliant speech, to gain our purpos'd will.
The foe may yet, be reason'd into right.
And if we fail in speech—we still may fight.
At least, one further effort, be our care,
I will myself, the daring message bear,
I give my body, to the mission free,
And if I fall, my country, 'tis for thee!
The wife and child, shall lisp my song of fame,
And all who value peace, repeat my name!

    'Tis well—Baimwáwa[165] placidly replied,
'To cast our eyes, with care to either side,
Lest in our pride, to bring a rival low,
Our own fair fields shall fall beneath the foe.
Great is the stake, nor should we lightly yield,
Our ancient league by many a battle seal'd.

No. 13. March 10th 1827

The deeds of other days before my eyes,
In all their friendship, love and faith arise,
When hand in hand with him we rov'd the wood,
Swept the long vale, or stem'd the boiling flood.
In the same war path, march'd with ready blade,
And liv'd, and fought, and triumph'd with his aid.
When the same tongue, express'd our joys and pains,
And the same blood ran freely thro' our veins?

'Not we—not we'—in rage Keewaydin[166] spoke,
'Strong ties have sever'd, or old friendships broke,
Back on themselves the baseless charge must fall,
They sunder'd name, league, language, rites and all.
They, with our firm allies, the Gallic race,
First broke the league, by secret arts and base,
Then play'd the warrior—call'd our bands a clog,
And earn'd their proper title, Fox and Dog.
Next to the false Dacota gave the hand,
And leagued in war, our own destruction plan'd.
Do any doubt the words I now advance,
Here is my breast'—he yelled & shook his lance.

'Rage'—interposed the sage Canowakeed,[167]
Ne'er prompted wit, or bid the council speed
For other aims, be here our highest end,
Such gentle aims as rivet friend to friend.
If harsher fires, in ardent bosoms glow,
At least restrain them, till we meet the foe,
Calm judgment here, demands the care of all,
For if we judge amiss, ourselves shall fall.
Beside, what boasts it, that ye here repeat,
The current tale of ancient scaith or heat,
Love, loss, or bicker, welcome or retort,
Once giv'n in earnest, or return'd sport
Or how, or when, this hapless feud arose,
That made our firmest friends, our firmest foes.
That so it is, by causes new or old,
There are no strangers present, to be told,

141

Each for himself, both knows & feels & sees,
The growing evils of a heartless peace,
And the sole question, of this high debate,
Is—shall we longer suffer—longer wait,
Or, with heroic will, for strife prepare,
And try the hazard of a gen'ral war!

INVOCATION
To My Maternal Grandfather
On Hearing His Descent From Chippewa Ancestors
Misrepresented

Rise bravest chief! of the mark of the noble deer,
     With eagle glance,
     Resume thy lance,
And wield again thy warlike spear!
     The foes of thy line,
     With coward design,
Have dar'd, with black envy, to garble the truth,
And stain, with a falsehood, thy valorous youth.

They say, when a child, thou wert ta'en from the Sioux,
     And with impotent aim,
     To lessen thy fame
Thy warlike lineage basely abuse,
     For they know that our band,
     Tread a far distant land,
And thou noble chieftain! art nerveless and dead,
Thy bow all unstrung, and thy proud spirit fled.

Can the sports of thy youth, or thy deeds ever fade?
     Or those ever forget,
     Who are mortal men yet,
The scenes where so bravely thou'st lifted the blade,
     Who have fought by thy side,
     And remember thy pride,
When rushing to battle, with valor and ire,
Thou saw'st the fell foes of thy nation expire.

No. 13. March 10th 1827

Can the warrior forget how sublimely you rose?
       Like a star in the west,
       When the sun's sunk to rest,
That shines in bright splendor to dazzle our foes:
       Thy arm and thy yell,
       Once the tale could repel
Which slander invented, and minions detail,
And still shall thy actions refute the false tale.

Rest thou, noblest chief! in thy dark house of clay,
       Thy deeds and thy name,
       Thy child's child shall proclaim,
And make the dark forests resound with the lay;
       Though thy spirit has fled,
       To the hills of the dead,
Yet thy name shall be held in my heart's warmest care,
And cherish'd, till valor and love be no more.

[1823]   Rosa

The Literary Voyager

No. 14.   *Sault Ste. Marie*   *March 28th 1827*

DIED,

On the 13th inst. at 11 o'clock at night, William Henry, only child of
Henry R. Schoolcraft Esqr. AE. 2 years, 8 mo. & 14 days. "Suffer
little children to come unto me, and forbid them not; for of such is
the kingdom of heaven."

NOTICE OF WILLIAM HENRY SCHOOLCRAFT

The month of May [1824] at the Sault Ste. Marie, was a month of
all the sweets of attractive northern climate and scenery. The harsh
winds of winter, had ceased with the opening of April. May introduced into the woodlands and glades of the St. Mary's valley, the
little pink bordered *miscodeed,* or spring beauty, the wild violet of
the north, with other well known blossoms of Flora's bounties. And
the month of June completed the botanical panorama, by contribut-
ing its flowering shrubs, with agreeable odors. The river ran ma-
jestically before our doors, on its proud course, to Lake Huron, and
the distant hills of lake Superior, and the white wreathed rapids of
St. Mary, with their ceaseless, murmuring diapason, led every heart
to be joyful. To these sweet and agreeable objects, there was added
on the 27th of the month the beautiful and bright-eyed, little stranger
William Henry. A smile was his first expression in joining the society
of the world. With a face of the purest Caucassian whiteness, eyes
with the brilliancy of a polished diamond, auburn hair, and features
of the sweetest amenity of regularity, he became at once an object of
the deepest love and affection. Physical traits of so attractive a kind,
were, however, only the tokens of an intellect, bright and precocious.
When but six months old, having gone with his parents to the City
of New York, his nurse in carrying him from the boarding house to
the Battery, was frequently stopped, to ask the name of the bright
and beautiful child. And when the reply denoted that his mother was
another Pocahontas, Chippewa blood by the maternal line, and a sire

from the coasts of Dalriada in the north of Ireland, where she was educated, additional interest, was felt in the bright American boy, and many visits were paid to see the mother and child, at their lodgings. The winter of '24 and '25 added to the rapid development of his manly traits and attainments in speech and decided manner, and the spring of 1825, before his first year closed, beheld him walk. His father, during this time, having occasion to visit Washington, and spend sometime at the Capitol, an invitation of Saml. S. Conant Esqr. and Mrs. Conant to the mother and child to spend the interim at their country residence, a few miles out of the city [of New York] on the Bloomingdale road, was accepted, and he continued to improve in growth and development. Born with a fine constitution and complete organization, no sickness ever detracted from his physical improvement.

In the spring of 1825, parting from the kind friends, who had rendered the winters residence in the city agreeable, he proceeded with his parents up the attractive valley of the Hudson, to Albany to the western parts of the state, where a season was spent at the residence of his grandfather and grandmother. Being accompanied from there by a young uncle and aunt,[168] just entering on the stage of active life, who sought their future homes in the west, the party proceeded to Buffalo, and thence by those fine line of palace steamboats, which mark the Lakes, to Detroit, & through the magnificent panorama of lake Huron and the sylvan St. Mary's straits, to the scene of his nativity at St. Mary's.

His first year had now closed. To see the infantile countenance expand with new life and hope, and the hearts of adult, re-illumined by the return of such joyous accessions to, and renewal of affectionate sympathy, constituted one of the brightest scenes of human life and social enjoyment. We are bound together in closer bonds, by every such exhibition. There is nothing sordid in it, and the heart is thus purified and exalted.

Elmwood,[169] the seat of his nativity, stands on the banks of one of the noblest of rivers, where the eye is constantly regaled with sights of vessels and Indian canoes, in their picturesque and native rig. His father being called to attend a distant council of native chiefs, at Prairie du Chien, on the Mississippi, he had left the wharf in front of the agency, in the light and rapid canoe, manned with the Canadian

145

voyageurs, with their gay feathers and allegoric songs and duetts, and thus passed out of sight, as a summer cloud driven by the wind. To walk along these banks with his nurse, watching the return of this canoe, to pick the wild flowers on its banks, to learn the art of casting pebbles into the water, these became his employments. Early autumn brought the expected return, and the following fall and winter, added to his little arts, and gave new proofs of a precociousness in every thing. The spring of 1826, brought new duties, which drew his father to a convocation of native chiefs, at Fond du Lac, on the extreme head of lake Superior. Willy was now two years old. His father had taught him the alphabet, by making twenty six wooden cubes, and putting the same letter on each of its six sides, so that whichever turned up, in his plays, the same letter of the alphabet appeared. This necessary absence, consumed the summer of that year. On returning in the autumn, he brought him a little bag of cornelians and agates from that lake as playthings. He found him improved by his walks, sports, and alphabetical studies, with improved health, and redolent joyousness of spirits. His voice and smile formed the charm of the domestic circles. He chased his shadow on the wall, as a phenomenon; he talked to his dog, as if possessed of reason, and he, manfully got out of his little carriage, on any little accident, offering to aid in repairing the mechanical interruption. The completion of the garrison saw mill, became a new and very exciting object of his notice. The roaring of the water, and above all, the action of the surf arrested his deepest attention. His grandmother, never failed to address him in the native tongue, and used both the Chippewa and English words, sometimes as synonyms, and sometimes by clipping the Indian of its initial, or terminal syllables. She invariably addressed him by native infantile exhibition for boys, of penaysee or little Bird, a term of manly endearment, birds being symbollically, referred to as figures of speech in war. And she, carefully made him a little pillow of swan's down, plucked from the game brought in by aboriginal friends.

The terms new and old, are wholly relative, without reference to any particular period of time. Old, was, to his mind, merely something that has transpired, so that when in the fall of 1826, a barrel of fine spitzenberg apples had been opened, he eagerly seized one, saying, "here is my *old* apple."

He had, from the earliest moments of his life, been made familiar with the existence of God and recognized that existence, pointing to His residence above. But what was noticeable as a physical phenomenon of no good omen, was his stopping often, in a still and clear day, and saying—"it thunders!" The autumn of 1826, and the winter of 1827, wore away heavily, and compelled us to keep more than the usual time within doors. March opened with a cloudy and humid atmosphere. Willy exhibited cataral symptoms, during which he was carelessly exposed by the nurse in visits, relying on his usual robust health. The night following this exposure, indications of croup appeared. Dr. [Zina] Pitcher from fort Brady was in attendance, at an early hour, but the developments of the disease, were so rapid, that only temporary reliefs were afforded that night and morning. The disease assumed a more violent form during the next day, which baffled every attempt of skill, and terminated fatally, on the afternoon of that day. (13th)

So sudden and rapid had been the disease, that no emaciation took place. In a vigorous development of every physical faculty, the repose and placidity of his countenance retained every sign of life. He appeared in death, as if but sleeping, and the ring of his charming voice, was still in the house, while he lay a lifeless embodiment of humanity. Expectation, as it gazed on his placid features, could hardly be persuaded, that he would not again speak.

Death in a family is ever appaling. Willy had lived every moment of his life to be loved and admired. Of a bright happy organization, physically and mentally, he was the source of perpetual happiness to others. His appearance and life in the world, appear like a happy dream, and when he was suddenly withdrawn, the hearts that loved him were desolate, and only desolate. The blow his death inflicted, was regarded as admonitory.

There was a hope, even in despair. The nucleus of his coffin pillow, was a bible—the only one his father had, up to that date owned. Over his shroud was spread a fold of white satin. On the third day, after his demise, his funeral took place. A wide road had been dug through, in the heavy snow plain, that intervened, between the south side of Fort Brady, and the garrison burying ground. His aged grandfather John Johnston Esqr. read the English service. And thus the jewel of bright hopes and warm hearts, was left under the wide winter mantle of snow which covered the whole country. In the spring a neat tombstone of marble was erected, containing under the dates, the words "Sweet Willy." His vase of agates were spread around the path, and the mountain ash, and the rose and wild violets planted, as a shade, over the sacred spot.[170]

LINES OF A FATHER ON THE DEATH OF HIS SON

Sad is the task, a father's hand essays,
To mourn thy fate in tributary lays.
These bitter sighs express my latent woe,
And bathed in tears, the verse must onward flow.
O ever loved! O ever beauteous son!
So fondly cherish'd, and so early flown
So sweet, so fair—so link'd in ev'ry part,
Thy dear idea clings around my heart.
I sought no joys but such as thou might'st see,
And lost a father's name, in losing thee!
Oh! can I blot away that dismal night,
That clos'd in death those eyes of beaming light,
Hush'd the small pulse, that warm'd thy lab'ring breast
And wing'd thy spirit to eternal rest.
I held thy tender arm as life fled fast,
Mark'd each returning throb, and felt the last,
Press'd in mute agony thy burning head,
And saw thee lie—pale, motionless and dead!

Still seems his form to gleam before my eyes,
I see his face—I hear his playful cries,
Still seem to bear him in my anxious arms,
And gaze enraptur'd on his infant charms.
Ah bitter fancy! cease to haunt my brain,
Too soon I wake to wretchedness and pain,
Too soon from slumber's mazy ties I start,
And all the father rushes to my heart.
Oft have I led his tender little hand,
On yonder hill—to take my airy stand,
Where gliding waters sweep its ample base,
And azure hills fill up the distant space,

No. 14. March 28th 1827

Pointing to earth, or to the starry plains,
Where God invisible, eternal reigns.
And oft, when sober evening streak'd the west,
And weary nature woed his cradle-rest,
Pleas'd have I watch'd his slumber sealed eyes,
And seen, in fancy, all the man arise,
I traced his course thro' academic cells,
Where genius lingers, and where learning dwells,
And fondly hop'd, youth's anxious perils past,
Fame, virtue, grace, should crown his life at last.
Fond dream of bliss—a shadow or a shade,
In one short night forever-ever fled!

And when dire sickness, seiz'd his little frame,
I watch'd intent, beside the midnight flame,
Laid my moist hand upon his fever'd brain,
And strove by ev'ry art to soothe his pain,
Oft gave the cup—I fondly wish'd to bless,
And gave it once, when he no more could press!
These throbbing veins, these heavy sighs declare,
How weak, how vain, was every human care!
Th' Eternal Power, ever good and wise,
Reclaimed the suff'ring cherub to the skies,
Such was his will, ere earth or heaven begun,
O be that will, not mine Jehovah, done!

EXTRACT OF A LETTER, DATED MARCH 22ND 1827[171]

"It has pleased the mysterious providence of God, to separate from us, our dear and only child. This event would have been one of the hardest trials to which our hearts could have been put, happen when it might, but has overwhelmed our feelings by the sudden and unexpected manner, in which our son was called away. He was carried off by that fatal disease, the croup, after an illness of only twenty six hours. And such was the blindness of our affections, that up to within the very hour of his disease, we were in momentary hopes of some favorable change, and could not admit the idea of death. So rapid was the transition from life to death, that the sound of his playful voice still seemed to ring in our ears, when he lay an inanimate corpse.

"You will recollect the picture of health which our dear boy presented during our visit to New York. His sparkling eye, and florid countenance, were the delight of every circle; but were peculiarly so, of our own. As he grew up, and his faculties developed themselves, he became every day more lovely and engaging, and took a deeper hold on our hearts. He began to speak early, and improved rapidly, and we had daily cause to observe a mind sensible and intelligent beyond his years. His interesting prattle, the vivacity of his manners, and those expressive, speaking eyes, in which the soul of love and affection beamed forth, rivetted our hearts. His well being formed the object of our fondest hopes, and we had formed no plan of future felicity, in which he had not the most conspicuous part.

"To his grandfather and grandmother, and to his affectionate aunts and uncles, he was equally endeared; & their sweetest enjoyments arose from those little offices of affection which they continually sought opportunities of paying. So endeared, so beloved, our whole souls were wrapped up in him, and we were suddenly awakened from this trance of bliss, by beholding his pale and cold limbs—those beaming eyes closed in death—that beautiful forehead cold as marble, and that lovely mouth closed with a placid smile in death. We retained his dear body with us as long as custom rendered proper, and we gazed upon his manly features with undescribable emotions.

"God saw that we had erected an idol in our hearts, and to the end, that we might fix our affections with less intensity upon sublunary objects, transferred him, to that bright, eternal sphere, "where the wicked cease from troubling, and the weary are at rest." The promises of holy writ are consolatory, and the maxims of Christianity, teach, as with words of fire, that the present scene is one of trial and affliction, in which no true happiness is permitted, and that we must look forward to a future state for that "peace, which passeth all understanding."

A Reminiscence of Domestic Scenes,
Dated, Prairie du Chien July 27th 1825[172]

"William Henry is thirteen months old this very day. He will probably be fifteen before I see him. Will he walk alone? Will he have added many words to his slender vocabulary of papa! and mamma! before that period? These are pleasing recollections. Let me see, how I can improve them."

"Lovely, smiling, prat'ling boy,
"Eldest born of hope and joy
"With thy sweet, expressive eyes,
"Where the jet with diamond vies,
"With thy sense-denoting face,
"Manly lineaments and grace,
"Fair in ev'ry trait and feature,
"Lovely, smiling little creature,
"Art thou still the same sweet Lilly,
"Say, my beauteous little Willy?
"Art thou, as when last I saw,
"Crying still, Papa! Papa!
"Clinging to thy mother's breast,
"Pleas'd whene'er by her carest,
"Portraiture of health and bliss
"Smiling to receive a kiss.
"Or, has time so quickly made,
"On thy face a manlier shade,
"Given thy limbs a greater length,
"Or thy muscles greater strength,
"Given thy voice a deeper tone,
"Or approaching more my own!
"Is thy tender infant mind,
"Still to happy play inclin'd!
"Or begins it to discover,
"Aught of little mad-cap rover,
"Daring, noisy, willful, vex'd,
"Pleas'd this hour, displeas'd the next!
"If so, spare him Dearest! rather
"Rule the son, as thou'st the father
"Not like Juno or like Jove,
"But by tender, winning love.
"Now adieu, heav'ns smile attend,
"The child, the mother and the friend."

151

The Literary Voyager

REFLECTIONS,

ON VIEWING THE CORPSE OF WILLIAM H. SCHOOLCRAFT
FEBRUARY 14TH 1827

Sweet child! how soon,
Thy cold and lifeless form, will be convey'd,
To the gloomy silent tomb! There,
To moulder and return to dust.
But hope bids me say; ere this,
Thy spirit rests, in the bosom of thy God
Where nought is found, but peace,
And happiness; when ages numberless
Shall have past away, thy bliss
Is just begun. Fortunate!
Thrice, fortunate, art thou! so soon,
T'escape the great—the numberless evils,
Of this ungrateful world.

Had thy life been prolong'd, thy tender heart,
Might have received—*wound* upon *wound*,
Hate, malice, envy, evil; all combin'd,
Thee innocent to destroy. But sweet Babe,
From all these evils, thou are free—
Entirely free! To parents and relatives,
Great indeed thy loss! but to thee,
Great the gain! Parents? has not the bliss,
Of your dear William, ever been your theme?
Why then lament so much? Why wish him back
To this vain world of sin and sorrow.
Oh! wipe away the drop that's forc'd to flow,
And kiss the hand that sore afflicts, and say,
With David—"He will not come to us, but we,
Shall go to him." If ye're possessed
Of innocence like his,—short—very short,
Will be your separation! Seek it then,
And a few revolving years, (at most!)
Will close your earthly trials, and duties,

And allow you, once more, to behold,
Your near and dear Willy.

J. H.[173]

Sonnet

The voice of reason bids me dry my tears,
   But nature frail, still struggles with that voice;
Back to my mind that placid form appears
   Lifeless,—he seemed to live and to rejoice,
As in the arms of death he meekly lay.
   Oh, Cherub Babe! thy mother mourns thy loss,
Tho' thou hast op'd thine eyes in endless day;
   And nought, on earth, can chase away my grief
But Faith—pleading the merits of the Cross,
   And Him, whose promise gives a sure relief.

J. S.[174]

Invitation,
To an Autumnal Walk

Come and walk on the bank—it is charming to see,
Come and walk on the bank, with my Willy and me;
Winds and rain now no longer disfigure the scene,
And the sad spreads a carpet of velvet and green—
Fleecy clouds fly above—like a veil drawn aside,
And the Sun's smiling out, like a golden hair'd bride.
Come and walk—come and walk—it is charming to see,
Come and walk on the bank, with my Willy and me.

The woodlands are fading—yet fading they spread
A beautiful liv'ry of yellow and red.
Hark! The plover comes up with his October cry,
And the river runs swiftly and murmuring by;
Yet think not of winter! but look on our son,
Who fills up the moments with beauties his own.
Come and walk—come and walk, it is charming to see,
Come and walk on the bank, with my Willy and me.

153

Away to the south, all our songsters have fled,
And the flow'rs of our garden are faded and dead,
Yet our green river bank—it is left us in bliss,
And the Sun shines to guild it, on evening's like this!
Come, enhance with thy presence, a season so fine,
And smile on the beauties that mark its decline,
Come and walk—come and walk—it is charming to see,
Come and walk on the bank with my Willy and me.

The morning flow'rs display their sweets,
  And gay their silken leaves unfold;
As careless of the noontide heats,
  And fearless of the evening cold.

Nipt by the winds unkindly blast,
  Parch'd by the sun's directer ray,
The momentary glories waste,
  The short liv'd beauties die away.

So blooms the human face divine,
  While youth its pride of beauty shows,
Fairer than spring the colors shine,
  And sweeter than the virgin rose.

Or worn by slowly—rolling years,
  Or broke by sickness in a day,
The fading glory disappears,
  The short liv'd beauties die away.

But then new rising from the tomb,
  With lustre brighter far shall shine,
Revive with ever during bloom,
  Safe from diseases and decline.

Let sickness blast—let death devour,
  If heaven will recompense our pains,

No. 14. March 28th 1827

Perish the grass—and fade the flower,
If firm the word of God remains.

E. K.[175]

DEATH AND FAITH

"Sweet Day so calm so bright,
"The bridal of the Earth and Sky
"The dew shall weep thy Fall tonight,
                    "For thou must die."

"Sweet Rose," that doth such fragrance leave,
On every gale that passes by,
"Thy root is ever in the grave,
                    "And thou must die."

"Sweet Spring" array'd in loveliest flowers,
Bright are thy days! but ah! they fly,
Time urges on the lagging hours,
                    And thou must die.

But thou, sweet Love, dear child of Faith,
With Christ shall reign in glory high,
Shalt prove triumphant over death,
                    And never die.

E. K.

TO A BOY AT SCHOOL, FROM HIS MOTHER

Dear object of my love, too fondly dear,
Still on my lip I feel thy parting tear,
Still hear the sobs that heaved thy little heart,
When from my fond embraces forced to part.
Alas! my child, how sorrow from our birth,
Is interwov'n with all the joys of earth!
E'en the fine feelings which warm hearts unite,
The noblest earthly sources of delight,
From which our dearest, best enjoyments flow,
Are still the sources of our keenest woe,
And warn us not to fix the feeling heart,
Or aught this transient being can impart.

155

But now advance the ever rolling year,
Thy glad heart bounds—thy holy days are near—
From all thy little cares thy thoughts now roam,
All fondly clust'ring round thy dear lov'd home.
How swiftly now the cheerful moments run,
How gaily thy remaining tasks are done!
Nought can disturb thee now, while to thine eyes,
The joys of home, in sweet idea, rise;
At length the welcome messenger is come!
Thy father sends him to conduct thee home;
Tho' rough may be the road, and chill the day
How pleasure wings thee on the joyous way!
Thus—thus my child may God his grace bestow,
When thou hast fill'd thy destin'd tasks below,
When the last summons to go home is giv'n,
And Death appears, the messenger of Heaven,
May'st thou, thro' whatsoever path he please,
The path of suffering, or the path of ease,
Thus gladly follow to that blest abode,
The home where dwells thy Father and thy God.

Dec. 15th 1818   E. K.

Say dearest friend, when light your bark,
Glides down the Mississippi dark?
Where nature's charms in rich display,
In varied hue appear so gay
To wrap your mind and gain your eye,
As light and quick you pass them by,—
Say, do thy thoughts e'er turn on home?
As mine to thee incessant roam.
And when at eve, in deserts wild,
Dost thou think on our lovely child!
Dost thou in stillness of the night,
By the planet's silvery light
Breathe a prayer—to the Spirit above,
For thy wife, and thy child, my love.

1825   Rosa

No. 14. March 28th 1827

To My Ever Beloved and Lamented Son
William Henry

"Who was it nestled on my breast,
"And on my cheek sweet kisses prest"
And in whose smile I felt so blest?
                    Sweet Willy.

Who hail'd my form as home I stept,
And in my arms so eager leapt,
And to my bosom joyous crept?
                    My Willy.

Who was it, wiped my tearful eye,
And kiss'd away the coming sigh,
And smiling bid me say "good boy"?
                    Sweet Willy.

Who was it, looked divinely fair,
Whilst lisping sweet the evening pray'r,
Guileless and free from earthly care?
                    My Willy.

Where is that voice attuned to love,
That bid me say "my darling dove"?
But oh! that soul has flown above.
                    Sweet Willy.

Whither has fled the rose's hue?
The lilly's whiteness blending grew,
Upon thy cheek—so fair to view.
                    My Willy.

Oft have I gazed with rapt delight,
Upon those eyes that sparkled bright,
Emitting beams of joy and light!
                    Sweet Willy.

Oft have I kiss'd that forehead high,
Like polished marble to the eye,

157

And blessing, breathed an anxious sigh.
For Willy.

My son! Thy coral lips are pale,
Can I believe the heart-sick tale,
That I, thy loss must ever wail?
My Willy.

The clouds in darkness seemed to low'r,
The storm has past with awful pow'r,
And nipt my tender, beauteous flow'r!
Sweet Willy.

But soon my spirit will be free,
And I my lovely son shall see,
For God, I know, did this decree.
My Willy.

Jane Schoolcraft

March 23rd 1827

To a bereaved mother (Mrs. Jane Schoolcraft) on witnessing the death of her son, from the croup,—a child of great mental promise, and uncommon manliness of deportment. By the attending Physician.

I've seen life's foe his arrows fling,
Swift from the bow with deadly spring,
Leaving behind his mortal sting,
With venom fill'd.

But never saw a warmer heart,
Made cold by death's insatiate dart,
(With whom it pain'd my soul to part,)
Than thy best child's.

As twang'd the bow the victim sigh'd,
He heav'd his breast convuls'd, and died!
The mother shriek'd aloud and cried,
"Poor Willy's gone"!

No. 14. March 28th 1827

The father's grief ran deep and still,
In forc'd obedience to his will
While others swelled the bring rill,
    For him that's flown.

I wail'd the impotence of art—
Then wept to see the foeman's dart,
Fix'd firmly in his bleeding heart,
    So fierce 'twas driven.

But we've a hope too pure to smother,
That b'yond this life there'll be another,
Where Willy and his pious mother,
    Shall meet in heav'n.

March 25th 1827   Z. P.

WOMAN'S TEARS

Woman's tears, are as the sunbeams,
Smiling through vernal showers.
Woman's tears are as the rain descending
From the murky cloud, char'd with the tempest,
Ere the resplendent bow gives sign of safety,
    And returning peace.

Woman's tears, are as the dew drops,
In the morning ray, warming to life,
    The early buds of spring;
But woman's tears, when meekly shed,
In resignation o'er the infant flower,
Untimely blighted; are drops so precious,
That attending angels collect them in their urns,
And at the footstool of the Savior's throne
With the bright, beauteous Babe, present them,
As a pure off'ring, worthy of Him alone—
Straight th'unfledg'd Cherub into Paternal
Arms is receiv'd and nourish'd to life
Eternal, in the warm bosom of Supernal love.

                                          J. J.[177]

THE DEAD SON

The babe within its coffin lay,
In its robes of innocent unite;
But his spirit had wing'd his early way,
To the regions of glory and light.

The glow of life had left that face,
Which late for breath had striv'n,
But his placid smile, and infant grace
Spoke only of peace and heaven.

Cold and dank were his icy hands,
Though not more cold than fair;
They form'd a vault, beneath the sands,
And left him to moulder there.

But not alone—oh! not alone!
The mother transpierc'd with care;
With frequent tears bedewed his stone,
And fondly lingered there.

But she shall dry her bitter tears,
And she shall smile again,
For lo! the Savior's word appear'd
To conquer death and pain.

That Word within his little tomb,
The parents trusting, lay
That they again shall see him bloom,
In everlasting day.

The Literary Voyager

No. 15.	Sault Ste. Marie	April 11th 1827

To those who have taken interest enough in our "Tale of the Creek War" to wish to see a development of the plot, we must observe, that the recent severe affliction, with which it has pleased an inscrutable providence to visit our domestic circle, has pressed upon our feelings and recollections, with too absorbing a sense of the reality, to permit us to dwell upon fictitious woe.

As a succedaneum, we present, in the ensuing columns, an *Indian Rhapsody*, which has lain in our drawer more than a twelvemonth. It will, at least, have the effect to direct the attention, to one of the most interesting periods of our frontier history; and to recal the name of one of the noblest of those Aboriginal Chieftains, whose exploits will embellish the future pages of American history.

PONTIAC'S APPEAL TO THE WESTERN TRIBES

Fort Niagara was captured by the British and provincials on the 24th July 1759; Quebec surrendered to Wolf on the 18th of October of the same year, and Montreal capitulated to Sir Jeffrey Amherst early in 1760. To all but the Indians, the fall of Canada seemed to be complete, although no treaty between the powers had yet been made. Pontiac, had assumed a tone of haughty defiance, when the first detachment of British troops came to take possession of the country in 1761.[179] On the 8th of May 1763, he invested the fort of Detroit, with his warriors and confederates, whom he had gathered, from tribes and united in a league against the British powers. By his eloquence and energy, he roused up the tribes to make resistance. On the 4th of June 1763, the English garrison at old Michilimackinac, on the peninsula, was surprized and carried by the Indians. The isolated little garrisons at Maumee, Presqu'Isle, and along the whole frontier line of the lakes, were taken by his allies. Detroit, the central, and strongest garrison of all, he reserved for his personal action. The treaty of the 10th of February 1763, between France and England, reached Detroit on the 3rd of June. He had then

been before the place twenty seven days. As the bold defender of
Indian sovereignty, his position is heroic; but the effort was out of
time, being made just at the era when he could derive no aid, from his
warm allies the French. But what this chieftain may have lacked in
diplomatic knowledge of foreign nations, or foresight of his actual
position, he had well nigh, made up, by appeals to their superstitions,
prejudices and customs, and by knowledge of combinations and means
of offence, which are truly remarkable. The following address is
assumed to have been made at this time.

> Now the war cloud gathers fast,
> See it rising on the blast?
> Soon our peace fires shall be quench'd,
> Soon our blades in gore be drench'd;
> See the red foe's legions pour,
> From Wyaunoc's[180] gulfy shore,
> Threatening woe to me and mine,
> Means and power, name and line—
> None may 'scape whose souls are free,
> None—who doat on liberty
> Who is true, or who is brave,
> Or who loathes to be a slave
> Warriors up! prepare—attack!
> 'Tis the voice of Pontiac.
>
> Hang the peace-pipe to the wall,
> Rouse the nations one and all,
> Tell them quickly to prepare,
> For the bloody rites of war—
> Now begin the fatal dance,
> Raise the club, and shake the lance.
> Now prepare the bow and dart,
> 'Tis our father's ancient art!
> Let each heart be strong and bold,
> As our fathers were of old
> Warriors up! prepare—attack!
> 'Tis the voice of Pontiac.

No. 15. April 11th 1827

Take the wampum warrior, fly!
Say a foreign foe is nigh,
On he comes with furious breath,
Speaking peace but dealing death—
Spreading o'er our native plains,
Forts and banners, fire and chains;
Death comes marching in his train,
With the family of pain—
Not the pain that warriors fear,
Ball or faggot, club or spear
Not fierce danger—that is sweet!
Not the red pine's burning heat,
But the bane from which we shrink,
Fiery, fell, destroying Drink.
Warriors hear! Be wise, be brave,
Rise to beat, and strike to save,
Rise to save a bleeding land,
From the rampart and the brand—
From the arts and from the crimes,
Bred in transatlantic climes—
From the thirst of sordid gains,
That ere long shall blast our plains,
And the cold, unpitying rush,
Name and rule that aims to crush.
Firmness now, is all that saves,
To submit is to be slaves!
Now or never! to the field—
Teach the lordly foe to yield,
Spurn his counsel, spurn his laws,
Strike alone for freedom's cause
Rally—rally for th' attack.
Drive th' invading legions back,
To their homes beyond the seas
Thus great Manito decrees.
Up—to arms—prepare, attack!
'Tis the voice of Pontiac.

Nursing vengeance in their hearts

They shall drive the legions back,
Like a thunder tempest, strong and black,
Tremble! 'tis the voice of Pontiac.

Heavens! and can ye live and burn,
And not on the insulter turn?
Have ye hearts, and have ye ears,
And not shape your vengeful spears?
Are ye men by God's decrees,
And can suffer taunts like these?
Rend, oh rend! the' impurpled sky
With your thrilling battle-cry,
Vengeance, valor, liberty!
Onward then, to the attack
'Tis the voice of Pontiac.

[Nov. 12, 1825]

The Indian Sheemaugun or lance, is of remote antiquity, and appears
to have been used contemporaneously with the bow and arrow. It was
formed of a piece of flint, hornstone or jasper, firmly attached to a
handle of wood, by means of thread composed of the cartilagenous
fibres of certain animals. This animal thread afterwards assumed
great hardness, and possessed a strength and durability far beyond
that prepared from the linum, or gossypium. The modern Indian
lance, or club-lance, pointed with iron, is the result of altered manner, and new means.

REQUIEM,
OVER THE GRAVE OF WILLIAM HENRY SCHOOLCRAFT

To gentle Willy's lonely tomb,
    Soft hands and tender hearts shall bring,
"Each op'ning sweet of earliest bloom,
    "And rifle all the breathing spring."

The leafy rowan there shall grow,
    And there the tender vi'let bloom,
And many a wild-flow'r early blow,
    To shed its fragrance o'er thy tomb.

164

No. 15. April 11th 1827

The robin "oft at evening hours,
   "Shall kindly lend his little aid
"With hoary moss, and gather'd flowers,
   "To deck the ground where thou art laid."

Oft there shall fond Affection go,
   And lonely sorrow thither stray,
To shed the tear of tender woe,
   And sigh the dewy hours away.

The snow that weils the dreary ground,
   Was not more pure and bright than thee,
The bow that gilds the heav'ns around,
   Not more of promise show'd to me.

That snow shall melt—that iris fade,
   All nature change to mortal eye;
But thy pure soul in light array'd,
   Shall swell immortal in the sky.

And when that month of vernal storms,[181]
   Shall pour again its wailing blast,
Fond hearts, whom love and pity warms,
   The tender thought on thee shall cast.

Each sunny bank—each early sweet,
   Shall but renew the smother'd pain,
For there I led thy tender feet,
   And hop'd to lead them oft again.

The dasied field—the wild-wood lawn,
   The stream that murmurs softly by,
Ah! what are these since thou art gone,
   But sad mementos to my eye.

Each varied scene shall thee restore,
   For thee the heart its sorrows shed,

Belov'd till memory is no more,
And Love and Hope and Faith are dead.

S.[182]

AGE OF TREES

It is probable that living trees, are the oldest of all organic forms in America, save fossil bones. This idea of the stable and lasting nature of forest trees, is sustained by reference to scripture. This symbol is seized on by Isaiah, who exclaims in describing the permanency of blessings yet in store for the remnant of the people, "as the days of a tree, are the days of my people; and mine elect shall long enjoy the work of their hands." The promise relates to the permanence and fixity of the houses, and vineyards, and the general prosperity, which, the accepted, shall plant. Isa. LXV.22. If the oak or fagus yet stands, on the hills of America, which by its nod, welcomed, Columbus, and Cabot and Verizani to its shores, we perceive the great pertinacy of this scriptural allusion.

Antiquarius

SAULT DE STE. MARIE

This name was first bestowed on the rapids of the river which connects the waters of lake Superior with those of lake Huron, by the early Catholic missionaries in New France. Having given the name of *Sault*, a leap, on the falls. The Chippewas who were seated here, called the passage of the river over a rocky bed, Bauwateeg. By a change of the terminal inflection, from *eeg*, to *ing*, the meaning of at, or by, was indicated. Having called the rapids *Sault*, they called the Indians *Saulteurs*. The term Chippewa itself, is the Anglicized form of O-jib-way.

The place appears to have been first visited in 1642 [1641] by two Jesuit missionaries named Isaac Joques and Charles Raymbault. Sagard had established himself among the Hurons in 1634. Thus St. Mary's was the second Catholic Mission in this country.[183]

Notes to "The Literary Voyager"

1. Schoolcraft's study of the Iroquois was originally published as *Report of Mr. Schoolcraft to the Secretary of State (New York) Transmitting the Census Returns in Relation to the Indians* (Albany, 1846). It was later reissued as *Notes on the Iroquois; or Contributions to American History, Antiquities, and General Ethnology* (Albany, 1847).

2. For a bibliography of Schoolcraft's better known works, see Chase and Stellanova Osborn, *Schoolcraft, Longfellow, and Hiawatha* (Lancaster, Pa., 1942), pp. 624-645.

3. *Index to Schoolcraft's Indian Tribes of the United States.* Compiled by Frances S. Nichols (Washington, 1954).

4. Walter Hough, "Henry Rowe Schoolcraft," *Dictionary of American Biography*, XVI (1943), p. 457.

5. See Vernon Kinietz, "Schoolcraft's Manuscript Magazines," Bibliographical Society of America, *Papers*, XXXV (April-June, 1941), pp. 151-154.

6. *Algic Researches, Comprising Inquiries Respecting the Mental Characteristics of the North American Indians*, 2 vols., (New York, 1839); *The Red Race of America* (New York, 1847); *The Myth of Hiawatha, and other Oral Legends, Mythological and Allegoric, of the North American Indians* (Philadelphia, 1856).

7. (London, 1838), 3 vols.

8. (New York, 1836), 2 vols.

9. The "Literary Voyager" was in great demand among Schoolcraft's friends in Detroit. Governor Lewis Cass and his wife requested to examine the copies of the magazine which were circulating in Detroit in 1829. See Henry R. Schoolcraft to Jane Schoolcraft, May 1828; and Henry Whiting to Schoolcraft, June 2, 1829. Schoolcraft Papers, Manuscripts Division, Library of Congress. See also Kinietz, "Schoolcraft's Manuscript Magazines," Biographical Society of America, *Papers*, XXXV (April-June, 1941), p. 153.

10. Stellanova and Chase S. Osborn, *Schoolcraft, Longfellow and Hiawatha*, pp. 444-445.

11. *Personal Memoirs of a Residence of Thirty Years with the Indian Tribes on the American Frontiers* (Philadelphia, 1851), xxxiv.

12. Even as a glassmaker, Schoolcraft pursued his scholarly interests. He experimented constantly and prepared a treatise entitled "Vitrology or the Art of Making Glass." A small bound manuscript volume of this study is in the Schoolcraft Papers in the Library of Congress.

13. (New York, 1819).

14. *Personal Memoirs*, p. 87.

15. The American claim to land for a fort at Sault Ste. Marie was based on a provision of the Treaty of Greenville of 1795.

16. A first-hand account of this episode is found in Schoolcraft's *Narrative Journal of Travels through the Northwestern Regions of the United States . . . in the Year 1820* (Albany, 1821), pp. 137-140, and the Journal of Charles C. Trowbridge, which was published in three installments in *Minnesota History*, XXIII (1942), pp. 126-148, 233-252, 328-348. The original journal is in the Burton Historical Collection of the Detroit Public Library.
Sassaba continued to oppose American authority even after Fort Brady and the Indian agency were established at Sault Ste. Marie in 1822. According to Schoolcraft, he never forgave the Americans for the death of his brother at the Battle of the Thames in 1813. He was drowned in the rapids of the St. Mary's River, September 25, 1822, while on a drinking spree with several companions. Schoolcraft, *Personal Memoirs*, p. 119.

17. War Department directives to the Indian agent are in the *Records of the Michigan Superintendency of Indian Affairs*, Bureau of Indian Affairs, Record Group #75, National Archives. See Lewis Cass to Schoolcraft, March 12, 1823, *Ibid*.

18. Schoolcraft, *The Indian in his Wigwam, or Characteristics of the Red Race of America* (Buffalo, 1848), p. 64.

19. An original copy of the questionnaire is in the Cass Collection in the William L. Clements Library, Ann Arbor. See also Elizabeth G. Brown, "Lewis Cass and the American Indian," *Michigan History* XXXVII (September, 1953), pp. 286-298.

20. Schoolcraft, *Personal Memoirs*, p. 89.

21. Schoolcraft's dictionary of the Chippewa was never published, except for a brief word list, which appeared in *Narrative Journal of Travels through the Northwestern Regions of the United States* (Philadelphia, 1856), pp. 203-210. A manuscript copy of the dictionary is in the Schoolcraft Papers in the Library of Congress.

22. Schoolcraft, *Personal Memoirs,* pp. 196-197.

23. Schoolcraft recorded the interviews of the following Chippewa leaders who visited him at Sault Ste. Marie during the 1820's: Chacopee (The Six), Snake River, Wisconsin; Monomine Kashee (The Rice Maker), Port Lake, Wisconsin; Chianokwaut or Tems Covert (The Lowering or Dark Cloud), Leech Lake, Minnesota; Shingabawossin (The Image Stone), Sault Ste. Marie; Shewabeketon (Jingling Medals), Sault Ste. Marie; Wayishkee (The First-born Son), Sault Ste. Marie; Guelle Plat (Flat Mouth), Leech Lake; Grosse Guelle (Big Throat), Sandy Lake, Minnesota; Catawabeta (The Broken Tooth), Sandy Lake; Wabishke Penais (The White Bird), LaPointe, Wisconsin; Miscomonetoes (The Red Insect or Red Devil), Ottawa Lake, Wisconsin; Mongozid (The Loon's Foot), Fond du Lac, Minnesota; Annamikens (Little Thunder), Red River, Minnesota.
The detailed notes on these interviews are in the Schoolcraft Papers in the Library of Congress.

24. The data on John Johnston's early history is taken from a series of "autobiographical letters" which he wrote at Schoolcraft's request shortly before his death in 1828. They were published in 1903 in the *Michigan Pioneer and Historical Collections,* XXXII (1902), pp. 328-353. Schoolcraft used these letters in his "Memoir of John Johnston" written shortly after the death of his father-in-law for publication by the Michigan Historical Society. It was not used at this time, however, but was published in the *Michigan Pioneer and Historical Collections,* XXXVI (1908), pp. 53-90.
For additional biographical information on Johnston and his family, see: Charles H. Chapman, "The Historic Johnston Family of the Soo," *Ibid.,* pp. 305-328; L. R. Masson, *Les Bourgeois de la Compagnie du Nord-ouest* (Quebec, 1889-90); Alice B. Clapp, "George Johnston, Indian Interpreter," *Michigan History,* XXIII (Autumn, 1939), pp. 350-366.

25. In 1810, John Johnston was offered the governorship of the projected Hudson's Bay Red River Colony. He declined because he felt the move would impair the education of his children and because he recognized the rival Northwest Fur Company would attempt to wreck the colony. His decision was wise, for the colony failed and its governor, William Semple, was killed and scalped in an Indian attack, inspired and directed by agents of the Northwest Company. See Alexander Ross, *The Red River Settlement* (London, 1856), and Schoolcraft, "Memoir of John Johnston," *Michigan Pioneer and Historical Collections,* XXXVI (1908), pp. 59-60.
Later, John Jacob Astor, the owner of the American Fur Company, hired Johnston to direct the Company's operations in the Lake Superior region. This agreement was terminated when Congress

passed legislation in 1816 restricting trade within the territorial limits of the United States to citizens. *Ibid.*, XXXVI (1908), pp. 73-74.

26. See "Account Book of John Johnston, 1814-1819," Schoolcraft Papers, Library of Congress.

27. The losses he suffered forced Johnston to abandon his plans to purchase a farm near Montreal where his children could enjoy greater educational advantages. Schoolcraft, "Memoir of John Johnston," *Michigan Pioneer and Historical Collections*, XXXVI (1908), p. 64.

28. George Johnston, "Reminiscences," *Ibid.*, XII (1888), pp. 605-608.

29. In addition to their own children, the Johnston's adopted in infancy Nancy Campbell, the daughter of a close family friend who was killed in a gun duel in 1808 or 1809. Schoolcraft, "Memoir of John Johnston," *Ibid.*, XXXVI (1908), p. 61.

30. The correspondence between these two men are in the Johnston Papers in the Burton Historical Collection of the Detroit Public Library, the Carnegie Library at Sault Ste. Marie, and the Schoolcraft Papers in the Library of Congress.

31. William Johnston was particularly helpful in collecting legends of the Chippewa and Ottawa for his brother-in-law. As a fur trader, he wintered often among the tribes of the Interior and had an excellent opportunity to interview Indians relatively uncorrupted by contact with white civilization. During the winter of 1833, for example, he lived among the powerful and warlike Chippewa band, the Pillagers of Leech Lake.
    The Indian materials he collected there are in the Schoolcraft Papers in the Library of Congress. Included in this material are the following: "Story of Me-she-ge-na-big-o: Manners and Customs of the Leech Lake Indians;" "Ottawa Stories;" "Shagwanabee;" "Ottawa Superstitions and Traditions;" "Story of Bokewauwag and his Brother;" "Ojeeg, or the Fisher, A Chippewa Tale;" "Manahbosho."

32. *Sketches of a Tour of the Lakes* (Baltimore, 1827), pp. 182-184.

33. Schoolcraft, *Personal Memoirs*, pp. 107-108.

34. Schoolcraft's interest in the "Literary Voyager" was more than an attempt to provide his friends with a weekly magazine. As early as 1825, he made plans to publish a magazine dealing entirely with the American Indian. The proposed title was *Indian Annals* and the format was to be similar to the *North American Review*. Although Schoolcraft and his partner in the venture, Samuel L. Conant of New York, solicited articles from leading Indian authorities, the magazine did not appear in print. See Agreement between Schoolcraft, Conant and the publishing firm of Wilder and Campbell, May 19, 1825;

Notes

Samuel Conant to Schoolcraft, July 19, 1825. Schoolcraft Papers, Library of Congress; Schoolcraft's *Personal Memoirs*, p. 207.
Similarly, Schoolcraft's plans for the journal, *The Algic Magazine and Annals of Indian Affairs*, never materialized. Planned during 1841, this publication had the support of Albert Gallatin, John C. Calhoun, William Woodbridge, Caleb Cushing, and Percy Du Ponceau. The Prospectus for this magazine is in the Schoolcraft Papers, Library of Congress. Schoolcraft's *Oneota*, which appeared in serial form in 1844, was slightly more successful. It was similar to the "Literary Voyager" in content, and indeed, contained many articles which were reprinted from the earlier manuscript magazine. After *Oneota* failed in 1844-45, the issues were republished in book form. John F. Freeman, "Pirated Editions of Schoolcraft's Oneota," Bibliographical Society of America, *Papers*, LIII (Third Quarter, 1959), pp. 252-254.

35. This legend was later published by Mrs. Anna Brownell Jameson, a well known English writer and traveller, in *Winter Studies and Summer Rambles in Canada* (London, 1838), Vol. III, pp. 218-221. Mrs. Jameson visited Mr. and Mrs. Henry Schoolcraft at Mackinac Island and the Johnston family at Sault Ste. Marie on her trip to the United States in 1837. During her visit, Schoolcraft offered her the use of his Indian materials, probably including the "Literary Voyager." Schoolcraft later re-published the legend "Pebon and Seegwun" in *Algic Researches* (New York, 1839), I, pp. 84-86; *Myth of Hiawatha and Other Oral Legends* (Philadelphia, 1856), pp. 96-98; and the *Indian Fairy Book* (New York, 1856), I, pp. 261-263.

36. Winter [H.R.S.].

37. The Claytonia Virginica [H.R.S.].

38. Schoolcraft later wrote about his experiences with the Indian, Wabishkipenace or "The White Bird," who had led Lewis Cass and his party to the site of the Ontonagon Boulder in 1820. His tribesmen claimed that he displeased the Great Spirit by taking white men to the Sacred Rock. According to Schoolcraft, the ostracism had a telling effect on Wabishkipenace, for in March, 1827, when he visited the Indian agency at Sault Ste. Marie, he was still dejected and melancholy and felt that he was being punished for his actions. Schoolcraft, *Personal Memoirs of a Residence of Thirty Years with the Indian Tribes on the American Frontiers* (Philadelphia, 1851), p. 260.

39. Jane Johnston Schoolcraft used the pseudonyms "Leelinau" and "Rosa" in the magazine. Her mother was undoubtedly the source of many of the legends which she submitted. In fact, the letter to the editor "Character of Aboriginal Historical Tradition," was dictated by Mrs. Johnston to Jane who translated it into English.

40. See note 39 above.

41. Schoolcraft later published an account of this episode in *Personal Memoirs,* pp. 104-5.

42. Rufus Anderson, *Memoir of Catherine Brown, a Christian Indian of the Cherokee Nation* (Boston and New York, 1825).

43. Pseudonym used by Henry R. Schoolcraft.

44. In 1822, the U.S. placed an Indian agency for the Chippewa at Sault Ste. Marie, at the foot of Lake Superior, in charge of Mr. Schoolcraft. This tribe had been arrayed against the Americans in the War of 1812 and was yet unfriendly. Shingabawossin was one of the first influential chiefs to espouse their cause, while his brother Sassaba opposed it. [H.R.S.].

45. Mr. Schoolcraft [H.R.S.].

46. The Chippewa name for the Sabbath [H.R.S.].

47. Schoolcraft later published this allegory, attributed to the "manner of the Algics," in *Algic Researches,* II, pp. 242-244. According to Mentor Williams, who edited the legends, "The Vine and the Oak" was "probably a Schoolcraft invention." *Schoolcraft's Indian Legends* (East Lansing, 1956), p. 238.

48. Osha-gus-coda-waqua or Ozha-guscoday-way-quay as it was often spelled, Chippewa for "Woman of the Green Valley," was the Indian wife of John Johnston.

49. Chequamegon is now the accepted spelling.

50. Foxes [H.R.S.].

51. William W. Warren, the Ojibway historian, presented a different account of the conflict between the Ojibway, the Fox, and the Sioux. In his *History of the Ojibway Nation* (pp. 95-107), published by the Minnesota Historical Society in 1885, he claimed that the Ojibway had to fight the Fox and Sioux "at every step of their westward advance along the southern shores of the Great Lake . . ." They chose the island of LaPointe because of its strategic position against surprise attacks from their enemies.

52. Continued in issue No. 3, January, 1827.

53. Schoolcraft is quoting from Antonio De Solis' *History of the Conquest of Mexico by the Spaniards,* published in London in 1724. A similar account is found in Schoolcraft's *Personal Memoirs,* pp. 160-161. Schoolcraft brought a modest library with him to the Sault in 1822 and added to it constantly through purchases from Detroit, Albany, and New York booksellers. Moreover, for the first two years

after the establishment of Fort Brady, the garrison library was housed in Schoolcraft's office, allowing the Indian agent unlimited freedom to use it. Among the books which he read between 1822 and 1827 were the following:

Benjamin Silliman, *Remarks Made on a Short Tour between Hartford and Quebec in the Autumn of 1819* (New Haven, 1820).

Jonathan Carver, *Three Years Travels through the Interior Part of North America, for more than 5,000 miles; containing an account of the Great Lakes* (Philadelphia, 1796).

Thomas Mante, *History of the Late War in North America and the Islands of the West Indies* (London, 1772).

Louis Hennepin, *Discovery of a Large, Rich, and Plentiful Country in the Northern America; Extending Above 4,000 Leagues* (London, 1720).

Sir Alexander Mackenzie, *Voyages from Montreal on the River St. Lawrence through the Continent of North America, to the Frozen and Pacific Oceans; in the Years 1789, 1793 . . .* (London, 1801).

Johann Forster, *History of the Voyages and Discoveries Made in the North . . .* (London, 1786).

Dieudonne Thiebault, *Original Anecdotes of Frederick the Great, King of Prussia, and his Family, his Court, his Ministers, his Academies and his Literary Friends* (Philadelphia, 1806).

Daniel Williams Harmon, *A Journal of Voyages and Travels in the Interior of North America . . .* (Andover, Mass., 1820).

Louis Armand Lahontan, *New Voyages to North America . . .* (London, 1735).

Samuel Johnson, *The Lives of the English Poets; and a Criticism on Their Works* (London, 1793).

Plutarch's Lives (New York, 1816).

54. George Yarns was Schoolcraft's first Indian interpreter whom he hired on July 9, 1822, three days after the Indian agent's arrival at the Sault. He described Yarns as "a burly-faced, large man of some five and forty who tells me that he was born at Fort Niagara, of Irish parentage . . . and has spent life it seems, knocking about trading posts, in the Indian country, being married, has *metif* children, and speaks the Chippewa tongue fluently . . ." Schoolcraft, *Personal Memoirs,* p. 96.

55. Erin Hall refers to the John Johnston residence at Sault Ste. Marie.

56. Schoolcraft is referring to his young dog, Ponti, who tore up some valuable papers in his absence. By soaking the "gnawed and mutilated parts in warm water," Schoolcraft was able to restore the manuscript. Entry of December 22, 1822, *Personal Memoirs,* p. 133.

57. The Crane Totem was the designation given the most renowned clan

of the Ojibway tribe of Lake Superior. Famous for its orators, this group claimed chieftainship over other clans of the tribe.

58. The Battle of the Falls of the St. Croix occurred about 1770. Ojibway warriors from Sault Ste. Marie, Grand Island, L'Ance, LaPointe, and other Chippewa villages participated in the famous battle. Despite strong support from the Dakotas, the Foxes were decisively defeated and retreated far to the South, never again to challenge the Ojibways. See William Warren, *History of Ojibway Nation* (Minneapolis, 1957), pp. 242-246.

59. Schoolcraft added the reference to the Treaty of Butte des Morts later.

60. New York Indians [H.R.S.].

61. The questions to the answers listed above by John Johnston are as follows:
    4. "To what other tribes are they related?"
    5. "What is the degree of relationship?"
    6. "What is the earliest incident they recollect in their history?"
    7. "Whence did they come?"
    8. "What migrations have they made, and when, and why?"

62. This poem was unquestionably written by Schoolcraft. Lake Dunmore, Addison County, Vermont, was near the glass-making factory which Schoolcraft managed from 1813-1814.

63. Betula papyrucae [H.R.S.].

64. Solomon Gessner (1730-1788) was a Swiss idyllic poet, landscape painter, and engraver.

65. This was one of Schoolcraft's favorite legends. He published it in *Algic Researches, Comprising Inquiries Respecting the Mental Characteristics of the North American Indians* (New York, 1839), I, pp. 221-225; *History and Statistical Information Respecting the History, Conditions and Prospects of the Indian Tribes of the U.S.* (Washington, 1852), II, pp. 229-230; *The Myth of Hiawatha, and the Oral Legends* (Philadelphia, 1856), pp. 109-112; and the *Indian Fairy Book* (New York, 1856), I, pp. 98-101.
    Dr. Chandler Robbins Gilman, a New York physician, who visited Schoolcraft on Mackinac Island in 1835, published the "Origin of the Robin" tale in his *Life on the Lakes* (New York, 1836), I, pp. 165-169. Dr. Gilman reported that Schoolcraft had recorded it from the "lips of an old Chippewa woman" and that "she has since been assured by very many of the oldest and most intelligent of the tribe that the 'Origin of the Robin-red-breast' has been current in the tribe from the earliest recollections."

Notes

Mrs. Anna Jameson also used the legend in her books, *Winter Studies and Summer Rambles in Canada* (New York, 1839), II, pp. 178-180 and *Sketches in Canada and Rambles Among the Red Men* (London, 1852), pp. 203-205. She credited Mrs. Jane Johnston Schoolcraft as the informant.

It is possible that both Dr. Gilman and Mrs. Jameson had access to the "Literary Voyager." Schoolcraft kept the issues intact and showed them to friends who visited him. The Reverend Peter Dougherty, for example, recorded in his diary (July 16, 1838) that he examined the "Literary Voyager." (Dougherty Collection, University of Michigan Historical Collections.) Moreover, Mrs. Jameson's published account of the legend, "Origin of the Robin," is almost identical to the version published in the "Literary Voyager." Only a few words have been changed.

66. The biographical sketch of Waub Ojeeg is continued in Issue Number Four, January 12, 1827. Schoolcraft later used this material for an account of Waub Ojeeg in *The Indian and His Wigwam*, or *Characteristics of the Red Race of America* (New York, 1848), pp. 134-144.

67. Schoolcraft kept a detailed journal of his observations of Indian life and customs while he was Indian agent. Episodes like the ones described here were recorded in minute detail and constitute one of the finest collections of Indian material in existence. They are now in the Schoolcraft Collection in the Library of Congress. This account of Chippewa superstitions also appeared, in slightly different form, in Issue Number One of "The Literary Voyager." Schoolcraft gave no explanation for the repetition.

68. Henry R. Schoolcraft.

69. This poem was written by Schoolcraft for the *Knickerbocker Magazine*. See Schoolcraft Papers, Library of Congress, Vol. 37, pt. 1, p. 8098.

70. A literal translation of the Chippewa name for this fish—Ad-dik-kum-maig. [H.R.S.].

71. Schoolcraft was not exaggerating when he extolled the edibility of the white fish. Scores of travellers who visited the Sault area have raved about this fish. Anna Jameson, for example, wrote: "I have eaten tunny in the Gulf of Genoa, anchovies fresh out of the Bay of Naples, and trout of the Salz-kammergut, and divers other fishy dainties rich and rare,—but the exquisite, the refined white fish exceeds them all . . ." *Winter Studies and Summer Rambles in Canada*, II, pp. 220.

72. There is no indication of the author of this piece. It may have been Schoolcraft, one of the Johnstons, or a member of the garrison at Fort Brady.

73. From December until navigation on the Lakes opened early in May, Sault Ste. Marie was almost completely isolated from the outside world. Mail was delivered by "Express" from Detroit three or four times during the winter. In January, 1831, it took the mail carrier and a party of citizens from the Sault five days to travel to Mackinac Island on snow shoes, a distance of 45 miles. Jeremiah Porter, Journal, *Michigan History,* XXXVIII (December, 1954), pp. 356, 359.

74. This statement may have been made by Mrs. John Johnston or one of her daughters.

75. This is one of the poems which Schoolcraft wrote to Jane Johnston during their courtship. The poems and love letters between the two are in the Schoolcraft Papers in the Library of Congress.

76. According to the Ojibway historian, William Warren, Waub Ojeeg and his force were saved from certain defeat by the timely arrival of sixty warriors from Sandy Lake who held back the Sioux until Waub Ojeeg could rally his men. Warren, *History of the Ojibway Nation,* pp. 246-251.

77. The original of this war song is in the bound volume, "The Poetic Remains of John Johnston Esq," in the Schoolcraft Papers in the Library of Congress. It was reproduced in Thomas McKenney's *Tour to the Lakes* (Baltimore, 1827), pp. 189-190; and the *Michigan Pioneer and Historical Collections,* XXXII (1903), pp. 345-346.

78. Waub Ojeeg's battle with the moose became part of the folklore of his tribe and was circulated widely. In fact, a figure of a moose was carved on his gravepost in memory of his "desperate conflict with an enraged animal of this kind." Schoolcraft, *Information Respecting the History, Conditions, and Prospects of the Indian Tribes of the U.S.* (Philadelphia, 1853), I, pp. 356-357.

79. The legend was later published by Schoolcraft in the *Columbian Lady's and Gentlemen's Magazine,* I (1844), pp. 90-91; under the title, "Moowis, or the Man Made Up of Rags and Dirt: A Traditionary Legend of the Ojibways," in *Oneota* or *The Red Race of America* (New York, 1844-45), pp. 381-384; and the *Red Race of America* (New York, 1847), pp. 175-178.
Schoolcraft added the following comment to the legend in the later published version:
"It is a characteristic of some of the Indian legends, that they convey a *moral* which seems clearly enough to denote, that a part of these

legends was invented to convey instruction to the young folks who listen to them. The known absence of all harsh methods among the Indians, in bringing up their children, favors this idea. This tale addresses itself plainly to girls; to whom it teaches the dangers of what we dominate coquetry. It would seem from this, that beauty, and its concomitant, a passion for dress, among the red daughters of Adam and Eve, has the same tendency to create pride, and nourish self-conceit, and self-esteem, and assure a *tyranny over the human heart,* which writers tell us, these qualities have among their white-skinned, auburn-haired, and blue-eyed progeny the world over. The term Moo-wis is one of the most derogative and offensive possible. It is derived from the Ojibway substantive, *mo,* filth, or excrement. [H.R.S.].

80. In his *Personal Memoirs,* p. 67, Schoolcraft reported that on one occasion when the waves broke "in a long series, above our heads, and rolling down our breasts into the canoe," Governor Cass remarked "That was a fatherly one . . ."

81. Henry R. Schoolcraft.

82. Nathan Bailey, *The Universal Etymological English Dictionary* (London, 1737).

83. Schoolcraft was the author of this article. From 1810 to 1817 he managed glass-making factories in New York, Vermont, and New Hampshire.

84. Governor Cass' address to the Legislative Council is found in *Messages of the Governors of Michigan,* edited by George N. Fuller (Lansing, 1925), I, pp. 27-33.

85. This tale was published by Schoolcraft in *Algic Researches,* II, pp. 91-104, and the *Myth of Hiawatha and Other Oral Legends* (Philadelphia, 1856), pp. 202-212. Mrs. Anna Jameson also used this legend which follows almost verbatim the account found in the "Literary Voyager" in her *Winter Studies and Summer Rambles,* II, pp. 166-177.

86. This is not the end of the legend. Schoolcraft planned to complete it in a later issue of the "Literary Voyager." It is possible that it appeared in one of the issues, now missing. The ending which is appended is taken from *Algic Researches,* II, pp. 98-104. It was written by Jane Johnston Schoolcraft whose Indian name, "Bame-wa-wa-ge-zhik-a-quay," meant "Woman of the Stars Rushing through the Sky."

87. Jane Johnston Schoolcraft.

88. The original of this poem, written by Mrs. Jane Schoolcraft, is in the Schoolcraft Papers in the Library of Congress.

89. Editor, writer [H.R.S.].

90. Abraham [H.R.S.].

91. Hosea, VII, 8. [H.R.S.].

92. Solon, as related by Plato from Egyptian. [H.R.S.].

93. See Milman's *History of the Jews.* [H.R.S.].

94. Buckland's Reliquae. [H.R.S.].

95. Henry R. Schoolcraft.

96. I speak. [H.R.S.].

97. The sixth issue of the "Literary Voyager" published about February 1, 1827, is missing, as well as Numbers ten, twelve, and the first part of eleven. A search of the voluminous Schoolcraft Collection in the Library of Congress did not uncover the missing manuscripts, nor were they located in Schoolcraft Papers in other leading research collections in the United States.

98. A flintlock gun.

99. Sault Ste. Marie.

100. The informant of this tale is not known, although it was probably one of the Johnstons.

101. Mrs. John Johnston.

102. The village of the Garden River Chippewa was located north of Sugar Island on the Ontario shore of the St. Mary's river.

103. Point aux Pins is on the Canadian shore about eight miles west of Sault Ste. Marie, Ontario.

104. Point Iroquois, now called Naomikong Point, is about thirty miles west of Sault Ste. Marie on Whitefish Bay.

105. Alexander Henry, *Travels and Adventures in Canada and the Indian Territories between the Years 1760 and 1776* (New York, 1809).

106. Hibernicus was a pseudonym for John Johnston.

107. See note 39 above.

108. Henry R. Schoolcraft.

109. White-man [H.R.S.].

110. The author of this poem is not known. It was probably one of the Johnstons, perhaps George.

Notes

111. Schoolcraft was probably the author of this poem. During his lifetime, he wrote hundreds of poems and judging from the size of his poetry collection in the Library of Congress, he never discarded any of them. Unfortunately, his zest for verse was never matched by ability to write in this medium.

112. This tale was also prepared for the "Literary Voyager" by Mrs. Jane Schoolcraft. There is no evidence to determine the identity of her informer, although it was probably her mother, Mrs. John Johnston. The story was published in *Algic Researches*, I, pp. 191-199; *Historical and Statistical Information Respecting the History, Conditions and Prospects of the Indian Tribes of the United States* (Philadelphia, 1852), II, pp. 202-204; *Myth of Hiawatha*, pp. 52-70; *The Indian Fairy Book*, pp. 98-101. Mrs. Anna Jameson published the legend in *Winter Studies and Summer Rambles*. Schoolcraft also permitted Dr. Chandler Gilman to include it in his book, *Life on the Lakes*, II, pp. 216-224.

113. *Narrative Journal of Travels* (Albany, 1821), pp. 211-212; *Summary Narratives of an Exploratory Expedition to the Sources of the Mississippi River in 1820* (Philadelphia, 1855), pp. 113-114.

114. *Narrative Journal of Travels*, pp. 282-283

115. Charles G. Haines was a personal friend of Schoolcraft whom he met while the latter was manager of a glass-making factory in Salisbury, Vermont. Schoolcraft wrote to him often describing his travels in the West. In this letter, he described his trip from Detroit to Chicago to serve as Secretary to the Indian Treaty Commission.

116. Hon. Lewis Cass. [H.R.S.].

117. Henry R. Schoolcraft.

118. Sampson Occum (1723-ca792), an Indian, was ordained in 1759 as a Presbyterian missionary. After two years of service among the Oneidas, Occum directed a fund-raising campaign for a school for Indians. The 100,000 pounds which he raised in England helped start Dartmouth College, which was founded as an Indian school.

119. Captain Hendricks was a "respectable Indian" residing with the Oneidas.

120. Henry Obookaiah escaped from the tribal wars in Hawaii and came to New England in 1810. He became a Christian, obtained an education, and attempted to reduce the Hawaiian language to writing. He died in 1817 before fulfilling this ambition.

121. Schoolcraft was referring to Roger or Eleazer Williams. The latter

was the first Protestant missionary to work among the Indians. During the seventeenth century, he served the Pequots and Narragansetts of Rhode Island and Massachusetts. Eleazer Williams later served the Oneidas after they went to Green Bay, Wisconsin, in the 1820's.

122. John Eliot was a missionary among the Indians of Massachusetts in the seventeenth century.

123. David Brainard served as a missionary to Indian tribes in Pennsylvania and New York. After his death in 1747, he was replaced by his brother, John.

124. Samuel Kirkland was a congregational missionary to the Iroquois.

125. Theodat G. Sagard, a Recollect lay brother, missionary, and historian, administered to the Huron Indians in Canada in the seventeenth century.

126. Schoolcraft quoted a section of a statement made by President Jefferson: "To Captain Hendrick, the Delawares, Mohicans and Munries," Washington, December 21, 1808. *Letters and Addresses of Thomas Jefferson,* Edited by William B. Parker and Jonas Viles (New York, 1909), pp. 188-191.

127. Zina Pitcher was army surgeon at Fort Brady in 1827. Before his retirement in 1836, he won distinction in the army and was close to the attainment of the rank of U. S. Surgeon General. He opened a private medical practice in Detroit and became active in the social and political life of the city. He served as Mayor of Detroit in 1840, 1841, and 1843, and in 1842, led a successful movement to authorize building of five public schools, which earned him the title, "Father of Detroit's Schools."
While at Sault Ste. Marie, he studied remedies used by Indians for illness and later provided Schoolcraft with material on the subject.

128. See Alexander Mackenzie, *A General History of the Fur Trade from Canada to the North-West* (London, 1802).

129. Claytonia Virginica. [H.R.S.].

130. The original of this poem written by Henry Schoolcraft to his wife is in the Schoolcraft Papers in the Library of Congress.

131. *Historical Notes Respecting the Indians of North America with Remarks on the Attempts to Convert and Civilize Them.*

132. All of the Indian chiefs mentioned were famous orators of Iroquois tribes. Skenandoah was an Oneida; the others were members of the Seneca tribe.

Notes

133. *Archaeologia Americana.* Transactions and Collections of the American Antiquarian Society (Worcester, Massachusetts, 1820), Vol. 1., pp. 273-76.

134. Lake Superior, so called by the Indian. [H.R.S.].

135. Take it away—take it away. [H.R.S.].

136. The account of the Papuckewis legend in Schoolcraft's *Myth of Hiawatha* (Philadelphia, 1856), pp. 52-70, is much longer than the one which appeared here.

137. Continued from Issue No. 3.

138. Claytonia Virginica [H.R.S.].

139. June [H.R.S.].

140. Means: print of the Loon's foot [H.R.S.].

141. The Mendawakantons were a branch of the Dakotah Sioux.

142. Schoolcraft had a special interest in the adoption of Indian names for topographical places. As a member of the Legislative Council of the Territory of Michigan, he worked devotedly on a plan to introduce Indian names for new townships and counties. In 1838, while Superintendent of Indian Affairs, he prepared a similar proposal for Governor Stevens T. Mason. Many of his recommendations were adopted by the Governor and the Legislature, including Iosco, Tuscola, Leelinau, Oscoda, and Alpena. *Michigan House Documents* (1838), pp. 559-562.

143. Shawandasee [H.R.S.].

144. Zebulon M. Pike, *Exploratory Travels Through the Western Territories of North America Performed in the years 1805, 1806, 1807* (London, 1811), p. 79.

145. The last twenty manuscript pages of this issue are missing.

146. The second installment in the series of letters to Charles Haines, "Sketches of Western Scenery," was apparently published in one of the missing issues of the "Literary Voyager."

147. Henry R. Schoolcraft.

148. This poem, written by Henry Schoolcraft, is in the Schoolcraft Papers in the Library of Congress.

149. The first installment on the "Fur Trade" probably appeared in Issue No. 10, now missing.

The Literary Voyager

150. Marquis Francois Jean de Chastelloux (1734-1788), a major general in Rachambeau's French Army in America from 1780 to 1782, was author of *Travels in North America in the Years, 1780, 1781, 1782* (London, 1787).

151. Comte de Constantin Francois Chaiseboeuf Volney (1757-1820), the French scholar, wrote *A View of the Climate and Soil of the United States of America* (London, 1804).

152. Vicomte Francois Rene de Chateaubriand (1768-1848), a French writer and statesman, was author of *Atala: or The Amours of Two Indians in the Wilds of America* (London, 1802).

153. H. M. Brackenridge, *Views of Louisiana; together with a Journal of a Voyage up the Missouri River in 1811* (Pittsburgh, 1814).

154. Amos Stoddard, *Sketches, Historical and Descriptive, of Louisiana* (Philadelphia, 1812).

155. David Drake, *Natural and Statistical View of Cincinnati and the Miami County* (Cincinnati, 1815).

156. William Darby, *A Geographical Description of Louisiana* (Philadelphia, 1816).

157. Thomas Nuttall, *Journal of Travels into the Arkansas Territory* (Philadelphia, 1821).

158. *A View of the Lead Mines of Missouri, including Some Observations on the Mineralogy, Geology, Geography, Antiques, Soil, Climate, Population, and Productions of Missouri and Arkansas and other Sections of the Western Country* (New York, 1819).

159. In 1819 under Calhoun's direction, Major General Jacob Brown, commander of the U. S. Army of the North, ordered Lt. Colonel Henry Leavenworth to establish a military post at the confluence of the Mississippi and St. Peters' Rivers. The fort was completed by Colonel Josiah Snelling who relieved Leavenworth in 1820. Another military detachment erected Fort Atkinson near the present city of Omaha on the Yellowstone River.

160. Schoolcraft gave the American public an account of this historical expedition in *Narrative Journal of Travels through the Northwestern Region of the U. S.* (Albany, 1822).

161. The packs of L'Ance are worth more than those of any other post in the Lake, from the unusual proportion of beaver. [H.R.S.].

162. Continued from Issue No. 12.

163. This poem was written by Mrs. Henry Schoolcraft about her grand-

Notes

father, Waub Ojeeg. The original poem, which differs slightly from this one published in the "Literary Voyager," is in the Schoolcraft Papers in the Library of Congress.

164. A past sound. [H.R.S.].

165. The passing thunder. [H.R.S.].

166. The North Wind. [H.R.S.].

167. He Who Takes After the Wind. [H.R.S.].

168. On his return trip to Sault Ste. Marie, Henry Schoolcraft stopped at Vernon, New York, and "took along to the West, which had been favorable to me, my youngest brother, James, and my sister, Maria Eliza." Both remained at the Sault. James worked for his brother at the Indian agency and later was employed as a trader at the Sault. He married Anna Maria Johnston, the sister of Henry's wife, Jane. James' private life was a continued source of worry to his brother—he drank excessively, associated with "bad company," gambled, and was involved in several scandals. He was mysteriously killed July 6, 1846, by an unknown assailant, probably by the notorious John Tanner. Maria Eliza later married John Hulbert, the post sutler at Fort Brady.

169. Elmwood was the name given by Schoolcraft to the Indian agency house at Sault Ste. Marie. Completed in 1827, it was situated in a beautiful grove of elms on the St. Mary's River. It was a spacious building, containing fifteen rooms, including an office. The building has been preserved and restored as an historical site by the Chippewa County Historical Society.

170. Many years passed before Henry and Jane Schoolcraft recovered from the tragic death of their son, William. Immediately after his death, they packed clothing and stayed at the Johnston residence until fall.

171. This letter was probably written by Schoolcraft to his friend, Samuel Conant of New York City, with whom the Schoolcraft's stayed while they visited the East in 1825.

172. This poem was appended to a letter which Schoolcraft wrote to his wife, Jane, while he was attending the Indian Treaty meeting at Prairie du Chien in 1825. The original is in the Schoolcraft Papers in the Library of Congress.

173. John Hulbert, the post sutler at Fort Brady, who was a close friend and later a brother-in-law of Schoolcraft, may have been the author of these lines.

174. Jane Johnston Schoolcraft.

175. The identity of "E.K." is not known.

176. Zina Pitcher.

177. The original of this poem dated December 8, 1825, and signed by John Johnston, is in the Schoolcraft Papers in the Library of Congress.

178. Probably written by Jane or Henry Schoolcraft.

179. Major Robert Rogers in command of a force of two hundred Royal Rangers occupied Detroit on November 29, 1760.

180. Chippewa name for Niagara. [H.R.S].

181. April [H.R.S.].

182. Henry R. Schoolcraft.

183. The remaining pages of this issue were lost.

Index

"Age of Science, A Satire" (Henry R. Schoolcraft), 90-93
Algic Researches (Henry R. Schoolcraft), xv
Algoma, meaning of, 2
"Algonac, A Chippewa Lament on Hearing the Revellie at the Post of St. Mary's," 87-89
Algonquin, language, 1, 31-33
American Board of Commissioners for Foreign Missions, 11
American Fur Co., xxii, 169-170 n. 25
Andaigweos, Chippewa leader at La-Pointe, 9
Anderson, Rufus, 12-13
Anderson, Thomas G., 98
Annamikens (Little Thunder), 169 n. 23
Assiguns, 1
Augussawa, father of Gitshee Iaubance, 134

Bad River, Wis., 26, 51
Baimwáwa (The Passing Thunder), 140-141
Bame-wa-wa-ge-zhik-a-quay (Woman of the Stars Rushing Through the Sky): *see* Schoolcraft, Mrs. Jane
Ba-wa-teeg: *see* Sault Ste. Marie, Michigan
Bear, as totem, 54
Big Throat: *see* Grosse Guelle
"The Birchen Canoe" (Henry R. Schoolcraft), 33-35
Bois Brule (Broulé) River, Wis., death of Indians at mouth of, 41
Brackenridge, H. M., 132, 182 n. 153
Brady, Hugh, 4, 10
Brainard, David, 109, 180 n. 123
The Broken Tooth: *see* Catawabeta
Brown, Catherine, Cherokee missionary, 11-14
The Buffalo (Pezhickee): *see* Gitchee Waishkee

Butte des Morts, Wis., treaty of, 31
La Butte de Terre (Sat-tooke-wang) at Sault Ste. Marie, 3-4

Calhoun, John C., xvii, xviii, 170 n. 34
Campbell, Nancy, 170 n. 29
Camudwa, brother of Waub Ojeeg, 41, 140
Canowakeed (He Who Takes after the Wind), 141
Carver, Jonathan, 83
Cass, Lewis, 106-107, 167 n. 9, 177 n. 80
acrostic to, 58
bravery of, xix, 57-58
expedition, 1820, xvii, xviii-xxv, 133-134, 168 n. 16, 171 n. 38
Indian culture, interest in, xx
Inquiries Respecting the History, Traditions, Languages, Manners, Customs and Religion . . . of the Indians Living Within the U. S., xx, 31, 168 n. 19, 174 n. 61
message to Mich. legislative council, cited, 61
and Henry Schoolcraft, xix-xx
Catawabeta (The Broken Tooth), 169 n. 23
The Catfish: *see* Mizi
Chacopee (The Six) of Snake River, Wis., 169 n. 23
Chastelloux, Francois, 132, 182 n. 150
Chateaubriand, Vicomte Francois, 132, 182 n. 152
Chequamegon Bay, Wis.: *see* LaPointe
Chianokwaut or Tems Covert (The Lowering or Dark Cloud), 169 n. 23
Chippewa beliefs, concerning phenomena of nature, 3-5, 42-43, 136, 171 n. 38
Chippewa County (Mich.) Historical Society, 183 n. 169

185

Index

Indians
  Americans, treatment by, 114
  British, treatment by, 114, 136-137
  burial ceremony and customs, 10-11, 108
  Christianity, effects upon, 108-109
  construction of earthen cooking vessels, 97-99
  depopulation, causes of, 110-111, 115-116
  education of children, xxiii
  extinction of, 110-111
  grave posts of, 86, 102
  hunting practices of, 52-56, 120-121, 135-136
  hunting, reliance upon, 110
  implements of, 97-99
  intertribal marriages, 39-41
  intertribal warfare of, xix, 1, 23-26, 39-41, 50-53, 134-135
  language of, 46-47
  medicine of, 108
  mental traits of, 107-109, 117
  missionaries among, 108-111
  picture writing of, 102-103
  pottery of, 97-99
  religious beliefs of, 117. *See also* Chippewa religion
  starvation among, 119-121
  totems of, 24, 29, 40, 54, 173-174 n. 57
  vocabulary of, xx
  See also Chippewas; Sioux; Outagamies
Inquiries Respecting the History, Traditions, Languages, Manners, Customs, and Religion . . . of the Indians Living Within the U. S. (Lewis Cass), xx
"Invitation to an Autumnal Walk," 153-154
"Invocation to my maternal grandfather on hearing his descent from Chippewa ancestors misrepresented" (Mrs. Jane Schoolcraft), 142-143
Iroquois, (Nadawas)
  cannibalism among, 82
  Chippewas, hostilities with, 1, 81-83

Jameson, Anna B., author of *Winter Studies and Summer Rambles,* xv, xxiv, 171 n. 35, 174 n. 65, 177 n. 85, 179 n. 112
Jefferson, Thomas, statement to Indian delegation, 109-111
Johnson, Sir William, receives Ma-Mongazida, 40
Johnston, Anna Maria, xxiii
Johnston, Charlotte, xxiii
Johnston, Eliza, xxiii
Johnston, George, 170 n. 28
  as informant of Indian culture, xxiv
  positions in U. S. Indian Bureau, xxiii, xxiv
Johnston, Jane: *see* Schoolcraft, Mrs. Jane Johnston
Johnston, John, 170 n. 26, 27, 29
  activities in War of 1812, xxii
  biographical sketch of, xxi-xxiii, 169 n. 24, 25
  courage of, 136
  education of children, xxii
  as fur trader, xxiii
  Hibernicus, as pseudonym of, 84
  informant of Chippewa war song, 51-52
  informant of Indian culture, xv
  at LaPointe, 24
  marriage to Ozha-guscoday-way-quay, xxii
  poem by, 159
Johnston, John McDouall, xxiii
Johnston, Mrs. John (Ozha-guscoday-way-quay or Woman of the Green Glade), 172 n. 112
  account of Chippewa, 23-26, 39-42, 50-56
  autobiographical sketch, 5-7
  education of children, xxiii
  Indian attack averted by, xxv
  influence of, xxv
  informant of Chippewa culture, xxv
  marriage to John Johnston, xxii
  sketch of Waub Ojeeg by, 23-26, 39-42, 50-56
  as source of Indian data, 171 n. 39
  translation of statement by, 5-7
Johnston, Lewis Saurin, xxiii

Index

Johnston, William, xxiii
  as collector of Indian data, 170 n.
  31

Keene, N. H., glass factory at, xvi
Keweenaw Bay
  Chippewa war party from, 50-53
  Indians of, 134-137
Kewikonce, Chippewa chief, 98-99
Kirkland, Samuel, 109, 180 n. 124

Lac du Flambeau, Wis., 26, 53
L'Anse, Mich.
  Indians of, 134-137
  fur trade at, 135, 182 n. 159
"Lament for the Race" (Henry R.
  Schoolcraft), 130-131
LaPointe (Madeline Island), 172 n. 51
  Chippewa band at, 6, 9
  as Chippewa capital, 9
  Chippewa chiefs of, 9
  Chippewa war party from, 50-53
  Chippewas of, 9, 23-26, 39-42, 50-
  56, 138-142
  fur trade at, xxi-xxii
  farming on, 53
  Indian subagency at, xxiii
  John Johnston at, xxi-xxii
  war dance at, 51
  Waub Ojeeg at, xxii, 138-142
Leech Lake, Minn., Indians of, 169 n.
  23
Leelinau (pseudonym): see School-
  craft, Mrs. Jane Johnston
Life on the Lakes (Chandler R. Gil-
  man), xv
"Lines of a Father on the Death of
  His Son" (Henry R. Schoolcraft),
  148-149
"Lines, on Coming to Reside at Sault
  Ste. Marie" (Henry R. School-
  craft), 17-19
"Lines to a Friend Asleep" (Mrs. Jane
  Schoolcraft), 71
"Lines Written under Affliction" (Mrs.
  Jane Schoolcraft), 84-85
"Lines Writen under Severe Pain and
  Sickness" (Mrs. Jane Schoolcraft),
  97

Literary Voyager (Muzzeniegun), xiv
  circulation of, xv, xxvi, 167 n. 9,
  174-175 n. 65
  contributors to, xxv
  format of, xxvi
  informants of data in, 121
  missing issues of, 178 n. 97
  production of, xxiv, 90
  re-publication of, xxvi, 170-171 n. 34
  significance of, xv
Little Thunder: see Annamikens
The Lowering or Dark Cloud: see Chianokwaut

McKenney, Thomas, xxiv
Mackinac Island, Indian grave posts
  at, 102
Ma Mongazida (Mashickeeoshe), xxiii,
  24, 40, 122-124
Manabozho, 118-119
Manito poles, 5, 42-43
Martineau, Harriet, xxiv
Mashickeeoshe: see Ma Mongazida
Meda (Medawin, Me-da-we-win) So-
  ciety, Chippewa ceremony of, 36-
  37
Me-da-we-win: see Meda Society
Medawin: see Meda Society
Menominees, 31
Miamis (Miamies), as warrior class, 31
"Michigan" (Henry R. Schoolcraft),
  126-127
Mikeengwun (stone chisel), 97
Miscogandic-a-ub (a prophet), 23
Miscomonetoes (The Red Insect or
  Red Devil), mentioned, 169 n. 23
"Mishosha, or the Magician and His
  Daughters," a Chippewa legend,
  64-71, 177 n. 85, 86
Missionaries, success among Indians,
  109-111
Mizi (The Catfish), 9
Mongozid (The Loon's Foot), men-
  tioned, 169 n. 23
Monomine Kashee (The Rice Maker),
  mentioned, 169 n. 23
Monroe, James, xvii
Montcalm, speech to Chippewas, 40
Montreal River, Chippewa of, 7-8

Index

Index

Wabash River, description of, 128
Wabasha, a Sioux chief, 39-40
Wabekonjeewona, as Chippewa warrior, 134-135
Wabishkipenace (Wabishe Penais or The White Bird), 169 n. 23, 171 n. 38
Wabunakies (Wabnakies), 31
War of 1812, effect on John Johnston, xxii
Warren, William W., 172 n. 51, 176 n. 76
Waub Ojeeg (The White Fisher), 6, 9, 176 n. 76, n. 78
 biographical sketch of, 23-26, 39-42, 138-143, 150-156
 death of, 56
 encounter with moose, 55-56
 exploits of, xxiii
 father of Ozha-guscoday-way-quay, xxii
 leader of war party, 134-135
 lodge at LaPointe, xxii, 138-142
 marriages of, 54
 as orator, 54-55
 physical description of, 54-55
 prowess as hunter, 52-56
 poem about, 138-142
 as trapper, 54-55
 as tribal storyteller, xxv

Waub Onng Aqua (The Morning Star), 78-81
Wauwaunishkum (Gitshee Gausenee), of Montreal River, 7-8
The Waving Plum: see Wawabegwonabec
Wawabegwonabec (The Waving Plum), 79-81
Wayishkee (The First Born), xxv
"The Weasel and Wolf," a Chippewa legend, 103
"The White Fish" (Henry R. Schoolcraft), 43-46
The White Bird: see Wabishkipenace
The White Fisher: see Waub Ojeeg
Whiting, Henry, 167 n. 9
Williams, Eleazer, 108, 179-180 n. 121
Winnebagoes, 31
Winter Studies and Summer Rambles (Anna B. Jameson), xv
Woman of the Green Glade (Ozha-guscoday-way-quay): see Johnston, Mrs. John
"Woman's Tears" (John Johnston), 159
Woodbridge, William, 170-171 n. 34

Yarns, George, 173 n. 54
"Yellow Isle" (Henry R. Schoolcraft), 99-101

193